Evel Knievel

An American Hero

Evel Knievel

An American Hero

Ace Collins

St. Martin's Griffin ⚜ New York

www.stmartins.com

Design by Maureen Troy

Library of Congress Cataloging-in-Publication Data

Collins, Ace.
    Evel Knievel : an American hero / Ace Collins.
      p. cm.
    ISBN 0-312-24390-1 (hc)
    ISBN 0-312-26733-9 (pbk)
    1. Knievel, Evel, 1938– .   2. Motorcyclists—United States Biography.
  3. Daredevils—United States Biography.   4. Stunt cycling—United States.   I. Title.
  GV1060.2.K58C65   1999
  796.7'5'092—dc21
  [B]   99-17000
                                           CIP

First St. Martin's Griffin Edition: November 2000

10 9 8 7 6 5 4 3 2 1

To all who have risked everything

to fulfill a chance at tasting

the sweetness of success

Contents

Introduction

Robert Craig Knievel is a throwback to a different era. He was probably better suited for another time. He could have been a warrior during the glory days of Rome, a scout for the U.S. Cavalry during the Indian wars, a barnstorming pilot during the Roaring Twenties, or a daredevil barrel rider at Niagara Falls during the Depression. Seemingly fearless, he would have relished the challenge of landing on the beaches of Normandy on D day or standing with Travis and his band at the Alamo.

It goes without saying that this American icon is cut from a different piece of fabric than most people. To go with his raw courage Knievel has been graced with a cunning mind, rare athletic ability, and a promoter's instincts. He was born understanding the arts of salesmanship and showmanship. He was and remains a combination of Ripley, Barnum, and Buffalo Bill. Long before he was making millions jumping motorcycles over cars and trucks, Bobby Knievel had found ways to use his natural flair for sales and promotion to sell insurance, motorcycles, and a hockey team.

The story of Evel Knievel is unique and special. The rise of this icon probably could have only happened in America. Yet more than just the story of a daredevil, Evel's story is the stuff of dreams and nightmares. His has been a life where every moment was a gamble to beat the odds and stand alone. His is a tale where every glory he earned carried a price far too high for any other man to want to pay.

Remembered more for his failures—such as the crash in Vegas or the jump at Snake River—than his successes, Evel Knievel has served to inspire millions. He has done so not with his glorious victories, but because every time he was knocked down, he never failed to get back up.

This is the story of a man who could have easily been a loser, who instead continually challenged the odds to find glory and be seen as a winner. As the greatest daredevil the world has ever known, Evel Knievel has made his mark. There will never be another like him.

In early 1999, a dying Evel Knievel was given a choice to grab an almost sure chance at a lifesaving transplant or risk it all in order to serve a higher cause. As he always had, Evel gambled. By betting against the house he became the very model of a hero by anyone's standards.

Evel Knievel: An American Hero is a book about a man who has surprised and enthralled everyone he's met since his youth. This is the story of one of the most unique individuals ever to find the spotlight's warm glow. Evel wouldn't have had it any other way.

Butte—The City That Created Evel

On May 26, 1863, six tired, scared, and haggard prospectors camped near a creek in the Tobacco Root Mountains in what is now Montana. The men were running for their lives, trying to elude a relentless and fierce band of Crow Indians. The natives resented the white men's presence on the tribe's hunting grounds. For days the English-speaking fugitives had stayed just one jump away from their pursuers and death. Exhausted, worn, and unable to go any further without rest, the men made a camp in a ravine that could be defended from a surprise attack. As they rested in what they would soon name Alder Gulch, they felt a sense of security for the first time in weeks. As the night came and no Indians raided their camp, they began to believe they might live to see home again.

The next day the six should have quickly packed up and headed to civilization. Yet the lure of the beautiful land beckoned them. Seeing no Crow braves, they decided to take one more stab at discovering the elusive dream that had driven them for months. Pulling out their equipment, the prospectors stole a few moments to pan for gold in the cool, clear waters of the stream by their camp. Not only did the morning sun reveal a few shiny nuggets in their first pan, but with each new pan more gold appeared. Soon the men who had been running for their lives were determined to hold their ground. The claim they uncovered not only more than paid for their months away from home and their brush with death, it started the Rush of '63. The

Crow hunting grounds were soon to be the filled with greedy white men.

Within a year more than fifteen thousand had joined those first six prospectors, and within five years combined forces of men who had come from all around the world in search of easy wealth had mined more than thirty million dollars in gold from the stream and area surrounding Alder Gulch. The vein of gold didn't end there either. More than a decade later those willing to gamble everything they had were still striking it rich. "Gold" was the cry, and thousands jumped at the chance to find some of their own.

When the precious yellow metal began to play out, there was something else to take its place. Huge quantities of silver were discovered in the hills around Butte. The silver was dug out of the earth in even greater bulk than the gold. It seemed to be everywhere. Then while looking for more silver and gold, a prospector discovered a mountain of copper. And just as the silver began to play out, the Anaconda Mining Company and scores of others cashed in on the next precious metal.

First with gold, then silver and finally copper, Butte exploded. Long before anyone had considered how to plan it, a rough-and-tumble city grew down the hill and through the valley and draws. Filled with men whose lust for life was almost as large as their lust for wealth, Butte became not only a center of mining, but a center for sin. Violence erupted as quickly as another prospecter found another deep vein. Men were shot over everything from jumped claims to cheating at cards. The millions that were made brought not only wealth, but trouble. Brothels, bars, and gambling dens lined street after street, and just as the Old West was dying, this Montana city was filled with the kind of lawlessness that Dodge, Tombstone, and other legendary Western communities had finally put behind them. In a land where harsh elements made living a challenge, the riches in the ground drew men who didn't mind pain, hardship, and facing death as long as there was a chance of glory and riches on the other end.

It might seem hard to believe today, but Butte was once unimaginable in its decadent splendor. There were the richly furnished "parlor houses" served by Chinese servants and well-groomed girls. There

2

were hundreds of prostitutes from all over the world who catered to the needs of those who risked their lives searching for wealth. Belle Rhodes, Mabel Loy, and Molly De Murska offered the most beautiful women of all races. During copper's boom it was not unusual for a man to spend several thousand dollars in a single evening on wine, women, and entertainment. New millionaires lit cigars with greenbacks and tossed gold coins around as if they were candy. For almost two decades the abundance of wealth and the dens of pleasure made Butte a millionaire's sinful playground. This was a city that believed in excess and living large. The community was filled with people who were anxious to play the part of the Diamond Jim Brady of the West.

Besides the brothels there were dozens of theaters such as Owsley's Hall, Renshaw Hall, Sutton's Union Family Theatre, Speek's Hall, Gordon's Comique Theatre, and McGuire's Grand Opera House lining downtown streets. Because of these fabulous music houses built by the mines' treasures, the city regularly drew entertainment troops led by the likes of Eddie Foy, William A. Brady, Rose Osborn, and Maude Adams. Under imported chandeliers and lit by the brightest of Edison's lights, Butte looked like a western Broadway. It was one of the grand entertainment capitals of the West. If you had the money, you could see the greatest entertainers of the time in Butte.

If you hadn't struck it rich or you had lost all your money in a card game, then there were horse and dog racing, bear wrestling, and cockfights. There were also dice games, blackjack, and poker. You could bet on anything and everything seemed to be sport. Along with thousands of amateurs, Butte welcomed the best players of the day. During the boom days Jack Dempsey even fought for the heavyweight title in the city. It was the city where big events were born and where dreams came true in big ways. It was a showman's paradise, and the lure of wealth, excitement, and the high life attracted as many suckers as it did high rollers.

Fistfights, illegal gambling, prostitution, and even the female slave trade were all practiced out in the open, and the law was not in place to keep the peace so much as it was to settle disputes between gamblers and prostitutes with as little death as possible. As it was generally accepted that might ruled and the weak perished, the "sinful" behavior practiced by even many of the town's most respected businessmen was usually ignored and at times even accepted. Yet the party couldn't last forever.

As the ore played out and prospectors gave way to big companies, life began to change. Instant millionaires became a thing of the past and the big players moved to other cities. By the twenties the frontier town founded on gold had become a blue-collar community trying to redefine itself. But Butte still couldn't completely shake off its wild past.

Those who continued to drink in the saloons, play poker at the casinos, and bet on the local horse racers were now copper miners. They still dreamed of making it big on one race or one lucky hand. They still tried to beat the odds. When they didn't win they drank and tried to forget the hard life that slowly sapped their strength and their health.

Just like the prospectors who had first discovered gold along Alder's Creek, these strong men gambled for the highest stakes every day they worked. Their lives were as uncertain as the ever-changing Montana weather. Climbing in a hole that went down for thousands of feet, surrounded by eternal darkness, working in conditions that made the image of hell seem almost friendly, the miners knew life didn't really offer any second chances. One mistake and they were history. One misstep and the money they had in their pockets would never be spent. Their lives were spent on the edge. They realized they could die in an instant. They also realized that before their bodies had even been dug out of the pit, another man would have signed up to do their job. Old miners were more fable than reality. Most believed that if you worked in the mines you would die young.

For a copper miner there was no time or motivation to dream, no time to plan ahead or reason to consider retirement and no reason to save money. Every month someone lost his life in the holes. Many times men died by the dozens. It was accepted. With cave-ins, explosions, floods, and sudden bursts of poison gases, the life of a miner was a life where death was a constant. With life so cheap, few blamed those who played out their extra hours gambling, drinking, cheating, and cussing as if those moments were their last on earth. It was a mentality brought on by the mines and it was the overriding attitude of almost everyone who called this city home.

Though the mines were still the heart and soul of the area's commerce, by the Depression the glory days of mining were fast becoming a part of Butte's history. Yet the spirit and attitudes created by those days were still very much a part of the town's life. In spite of attempts by countless clergymen to "save" the people of Butte, in spite of civic leaders who again and again tried to clean up the city's image, many citizens still drank hard, partied long, and lived life as if death was just around the corner.

So on October 17, 1938, the day Robert Craig Knievel was born, Butte's western heritage was very much alive, and the wild elements of the frontier days were not as much a part of the past but of the present. Evel Knievel probably couldn't have come out of anyplace else but this Montana town. In everything he would do, he represented the city's history. He would have easily fit in with that first band of prospectors, the rich mining barons, the lowly miners, and even those who tried to clean the town up. And as impossible as it sounds, at one time or another, he would have made all those groups proud.

Evel's story, born in the Big Sky Country and taken to the world, is unique, unbelievable, and truly American. Yet without Butte, the daredevil probably would have never captured the world's spotlight and become the last gladiator of a modern Rome. It was this city that gave him his name and gave him the stuff that made him a star. Here, surrounded by history and the cruel life of the mines, the boy would grow into a man. And the stubborn courage this man would exhibit in arenas around the world, the constant excesses he embraced at every stage of his life, his thirst for adventure and fame, were born of the fabric of those who grew up in the shadow of Butte's colorful history.

2

The Evil Eye

Life was never easy in Butte, but things were very bleak during the late thirties. The Great Depression had hit the town and the mining industry hard. Faced with limited employment opportunities, many people were fleeing the area to look for work. Others were getting by on handouts. Only a very few were untouched. Sadly, the harsh times brought out the worst in many of those hit the hardest.

With jobs few and far between, with no one willing to lend money, and with FDR's job programs giving aid to only a few, many people were suicidal. Others, overcome by hopelessness, turned to drink. A handful even turned to crime. During this dark period of American history it was often tough for a single man to eke out a living in Montana, but it was especially difficult for a newly married couple. Divorce rates were high and love that survived those trying times was strong indeed.

On October 17, 1938, Robert and Ann Knievel may have welcomed the new baby boy who came into their lives, but they were hardly ready to raise him. Though Ann quickly became pregnant again, the bad times had already taken a heavy toll on the couple. The pressures of feeding and taking care of a baby, combined with the knowledge that another child was on the way, made the Knievels feel unprepared and ill-equipped. Hopelessness was all around them. For most people during this time, seeing the future meant little more than making it through that day. That was all Robert and Ann tried to do. Yet filled with questions and lacking answers, the newlyweds drifted apart. By 1940, they could see no way to salvage their union and they divorced. Leaving Butte to start rebuilding their lives indepently of each other, Robert and Ann gave Bobby and newborn son Nic to their paternal grandparents. Both parents felt this was the right thing to do. The older couple could give the boys a home, stability, and a chance at a normal life. Neither of the parents could offer that kind of promise at this time.

Just a year and a half old, Bobby Knievel was in a way alone. Though he would never blame his parents for leaving him, their absence would certainly leave a void that his grandparents couldn't completely fill. Yet Bobby's grandparents tried very hard.

Ognatius and Emma Knievel did everything they could for Robert and Ann's children. Though well past child-rearing age, the tire store owner and his wife devoted hours to the kids who called them Mother and Father. Even though times were tough and the couple and their store weren't doing that well, Bobby and Nic never lacked for toys, bikes, fishing equipment, clothes, and books. The Knievels constantly sacrificed to give the boys whatever they could. And material things were not the only gifts the older couple freely presented to their grandchildren. They also gave their time.

Some of the boys' best memories were of weekends hiking, fishing, and camping. Their grandparents taught them all about the wildlife in the barren lands around their hometown, and they made sure the boys came to appreciate the beauty and majesty of nature. There was never any doubt that the grandparents deeply loved these two boys. It was also obvious to all who saw this Knievel family together that Bobby and Nic loved and respected their grandparents dearly.

With her husband often working long hours at the store, most of the child-rearing fell to Emma. She did her best with the high-energy Bobby. Yet in truth a woman half Emma's age couldn't have kept up with him. Even before he was in school Bobby was exploring every part of Butte. Embodying the town's living-on-the-edge philosophy, the boy would jump on unbroken horses and try to ride them, race his bike down long steep hills, and fight anyone who said he wasn't tough. He was a child with enough spirit for an entire hockey team and enough energy to fuel a locomotive on a cross-country run. In the right place and time this could have been a wonderful combination of personality elements, yet in Butte during the Depression these traits were explosive. Those who had this much fire almost always ended up in trouble.

As an adult Bobby would remember Butte as a mean town. It was too. Butte had been a wild open place when times were good, but now that people were just barely scratching out a living, it was often openly hostile. Even before he could read Bobby had grown familiar with pimps, whores, and gamblers. He saw them all the time. All around him he watched con games and con artists. Early on he was sharp enough to observe that those who lived a bit outside the law had a much better life than those who worked in the mines and followed the words written in the Good Book. It was easy to understand how any child brought up in this environment would believe a strong person took what they wanted when they wanted it. That was the way of life.

The heroes of Butte where the same ones that children lionized in rural Oklahoma—Bonnie and Clyde, Pretty Boy Floyd, and Machine Gun Kelly. Though they were no longer terrorizing banks, the men and women who had once blazed across the nation defying the law were very real to those still suffering after a decade of hard times. Many here believed that it was better to go out famous in a blaze of glory that simply waste away in a backwater town. In their minds heroes died young but lived well during their short lives. In the bleak days of the Great Depression, there were few people who looked like heroes to the town's youth. Certainly the policeman didn't look like heroes.

Yet it wasn't that the cops were seen as the bad guys either. In Bobby's young eyes the police were friendly people who tried hard. He knew these men were concerned with people's lives, but by and large they were helpless to stop the will of the people. In Butte this meant that disputes were settled with fists or guns. It had always been a man-to-man, in-your-face kind of place that bred generations of the same kind of people. Vigilante justice was encouraged. If someone wronged you or your family, then it was your right to call them out.

The courts were therefore seen by many as places to settle traffic fines, not rule on acts of violence.

Emma had seen far too many of Butte's children grow up and embrace the barbaric rule of the Old West. She didn't want her own grandkids to fall under this spell. She knew that the kind of thinking that ruled the bars of Butte would only bring pain and bitterness to those she loved. Yet with so many reinforcing this view, it was hard for the woman to present an alternative to her grandchildren.

To balance the lessons he was getting on the street, Emma spent time with Bobby every chance she had. She preached kindness and generosity. She spoke of loyalty and living within the law. She told him that doing what was right didn't mean a person was weak. Bobby listened, but to a large degree what he observed around him had more impact on his life than Emma's words. Yet there was one area where her dedication and devotion took root and grew.

Emma Knievel loved her country. During World War II she was a flag-waving patriot. Even though Bobby and Nic were too young to understand what was going on in Europe and the Pacific, Emma shared with them why being an American was so dear to her. She taught them respect for the flag and the people who fought for it. Through example she gave them both a deep abiding love of everything that was red, white, and blue.

Even as young as five years old, Bobby fully embraced what his grandmother had taught him about loyalty to his nation. In the neighborhood war games the children played, he was always the soldier fighting for his country and his flag. He saw himself as the guy who could take any hill or beach for the United States. He was never the private or the common G.I., he was always the hero. In his mind he was Gary Cooper and John Wayne all rolled into one. He could beat anyone who dared insult the U.S.A. He thought that if you would just leave him alone in a room with Hitler, he could end the war in a few minutes.

Yet in truth it was hard to be the kind of hero Bobby heard about on the radio or watched in the movies. In Butte, the Lone Ranger and Superman were great guys, but they would have flopped in the Knievel neighborhood. Like most in Butte, Bobby's street was filled with tough, hard people. Many had chips on their shoulders against not only those they saw as their personal enemies, but against the police, banks, stores, and government. These people were often on missions of revenge. They wore their attitudes on their faces. They would cuss and fight for no reason. Many of them took pleasure in trying to beat children. They were bullies fueled by a lack of understanding of the world. Caught out of time, the world passing them by, unprepared for change they were hanging onto the past and its ways and everyone had to watch out for them.

Though America was still a man's world, it was probably more so in Butte. Women were often seen as nothing more than servants. They were to do what a man wanted. They had few rights and many received no respect. Abuse was open and rarely questioned. With women looked upon as frail servants, it was little wonder that the worst insult a boy could give another boy was to call him a sissy. No one would ever call Bobby Knievel that and get away with it. Yet even though they ruled this man's world, the men of Butte had it rough too.

There seemed to always be a fight for control taking place in some section of town. On every street corner there always seemed to be someone trying to be the toughest guy in town. The scuffles the kids had in their backyards were only practice matches for adulthood. Most of the fights weren't broken up either. Two men battled it out until only one was standing. Then the winner bought everyone a drink. Fighting was not to be avoided, it was the kickoff to partying.

Alcoholism was also a big problem in Butte. When Bobby was a child there were more bars in Butte per capita than in any other town in the nation. Many all but lived in those establishments. On his trips exploring town Bobby would often step over drunks in the street or see them passed out in alleys. These scenes were not viewed as a sad commentary on life, but as just a part of the landscape. Many who lived in Butte might have even thought every American town was like this.

The abuse, drinking, and lawlessness were hardly the kind of images that promoted a positive attitude. The fact was, even in the eyes of an imaginative child, Butte had to be seen as a depressing place.

11

Yet for some reason, Bobby usually had a smile on his face and a bright outlook. In his mind, life was a show put on for his benefit. And he was enjoying that show.

A part of this attitude had to come from his being so bright. Even in grade school Bobby had more common sense than most adults, and his teachers knew he had the innate intelligence to do anything he wanted. Yet even though Emma tried to get him interested in studies, school didn't really interest him. Bobby could see that schoolteachers were usually poorer than miners. They drove old cars and wore out-of-style clothes. If having an education meant living in near poverty, then what good was it?

Sensing that as he grew older his undirected energy would get him into trouble, Emma tried to direct Bobby into organized activities. She attempted to interest him in the Boy Scouts and vacation Bible school. She also tried art. With a pen or brush in his hand, Bobby was a natural.

Long before most of his peers could read, Bobby was drawing beautiful pictures. He could sketch almost anything. Emma so wanted Bobby to use his talent to escape working in the mines. When she discovered he could draw she bought him art supplies and praised his efforts. She constantly urged him to do more, but Bobby had other things on his agenda. While he like to create images on paper, he really wanted to be outside. He wanted to see the world, even the bleak one around Butte.

When she failed at getting Bobby motivated to study his books or continue with art, Emma tried sports. Though small for his age, he was a natural at everything from skating to hitting a baseball. Always the star of his teams, he really seemed not to care much about the team concept. In basketball he wanted to score every basket. In hockey he wanted to score every goal. In baseball there was simply too much dead time waiting for something to happen to hold his interest. Yet when the spotlight did shine on him, young Knievel always delivered.

During a baseball game, the skinny kid once pulled a Babe Ruth trick out of his hat. Looking into the face of the area's best pitcher, Knievel stepped out of the box and stared the boy down. As their eyes locked, Bobby fixed his steely gaze on the older boy until the hurler turned away. When he stepped back into the box, Knievel looked toward the fence. Digging in as he waited for what he knew would be a fastball, Bobby continued to stare into the pitcher's eyes. From the dugout his teammates took note of the eye-to-eye duel and starting baiting the opposing player.

"Bobby's giving you the *evil eye*, pitch."

"Knievel's *evil eye* is on you, boy."

"Knievel's evil and he is going to get you."

As the pitch was delivered, Bobby crushed the ball. As he rounded third base he gave the pitcher one more evil stare. By knocking a ball far out of the park, Bobby backed up his actions. This backing up is what he stood for, first publicly displayed in a child's baseball game, would become one of the hallmarks of his adult life.

Though this first use of *evil* and *Knievel* together wouldn't last, it was a bit of foreshadowing of what was to follow. And though his grandmother often missed it, there was a lot of devil in Bobby Knievel.

It may have been caused in part by his small, skinny frame, but even in grade school Bobby was always testing his limits. He would do anything on a dare. If someone dared him to steal something, he would. If they challenged him to a race, he would run it. Though his mouth was often the loudest, he also backed up every one of his brags. Even if he couldn't land on his feet after jumping off a roof, if he had said he could do it, he tried it. He discovered early that people respected you if you tried. Yet more than respect, Bobby liked attention. He often went to great lengths to get it too.

Bobby was soon not only known for his evil eye in baseball. His grandparents' neighbors were starting to shake their heads every time they saw the kid. Many of them thought of Bobby as the original dead-end kid. They sensed that Mr. and Mrs. Knievel had been put in charge of a force that was a lot more devil than angel. Everything he did, from "borrowing" anything he wanted without asking to racing through flower gardens on his bike, got on the neighbors' nerves. Eventually, when talking about the problem child who lived on their street, the residents began using the term that evil Knievel kid. Bobby laughed it off, but his grandmother couldn't.

Emma knew there was an energy in the boy that defied both logic and authority. She knew that her biggest challenge in life was trying to keep Bobby focussed. She never quit looking for ways to keep him out of trouble. Yet for every step he took in the right direction, he always seemed to take one the wrong way too. He was always getting into scrapes or doing something that riled someone. Even when he was by himself trouble just seemed to find him.

The hills around Butte were honeycombed with mine shafts. At times and without warning whole homes would simply fall a few feet into the earth as one of the shafts collapsed. Everyone knew where there were homes whose roofs were the only thing left above ground.

One day when Bobby was walking home, he crossed an old dirt road. Halting in the middle to look at something or play with a toy, he forced a man in a car to come to a screeching stop to avoid hitting him. As the man blew his horn and cussed, demanding that the boy move, Bobby just grinned and stared him down like he once had that youth league baseball pitcher. Finally, just as he was about to start walking and let the man drive by, Bobby heard a load roar coming from beneath the ground. Looking back at the man still blowing the old sedan's horn, Bobby watched as the earth disappeared under the auto. Suddenly the car was gone! The earth has swallowed it.

Most children would have been horrified to witness such a tragedy and would have immediately run home to tell their families. The story the old-timers in Butte still tell is that Bobby walked up to the edge of the hole, peered down to see it could find the car, then dropped a rock down the shaft to see how far the car had fallen. After he had fully taken in the scene, he finally found an adult and told him about the accident.

Though this scene was included in a 1971 movie about Knievel's life, there is some debate about if it really happened the way legend has it. Yet fact or fiction, the story correctly presents the attitude of Butte at the time. Because of mining, life was cheap. Even a child was not shocked by death occurring right in front of him. This was Bobby's world and it had a profound effect on him.

Yet while Bobby couldn't have ever become an American icon or a life-risking daredevil without Butte's influence, the city alone didn't make Evel Knievel. A great deal of it had to with Bobby's own God-given talent.

As he grew, so too did his ability to talk. Even when he was just eight years old he was a dynamic conversationalist. Because of his gift of gab, those around him did what he wanted them to do. He was their leader. He could sell anything to anyone. He could convince his friends to buy old bicycle parts they didn't need or even purchase a half-eaten candy bar they didn't like. He could even talk them into paying to watch him roll down a hill or ride a bike on a busy road. He was a natural salesman. Many believed he could sell a deserted mine shaft to the president of the Anaconda Mining Company. Given a chance, he probably would have tried too.

Bobby was not only a salesman, he was cool even before anyone knew what that meant. Like another future icon growing up at the time, Elvis Presley, Bobby wasn't afraid to be different. While his friends were dreaming of playing baseball with the St. Louis Cardinals or New York Yankees, Bobby was much more focused on sports that involved individual effort. As had been proven in his early outings in sports, he didn't want to stand with a team, he wanted to stand out by himself. He found out early on it took courage to earn cheers in this kind of arena.

He loved rodeos. Bobby thrilled at watching a man get on the back of a huge, unruly bull and hang on for dear life as the animal attempted to break every bone in the rider's body. He would have eagerly traded places with even the men who were tossed to the ground and kicked by the bull that had thrown them.

He also loved to go out to the ski-jump ramps in the winter and see the skiers risk life and limb leaping off the ramp and flying through the air. Like many of the adults who watched with him, he gloried in their crashes even more than their perfect flights. While a safe landing was to be applauded, the men who missed their landings and were thrown head over heels down the mountain were the ones who thrilled Bobby the most. He was awed by their courage.

Rodeo riders and ski jumpers fell as often as they hit their marks. Yet what Bobby saw that so many others his age missed was these men always got back up and tried it again. In their sports failure wasn't measured the same way it was in the busy world. In rodeo and ski jumping, winning was not as important as trying. This concept would later play not only a large part in Bobby's athletic experiences in high school, but it would also come to direct the boy's dreams and energy as a young man. Yet even with these insights coupled with his flair for salesmanship and obvious leadership abilities, Bobby Knievel the boy probably wouldn't have evolved into Evel Knievel the daredevil if his grandmother hadn't taken him to a traveling thrill show.

Joey Chitwood was a legend to many rural Americans. His auto daredevil shows were like no other traveling entertainment events in the world. In the 1940s Chitwood and his team were using Ford flathead V8-powered cars to jump from ramp to ramp, race through walls of fire, do balletlike high-speed criss-cross patterns while just missing human cones, as well as other assorted death-defying feats that included planned crashes, choreographed rollovers, and fiery wrecks. Crowds at county fairs and local stock car races ate up these shows. So did an eight-year-old Bobby Knievel.

Initially Emma must have thought Chitwood's daredevils had given birth to a miracle. She had never seen Bobby stay still for that long before. Fascinated and awestruck, he was all but stonelike. Yet this trancelike state didn't mean he wasn't taking it all in. One of the things the child observed was the reaction of the crowd when it looked like someone was about to kill themselves in a stunt. Everyone was excited, giddy, scared, and happy all at the same time. Their focus was given completely to the men and the event. Nothing else mattered. They forgot about their problems, the sorry state of Butte's economy, and their own dead-end lives. The only thing that interested them at that moment was watching some fool try to kill himself doing something they knew couldn't be done. Yet when that fool completed the stunt and didn't die, they weren't disappointed, only impressed. They cheered him like he was a hero.

Emma had hoped that Bobby would enjoy the show. She thought it would give them something to talk about. Yet what the older woman couldn't have guessed was that her grandson would see this show as an inspiration. If she had known her Bobby was going to seize Chitwood's performance and try to make it a part of his own life, she probably would have kept the boy at home that day. Yet more than just talk about the show all night long after they returned home, Bobby got up the next morning and literally tried to relive it.

"I got a couple of doors out of my grandfather's garage and propped them up on buckets," Knievel later told *Sports Illustrated*. And that was just the beginning. Getting his bike out, he raced up one home-made ramp and flew through the air until he landed on the other ramp. Nothing he had ever attempted had given him such a rush. He must have felt freer than he had ever thought possible.

Once the jump became routine, Bobby moved the doors further apart. He kept moving them until he had a gap of several feet between his homemade ramps. It was then Bobby ran out of speed and luck. Placing the doors too far apart, the young daredevil sailed through the air and came down with only his front wheel landing on the far ramp. When he crashed to the ground he had nearly torn his bike's frame in half. Just as he pulled himself to his feet, his grandfather appeared. Scared the boy was badly injured, the older man rushed up to comfort the third grader. When he discovered Bobby was unhurt, his concern quickly evolved into anger. Turning Bobby over his knee, he spanked the boy until tears of pain welled up in his eyes. Yet Bobby was too proud to cry out. He took the licking like a man.

With the spanking and the lecture that followed, the elder Knievel probably thought Bobby's days of jumping were over. Yet as soon as he got another bike, the kid set up the ramps again. Learning from not only his first bad jump, but the dozens that followed, young Knievel began to understand just how far he could push his luck. He also discovered that while his friends were impressed with his stunt the first few times, they grew bored when he did it again and again.

Sensing he needed more than just a couple of ramps and a gap of bare ground, Bobby put his mind to work. Remembering how Joey Chitwood's show had used fire, he piled up sagebrush, lit it with a match, and jumped the burning bush. Now his friends saw the risk. This was something they wouldn't try.

Armed with a gimmick that set him apart, Bobby organized his own show, talked his friends into paying a few dimes to see him possibly hurt himself, and then jumped everything from water to fire. Though he would eventually total four more bikes, the thrill of wowing other kids proved worth the bloody knees and elbows created by all the bad landings. For a few moments, as he flew through the air, Bobby was the only person in the spotlight. He not only had his friends' money, he had their respect too.

What began with bikes and fire would evolve into powerful motorcycles and long rows of cars. Yet before Bobby Knievel could find a real spotlight, he would have to survive his teen years in Butte. And this would prove a challenge not only for young Knievel, but for most of the town.

3

Bobby Embraces Evil

Even in Butte, a town where everyone seemed to have a rebellious streak, Bobby stood apart. He might have been short and skinny, but what he lacked in size he made up for in guts and gall. Knievel's younger brother, Nic, often says that his brother did everything to excess. In his many conversations with the media, Bobby always seems to agree with that assessment. He never knew when to quit.

Even before he was a teenager, Bobby was stealing hubcaps. He wasn't just taking a few here or there to sell for pocket money; once he got started he would swipe every hubcap on the street. Like jumping his bicycle between two barn door ramps, the kid always seemed to want to know how far he could take each new adventure. He seemed forever in search of his limits.

Most of his early efforts at hubcap thievery took place in the daylight. The cover of darkness might have made his pranks a lot easier, but Bobby just loved to live on the edge. He seemed to relish the thrill of taking a risk. He didn't really have a criminal mind, just a personality that thrived on the special high brought on by stress and danger.

In Butte there were a lot of ways besides stealing hubcaps for Bobby to experience this kind of rush. In the bleak terrain around his dusty hometown, there were many steep hills. A sane person wouldn't even attempt to climb down most of these drop-offs, however few people believed that the Knievel boy was sane. This assessment seemed to be constantly proven true as Bobby regularly challenged most of the steepest grades on his bicycle. Rarely was he able to make it from the top of the hill to the bottom without crashing. Skinned knees, cut arms, and bleeding gashes in his head were almost always the rule, but in spite of the pain, what most people thought was crazy, he relished as the ultimate in fun.

For almost everyone there is something appealing about being at the top of a steep grade, being able to see for miles. Though it was often a challenge to get to these places in Butte, most of the kids in town loved to ride their bikes up to the "top of the world." Yet after seeing the view, all except Bobby would then retrace their original paths back to the bottom via a road. Knievel was different. While his friends began to glide easily down the hill on a road, he would linger at the top until he had found the steepest grade, then holler and wave to his friends, before tossing caution to the wind. As the other kids watched his wild hillside rides, they were in awe. Their parents may have warned them about Bobby—the adults almost always called the kid insane—but the young daredevil's friends knew different. Bobby wasn't crazy, he just had more guts and wanted more glory than anyone they knew.

When he wasn't stealing hubcaps or flying down hills on his bike, Bobby found other ways to seek challenges. A favorite was throwing rocks at prostitutes. One of Butte's echoes from the past were the many streetwalkers who still lived in the city. When the kid would spot one of them, he'd throw rocks at them. He didn't cast stones to make a moral statement, or even to hit and hurt the women, he just wanted to begin a game that could be almost as large a challenge as speeding down a hillside. As he watched the gilded ladies race down the streets in their outlandish clothing, cussing him as they ran, he would stand out in the open waiting for the next phase of his game— the chase.

Within minutes of his initial assault, the prostitute's pimp would come flying down the street looking for the kid who had tossed the rocks. With courage far beyond reason, Knievel would wait until the man saw him, wave, and then take off jogging. While the kid was well aware of what would have happened to him if he had been caught, he felt the thrill of the race was worth the risk. Though incredibly quick for his age, Bobby would only run fast enough to allow the angry man to believe he had a chance at cornering the boy. By keeping the opponent in the match, the fun would last longer. Finally, when the pimp wore out and stopped, his chest heaving and breath coming in gulps, Bobby would give a final salute and jog on home.

The local coaches knew that Bobby was an excellent track prospect, as he had proven time and time again on the back streets of Butte. While it was easy for him to defeat opponents much older and stronger than he was, Bobby couldn't stay as focused on cinder tracks as he could on Butte's streets. Even in big track meets there just wasn't the same thrill as there was when a pimp or a local cop was hot on his trail. If he won a race, he got a ribbon. But even if he didn't finish first, he lost nothing. It just wasn't a trade-off that excited him very much. With no risk involved, there was little thrill in the activity. Track and field, a sport he could have dominated, thus seemed boring to the boy.

Hockey was another example of how Bobby's concept of life was far different than that of his friends. A very good defenseman, he could wow the crowd with his reactions and speed. Yet when he intercepted the puck on the far end of the rink, he wouldn't think of passing or looking for help, Bobby would try to take the puck all the way to the other end of the ice and attempt to score all by himself. He just wouldn't think of looking for an open teammate. And if you tried to stop him he would run you over in a heartbeat. It was almost as if he wanted to hit someone even more than he wanted to score. And the Knievel phase of the game meant that when bodies collided, even if he wasn't one of those who had tumbled to the ice, the gloves came off and Bobby would be in the middle of the brawls.

Emma, his grandmother, attended all of Bobby's hockey games. She watched him push, shove, and slash. She knew that eventually there would be a fight. She was also aware that at some point an opponent who was bigger and stronger than Bobby would pick him up and dump him over the side of the rink. Countless times she watched her grandson land headfirst against the concrete floor. Everyone in the crowd would rise as one, fearing the boy had been seriously injured. Many of the men would get ready to pick him up and rush him to the hospital, however Emma never seemed to worry. She knew that Bobby would bounce up, wipe the blood away from his eyes, and jump back into the game. He would also jump back into the fight, going after the kid who had dumped him out of the rink.

With his abrasive attitude it was hardly surprising that young Knievel was assigned to the penalty box more than any other player on his team. On many nights he spent more time in the box than all the other players on both teams combined. Yet his love of winning, his fiery spirit, and his competitive drive inspired his teammates and struck fear in his opponents' hearts. Though at times they didn't like his attitude, coaches saw the promise of professional potential in the boy. He had the speed and the stick ability; the challenge would be getting him to respond to the team concept.

Even when he was not playing hockey, basketball, or running track, Bobby was finding other ways to display his seemingly endless supply of God-given abilities. One of his most incredible abilities was a product of his quick smile and real charm. He was not just outgoing, he was friendly and smooth. In a world where most adults were rough and raw, Bobby was as polished as a seasoned politician. He could talk to adults as well as kids, and was intimidated by no one.

By the time he was a freshman in high school, he was using his talents to con adults and line his pockets with cash. He was a natural salesman, and at Bobby Knievel's "store," inventory was never a problem.

Countless times Bobby would steal the hubcaps off a new car, then a few minutes later come back to the scene and point out to the victim that his wheel covers were gone. After trying to help the man find them, Bobby would explain he might have some that were almost like them at home. The boy would then volunteer to race home and check it out. A little while later he would bring back the caps he had stolen and show them to his potential customer. Bobby would then name his price, usually the grateful man would pay the kid a few dollars, watch the friendly salesman fit the hubcaps back on his car, then, smile as the boy walked away. Amazingly, even though almost everyone in Butte was aware of the scam, he was so charming and convincing that few of Knievel's pigeons ever figured out they had been taken by the teenager.

Bobby got so good at the hubcap con that he moved it up a level. Rather than just stopping with the hubcaps, Bobby would jack the car up, taking the caps, wheels, and tires, leaving the auto resting on the ground without any "shoes." Butte old-timers still laugh about the way the young con man would approach an angry out-of-towner who had just discovered he had been ripped off.

After a friendly greeting, Bobby would inquire what was wrong. When he was shown the car, the kid would become very sympathetic. He would feign surprise that something like this could happen in such a friendly, law-abiding place as Butte. Then, after convincing the victim how sorry he was about the loss and lamenting how much it was going to cost the poor guy to replace the wheels and tires—if he could even find any that would fit in Butte—Bobby would say good-bye and start to walk away. Then, after only a few steps, he would turn back as though he had just remembered something. Pointing out that his grandfather owned a tire business, Bobby would explain that he believed at the store there were some wheels that already had tires mounted on them that might fit this car. He further stated that because the victim was from out of town and had been wronged right in the heart of Butte, Bobby thought he could convince his grandfather to let the whole set go for thirty dollars. The overjoyed man would usually jump at the deal. After Bobby retrieved the stolen goods and mounted them back on the car, the gentleman would quickly pay him, look both ways to ensure no one had seen him deal with the boy, then jump into his car and race away. Usually the victims got out of town as quickly as they could because they thought the tires and wheels they had bought from the kid were so cheap they had to have been hot. They would never discover that all Bobby had really given them was a full tire rotation.

In truth the con games just began on the street. Bobby was always looking for an angle to exploit people's ignorance and greed.

When Knievel was in high school, Marsh's Jewelry in Butte was robbed. The local store carried the finest jewelry in the area. It was a place where the rich bought and the poor dreamed of buying. Needless to say, the theft created a great deal of excitement in the area and everyone had his own thoughts as to who pulled the job. However, the police had no clues. All the cops knew for sure was the bandits had walked away with a large cash of necklesses, bracelets, and rings.

At school, like everyone else, Bobby began to talk about the heist. Yet the things he said seemed to indicate he knew a lot more about how it was done than even the police did. Sensing that Knievel just might have had the guts to do something really big, his friends finally worked up the nerve to ask the boy if he had done the deed. Rather than reply, Bobby just smiled. At first only a few kids thought their friend had pulled the job. Yet the way he was acting and the smug look on his face caused the whispers to grow louder. It didn't take long for a majority of those who knew Bobby to buy into the fact that he was the man behind the robbery. This belief was sealed when Knievel showed up a few days later with some jewelry he wanted to sell cheap.

For several weeks Knievel sold necklesses and bracelets at bargain basement prices and his friends bought all that they could afford. For the folks who had never had the money to buy the "good stuff" from Marsh's, knowing what they were purchasing was hot meant nothing. As a matter of fact, many of them actually wanted to own the jewelry because it was hot. It made them feel as they were rebelling and very proud of it. For a while anyway.

About the same time Bobby quit talking about the robbery and stopped selling his wares, his customers discovered they had bought nothing more than cheap, costume jewelry. The young con artist hadn't robbed the store, only taken advantage of a profitable situation by letting people think he had. The morning after Marsh's had been hit, Bobby had gone to the dime story and bought every cheap bit of jewelry he could find. He then allowed his attitude to influence the way people looked at his wares. He knew that they would see what they wanted to see, not what was really in front of their eyes.

Using some of the money he had made from his various scam games, Knievel purchased a Triumph T-120 motorcycle. Though it had no lights or brakes, and though he had little experience with motorbikes, within minutes of its purchase, Bobby was racing it up and down streets and hills at breakneck speed. He probably would have ridden the bike until it ran out of gas if he had not hit a parked car. As he lost control of the Triumph, it tossed him to the ground, hit a curb, and caught on fire. The bike was destroyed and Bobby broke his leg. Yet despite the painful introduction to the world of motorcycles, and maybe because of it, Knievel was hooked. As soon as he recovered, he bought another cycle. This second one, and all those that followed, would have not only a dramatic effect on the Butte police force, but on the way the world would come to look at Bobby.

Since his days tossing rocks at streetwalkers, Knievel had always enjoyed playing games of chase. Especially when there was some risk involved. As soon as he got a feel for riding his cycle, he traded pimps for police officers and began a cat-and-mouse game with the local cops. In this contest the winner walked free, the loser took a trip to the station house.

As part of his game plan, Bobby regularly baited the police. He would spot a squad car, then devise a plan to catch the cop's attention. He would often just roar by at well over the speed limit. Other times he would jump his bike up onto the sidewalk and create enough havoc for the authorities to become interested. At times he would pop and hold a wheelie for blocks. He would do whatever it took to taunt and provoke the policeman.

However the game of cat and mouse began, the remainder of the exercise was played out with Bobby managing to keep just far enough ahead of the squad car to make the officers feel they had a chance to catch him. Whenever they would get too close, he would turn down an alley or jump off the road and cut across a field to the next street.

Knievel and the police knew there were countless places in Butte where Bobby and his bike could go that a car couldn't. Most of the officers were also well aware that chasing the boy was fruitless. It would have been far more practical to have simply driven back to his grandparents and wait for him to come home. Yet when Bobby got them involved in the case, their competitive juices always began to flow. Over time this game of tag took on a life of its own and each of Butte's finest were bound and determined to be the first ever to catch Knievel while he was still astride his bike.

Bobby knew after his first few chases he was viewed in much the same way as the Warner Brothers' cartoon character the Road Runner. He also realized that the other parties in the chase were a great deal like Wile E. Coyote. Thus, in almost comic fashion, the good-natured chases became a diversion for the high-energy high schooler and the local men in blue. For Bobby, the cops, and everyone who watched, these races up and down the hills and back roads of Butte were a highly entertaining diversion in a very boring daily routine. Many locals even made bets on how long the police would chase Knievel before they gave up. Others were betting that even if the boy was caught, the cops would let him off with nothing more than a warning and a handshake.

On occasion the officers would get close to trapping the slippery cyclist. Once Bobby had taken a turn up a street with no outlet. Rather than chase him to the dead end, the cops simply blocked the road with the car and waited for the boy to turn around and come down the long hill. Seemingly having no way out, Knievel nevertheless headed back down the hill at top speed in what appeared to be a game of chicken. The officers were worried he was going to smash headlong into their car and kill himself. They were screaming at him to stop. Yet just before he got to the point where the car blocked his exit, Bobby swerved to his right and headed for a large pile of dirt that had been unearthed during recent city road work. Locals still claim he was going more than fifty miles an hour when he hit the dirt pile. Pulling his front wheel off the ground with his strong arms, Bobby used the piled-up earth as a ramp and sailed over the police car. Landing on his back wheel just a few feet beyond the vehicle, Knievel set his front tire down, slowed, looked over his shoulder, and waved farewell. Laughing, the awed cops waved back and vowed to get him the next time. And they realized there would be a next time, because it was obvious to them the restless kid would never settle down.

By the time he was sixteen, everyone in Butte was doing everything they could to get Bobby under control and keep him in school. Though he was bright, Knievel was impatient, independent, headstrong, and unfocused. He had problems sitting still for more than a few moments at a time. His gaze seemed always on what was going on in the world, not in the classroom. A star athlete in literally every sport the school offered—basketball, baseball, hockey, football, and track—Bobby was seen by students and faculty as a young man who could help Butte High win some area and state titles. However, the kid just didn't seem to care that much about team sports or a high school diploma. He couldn't see how either would take him away from the abject, depressing life that surrounded him. It seemed just a matter of time before he checked out of class and education for good.

At first, Bobby would stay away from school every once in a while. Soon, he would just be gone for a long stretch, then show back up. Finally, less than two years short of graduating, he just didn't come back.

As Bobby would quickly discover, a high school dropout had few opportunities in Butte. His father offered him one bit of salvation. Having just moved back to town with his second wife and their daughters, Jeanne, Christie, Renae, and Robin, Robert, Sr., wanted Bobby to work for him at his VW dealership. The "people's car," as the Bug was then called, had recently arrived on the American scene. So ugly they were considered cute, easy to drive and repair, cheap to buy, and very inexpensive to use, VWs were quickly becoming a cult favorite and the first really successful import car in U.S. history.

Robert had seen his son work on his motorbikes. He knew the boy could help his dealership with his mechanical skills. He also knew that Bobby could sell anything to almost anyone. Pushing new cars would have seemed to fit the boy to a tee. Yet rather than jump at the chance, the younger Knievel looked elsewhere for a job.

The years of separation with only occasional visits from his dad had been harder on Bobby than even he could admit. Now that Robert, Sr., had a wonderful new family and a happy life, his elder son just didn't have much in common with him. More than that, he didn't want to rebuild a relationship at this moment either. He had grown up without a father, or at least with a grandfather who seemed like a father, and now that the real father had returned, Bobby considered himself to be too old to need him.

After walking away from what should have been a fairly easy job at the Knievel VW dealership, Bobby ended up where almost all of Butte's men found work—the Anaconda Mining Company. At sixteen years old, the teenager was sent underground in the copper mines. A diamond drill operator, Knievel would handle a powerful hundred-foot drill bit and brace and use the tool to drill holes to allow water to escape from areas vital for mining operations. It was hard, dark, and dangerous work. Many drill operators had died in cave-ins and by suddenly being trapped by gases or floods. Yet it was an honest job that paid an honest wage and the kid did it well. For the few months Bobby pursued it, it also kept him pretty much out of trouble.

From underground, Knievel was promoted to surface duty. He drove a large earth mover and hauled dirt from the mining operation out to large man-made hills. One day, when Bobby had just loaded six tons of rock into the "Yuke's" bed, he decided to have some fun. Gunning the engine, he popped the huge vehicle's front wheels off the ground and did a motorcycle-type wheelie. Scores of tired men stopped their hard work to watch the kid perform, and smiles and applause broke out from all corners of the area. As Bobby fought to control the machine's wheelie and amaze his growing audience, he failed to notice a power line in his path. Striking the 4,800-volt line with the front of the "Yuke," Knievel literally turned the lights out all over town. With Butte's main power line cut, the community's citizens wondered what had happened. So did those who ran Anaconda. It took only seconds for Bobby's foreman to leave his office and storm up to the boy. After dressing him down with every curse word in his vocabulary, he fired Knievel on the spot. In less then a minute Bobby had gone from exalted hero to humiliated goat.

In truth Knievel was not all that upset about losing the job. He hated working for Anaconda. He didn't like the routine, the long hours, or the demands of a daily work grind. Yet while being unemployed did not bother him, he was troubled by the way his boss had verbally assaulted and embarrassed him in front of the employees.

This feeling must have built up in his mind until the day came for him to return to the mine offices and pick up his final paycheck.

If the foreman had expected a confrontation, it didn't appear to be coming. A silent Knievel got his money, placed it in his pocket, and headed outside. Yet before getting on his motorcycle and heading back downtown, he climbed aboard his old trusty "Yuke" for a final time. Starting the huge earth mover, he repeated his work routine one final time, loading it with seventeen cubic yards of dirt. This time, rather than dumping the earth on the pile, he drove back to the foreman's hut. Lifting the dirt dumper, a smiling Bobby dropped all the dirt onto the office of the man who had humiliated him. Satisfied that he had now completed his last obligation to Anaconda, he parked the "Yuke" and left the employee parking lot for the final time. Though he appeared to come out on top in this battle, and even though he was applauded by scores who had been injured or ruined in the mines, the mining company had built a trap that would soon catch the kid.

With time on his hands, Bobby and Butte's finest again picked up their cat-and-mouse tag games. Initially, Knievel won them all. Yet the cops were getting better and closer. One day, as a hauntingly stiff breeze blew dust down the city's quiet streets, Anaconda and the cops got their revenge all at once. After leading a squad car on a long chase, Bobby raced up the side of one of the mining operation's huge man-made dirt mountains. Having never been on this hill before, the kid didn't know that the only way down was the way he driven up. Trapped, this time he had no dirt mound for a ramp. Rather than give himself up to the two officers sitting in the car waiting for him, Knievel decided to try to snake down the steepest side of the hill like he once had done on his bicycle. This time the drop was too long and too dramatic.

As he popped a wheelie to jump the hill's crest, Bobby realized he had made what seemed to be a fatal mistake. Butte bar patrons reported that he somehow managed to ride the bike most of the way down before the machine's front wheel found a large boulder. Flying over the two-wheeler's handlebars, Knievel rolled like a sack of potatoes to the bottom of the hill. By the time the police had driven down the road that wound from the top to the base of the Anaconda pile, Bobby was up, but in obvious pain. His bike was busted up even worse than he was.

After placing him in the back of the squad car, the officers drove the teen to the local hospital. Once his wounds had been patched and his arm placed in a sling, Bobby was given back to the cops. Now that Butte's Road Runner had finally been caught, he was ordered to spend the night in the city jail.

Hurting, his ego and body broken by his fall and capture, young Knievel was not at all thrilled with the prospect of spending the evening with drunks and thugs. He couldn't believe his friends on the police force would do this to him. Yet as they locked him up, laughed, and walked away, the freewheeling Bobby found himself confined like never before. It was not only humiliating, it was unnerving too.

A few hours after he been locked up, the night jailer came into the cellblock to check the role and make sure no one had escaped. After he had become a nationally known stunt performer, Knievel described to *Esquire*'s David Lyle what took place as the man read through the list of new prisoners.

"Hey, we got a guy named Knievel in one cell and another named Knoffle in the other." Knievel described the moment. "This guard thought it was funny as hell and he shouted, 'Goddamn! Double the guard! We got Evil Knievel and Awful Knoffle here tonight.'"

Though it was not the first time Bobby had been called Evil, this time it seemed to stick. Even though he only spent one night in jail, soon everybody on the police force was calling Knievel "Evil." Though it was meant as a joke, Bobby was soon falling into areas where he would have the chance to live up to his new nickname. He was driven to take new risks by hard times.

Though he had been able to earn some spending money by participating in local professional rodeos and ski-jumping events—Knievel even won a state ski-jumping title in 1956—his lack of employment began to cramp Bobby's style. Needing money for everything from dates to fixing his motorcycles, and realizing that there were few opportunities for a dropout in Butte besides mining, Knievel turned his thoughts to crime.

As an adult Bobby admitted to robbing a few businesses in his youth. He also emphasized that he never hurt anyone during these escapades, nor did he rob individuals. Yet how many times and in what fashion he pulled his jobs is now open to debate.

In Butte, Knievel's early days of crime are remembered as larger-than-life adventures. In a scene in the 1971 movie about his life, Bobby supposedly stole a case of dynamite from the Anaconda Mining Company explosives shack, broke into the county courthouse, and then tried to blow up the safe. While the explosion woke up half the town, the safe held tight. Never one to give up, Knievel returned to Anaconda, picked up more dynamite, and returned to a courthouse that was now a crime scene. As local authorities cleaned up the mess and looked for clues, Bobby supposedly waited for them to finish. After they left, he returned and finished the job he had started earlier in the evening. This time, using twice as much dynamite, the safe blew. Supposedly Bobby left with the take.

Much like he had done when Marsh's Jewelry had been robbed, Bobby allowed many people to think he had knocked over the court-house vault. In a town where many still thought of Bonnie and Clyde and Pretty Boy Floyd as American heroes, this kind of gall was to be respected. Because of the aura created by the daring robbery, Knievel became a local star. Many bar patrons bought him drinks and meals just to hear him not deny that he had done it.

Even while others were patting him on the back, there was little doubt that both Bobby's grandparents and his father were becoming increasingly concerned about the young man's lack of direction in life. They were worried he would end up in jail or dead. Unable to control him, seeing no future for him in Butte, they hoped the teenager would find some kind of direction for his life. As it turned out, Knievel didn't have to go looking for guidance, it came to him in the way of an invitation to join the United States Army. As Bobby Knievel left for basic training, Butte could breathe a little easier. However, for a while, the wild town grew a lot more boring too.

4

Evil Days

In truth, Private Robert Craig Knievel was not cut out for military life in the late 1950s. The routines of a peacetime soldier were not varied or challenging enough for him. He would have been far better suited to serving in World War II. During that era Bobby would have gladly stormed the beaches at Normandy or dueled Japanese Zeros in one-on-one dogfights from the cockpit of a P-51 Mustang. In the time of crisis, he would have been the man of the hour. He would have relished the chance for glory. The grim odds, scathing enemy fire, and exploding bombs would have only stoked his enthusiasm for he job. The young man lived for moments when there were real questions to be answered and genuine risks to be faced.

The closest Knievel came to danger in his military tour was when he jumped out of airplanes. Because the army made him wear a parachute on all of his thirty jumps, Bobby hardly felt challenged at all. While many in his group grew sick, their stomachs churning as the jump time approached, the free-spirited soldier from Butte was the laid-back picture of calm. For a man who had charged down countless hills on both bikes and motorcycles, as well as worked in the mines and perhaps blown up a safe or two, leaping out of a moving plane ten thousand feet above the ground was child's play.

Though he kept his nose fairly clean during his days in uniform, the almost two years in the service failed to accomplish what his family and most of his hometown's police force had hoped they would.

Bobby would not leave the army with any more clean, upright American values than he had on his first day of boot camp. He wouldn't change his ways or temper his attitude. He wouldn't realize the risk of walking on the wrong side of the law or taking unnecessary chances in life. His ego would not shrink and his wisdom would not grow. As a matter of fact, his entire tour of duty might have been wasted altogether if the military brass hadn't discovered what Knievel's high school coaches had once noted—the guy was an incredible athlete.

From boot camp to regular exercises, Bobby was at the top of his unit in anything that involved speed and agility. He could scale walls, jump ditches, and win hand-to-hand combat contests against bigger and stronger men. And while there were many who were bigger, there were now few who were stronger. Sporting 180 pounds spread over a well-formed six-foot frame, Knievel could have been the model for a fitness poster. With his blue eyes and blond hair, the teenager was also as handsome as he was agile. At times his buddies wondered if he had a Superman suit under his uniform. He stood apart, unchallenged and almost invincible.

Because of his physical attributes and competitive nature, the army took Bobby away from many of his daily chores to place him on their track team. Shoving a heavy aluminum pole in his hands, they taught Knievel the basics of how to vault. As always he was fearless. He worked so hard and learned so quickly that he had soon leapt past everyone on the team. Those instructing thought he was born to fly through the air.

At a meet, when Bobby was readying to race down the track to the pit, his eyes fixed on the bar, he seemed like a stone statue. Silent, intent, and focused, he was the picture of mind over matter. It was as if he were about to will himself over. So powerful was that will that some of his friends felt that he really didn't need the pole. If Bobby tried hard enough, he might just be able to fly. When he sank the pole into the box and lifted off the ground, it was almost as if he was not of this earth. Joy etched across his face, his eyes lit up with a fire, his muscles rippling, Knievel not only made vaulting a thing of immense grace and beauty, he grabbed the attention of everyone who was there. All eyes were fixed on him. In unison every head followed his flight. When he cleared the bar and tumbled to the ground, cheers erupted and a few coaches even shed a few tears. For a few moments, a time when he owned everyone in view, he was the star. Before Bobby left the service he was winning pole vault competitions against men from all branches of the service, colleges, and track clubs. His 14' 6" record was all but unheard of in the days before fiberglass poles. He was a champion literally on his way up and he had the marks and medals to prove it.

Many of the brass and his army coaches were hoping Knievel would re-enlist. They wanted him to stay around for the good of the army track and field team. Some seemed to believe that with enough time and work, the young man could suit up for his country in the Olympics. Yet the wishes of military officers would have no more impact on the young man than his high school coaches had once had. Bobby didn't care much about what he could mean to a track program or what benefits the army could give him if he re-upped, he was ready to get back to Butte. He was ready to trade in the military routine for the lazy days of carefree life in his hometown.

Bobby's homecoming must have been a nightmare for both the local police and the parents of every teenage girl in the area. The veteran not only remained untamed, but had grown into a powerful figure, well built and handsome. Worst of all, his old charms had matured as well. Knievel still might have been full of energy and mischief, but now he was a lady killer too. He represented the kind of trouble the town hardly needed.

Among the first to discover Bobby's return were the police. Even before he had time to unpack it seemed that he was back on the streets popping wheelies, riding on sidewalks, and driving up and down the steps of city buildings. With the wild man back in town and ready to make up for the years he had been out of circulation, the police dug in. They knew Knievel would be leading them on more wild-goose chases in his first week home than they had seen in the two years he had been gone. With cars gassed up and engines warm, they were determined to shut the boy down before he did some real harm or got into very serious trouble.

For a few weeks the cat-and-mouse games with the cops and catching up with old friends seemed to be Bobby's main focus. Constantly seeking fun, often getting into minor disturbances, abusing most of Butte's traffic laws on a daily basis, the boy was a holy terror on the streets, but the cops had come to the conclusion that he was not an evil or mean kid. In fact, he was usually nice and accommodating. In general, the men in blue liked him. Yet he still made their lives miserable. To many of these men it seemed that every other call that came across their switchboard was a complaint of some sort about Knievel.

The origin of many of these calls was the local high school. Though he had dropped out years before, Bobby was now spending more time on campus than he had when he was enrolled. He loved riding his cycle up the main building's long front steps, occasionally even pulling the bike through the front doors. He would also pop wheelies up and down the street in front of the campus, gunning his engine and disrupting class. Even though he was twenty, he was still acting like a teenager.

School officials soon discovered that Bobby had taken an interest in education because Linda Bork had grown up and he had noticed. Linda, who had been a cute little kid when he left school, was now a pretty high school senior. A nice girl from a good family, she knew better than to run around with Knievel's type. She was a good student, apparently headed to college, one of the most popular young ladies in town, a cheerleader, and not the least bit wild or rebellious. For many of the students and all the teachers, it seemed unfathomable that Bobby Knievel would be attracted to someone as classy and sweet as Linda. After all, every wild girl in the school would line up to do his bidding at any time. Why would he want someone this sweet and moral?

Linda was an unreachable prize, but Bobby had always tried to accomplish the impossible. He had never been interested in doing something that was easy, rather he wanted to do what most said couldn't be done.

Linda certainly qualified as the impossible dream. Her folks were not going to let her date the town rebel even if she wanted to. And she didn't want to. Bobby was nothing like the young men who attracted her. She wanted to go with the type who could give her a home with a picket fence and family. She wanted to find a boy who was stable and had solid plans. She didn't want to wind up with a guy who had dropped out of high school, wasn't interested in working a job in the nine-to-five world, and whose idea of dressing up was wearing clean jeans. Yet try as she might, she just couldn't seem to get this message across to her unwanted suitor. Even when she told him to get lost, he didn't.

Linda was taking a lot of teasing from her friends about Knievel. It didn't help that almost everyday when school let out, he was there on his bike. If she ignored him, he followed her. If she wouldn't talk to him, he would talk for both of them. If she was at the top of the steps, he would ride his cycle up the steps to her. Bobby was not hiding the fact that he was after the Bork girl; he was advertising it with his every action.

For a while this adventure in dating looked a lot like Knievel's cat-and-mouse games with the local cops. Except the roles had been reversed. Now it was Bobby doing the chasing and failing again and again to catch Linda. It seemed she knew all the moves to keep herself just out of his reach. Yet over time, the handsome young man's attention and his direct approach began to fascinate her. Probably his bad boy image did too. Soon, over her parents' objection, and sometimes without their knowledge, she was going out to eat or to a movie with Bobby. She was also riding with him on his motorcycle.

Knievel might have finally been able to convince Linda to date him, but his salesmanship failed in another area. The high school girl had a strict moral code and she was not going to bend it even for a man as good-looking and charming as Bobby Knievel. There would be no sex until after the two of them were married. As the chilly winter winds blew through the town, and as Linda's high school activities began to take her away from Bobby more and more, the crazy biker hatched a plan that he thought would answer all his problems.

If it hadn't been love at first sight when he returned from the service, it hadn't taken very many evenings with Linda to convince the young veteran he had to have her. Yet with her parents against him, with her school activities constantly pulling her away from him, and with her telling him he would have to wait on sex until after they were married, he seemed to have very little control over the woman he loved. Her parents were not going to allow a union until he changed, he wasn't going to change, and even as cold as it got in Montana, Hell wasn't going to freeze over. Frustrated, Bobby decided to do what had always worked for him, to take matters into his own hands.

On a late winter afternoon, when Bobby knew Linda would be skating with friends at the Butte rink, Knievel convinced a friend of his to help him kidnap the girl. Marco discovered this was no joke. Knievel really did intend on snatching the young woman and eloping with her. Telling his buddy to keep a truck running, Bobby skated onto the ice, spotted the pretty cheerleader, and put his plan in action.

"She couldn't get away from me," Knievel later told *Sports Illustrated*'s Gilbert Rogin. "I drug her by the hair and threw her in the back of the truck."

With Linda in the truck, Bobby jumped into his own car and followed Marco. Meanwhile, scores of Linda's friends were wondering if this was another of Knievel's pranks or if something unlawful had just happened. At the first chance he got, Knievel pulled up beside his friend's truck, got Linda, placed the protesting and shocked teen in his car, and raced off. Though she had a strong idea, she still hadn't been told what her boyfriend had in mind.

For one of the first times in his life, Knievel appeared scared. He knew he had to evade what would soon be a growing search party made up of both families and the police. He also had to convince Linda that running away and marrying him now, before she got her high school diploma, was the right thing to do. To complicate matters, as he was driving out of town, a snowstorm roared across Montana and hit the area with the biggest blizzard in years. Bobby had been in such a hurry to get away from the rink, he hadn't bothered to take off his skates. With snow flying and patches of ice threatening to slide the car from the road, he was having to operate his clutch, brake, and gas pedals with the blades of his skates. As the puffy flakes fell faster than his car's windshield wipers could swipe them away, it looked as if even God was against him.

One of the main problems with Bobby's plan was that he really didn't have much of a plan. The main thrust of the operation had begun and ended with the kidnapping. After that he was just flying by the seat of his pants. He hadn't considered the weather or the fact that he was breaking a very major law. His friends at the police force would not consider this a prank. Knievel had finally stepped over the line.

If he had assumed that it wouldn't take long for the city of Butte to come out in force to save the Bork girl, Knievel would have been right. The city police and the county sheriff's department were looking for the couple just minutes after Linda was dragged from the rink, and they were putting bulletins out over the radio and television. No one was treating this as a silly and meaningless joke. If he was caught in this game of chase, Bobby was going to have to spend some serious time in jail.

Hampered by the heavy snow, often unable to see more than a few feet in front of the car, Knievel stopped in front of an empty church and convinced Linda to go inside. As they hid in the sanctuary, the magnitude of what he had done must have begun to sink in. While he was worried about evading the law, Linda was lamenting the fact that she was supposed to cheering at a basketball game and was missing it. They were in two different worlds, even though they were sharing the warmth of the same physical environment.

For the moment Bobby didn't know if the cops were on his trail. Yet he realized that when Linda didn't show up for the game, no one would be able to convince her family that this had been another one of Bobby's crazy but harmless pranks. The Borks would be worried. They might even insist on calling out the FBI.

Feeling he had to get farther away from Butte, when the snow appeared to be slackening, Bobby hustled the young woman back into his car. They managed to drive in blinding conditions for several more miles before becoming stuck in a drift. Unable to dig out, Knievel gave up for the moment. The two spent the rest of the night, cold, hungry, and lost, as snow piled up around the car. It was a wonder they didn't freeze to death.

When the sun came up and the snow stopped, Bobby hiked through huge drifts to a farmer's house. Using the man's telephone, Knievel called a wrecker to come tow them out of trouble. When the truck arrived, Bobby had Linda hide in the backseat in order to mask who they were. After pulling them out of the ditch, the driver got back in his truck and watched the car drive away. When Knievel was out of sight, the tow truck operator radioed police. He told the authorities that Bobby was alive and well, but the girl was not with him. When she was told this story, Linda's mother assumed Bobby had killed her daughter and tossed her in a snowbank. Now it appeared that not only was Knievel a kidnapper, but a murderer too.

Because of the two feet of snow that held the whole state in its icy grip, Bobby couldn't manage to get very far from Butte. Every road he took was blocked. It would have been impossible to make it over the mountains to another state, and Canada was just too far away. As the hours ticked by and he found himself running out of options, it became obvious to the swaggering biker he was not going to be able to pull this off. By midday, less than twenty-four hours after he had plucked Linda from the rink, Knievel drove into a roadblock. This time he didn't try to run. As he got out of his car, he was searched, read his rights, and handcuffed. Linda was hustled back to her relieved and still very angry family.

Thanks to Linda convincing the Borks that Bobby hadn't meant to hurt her, the family didn't asked the prosecutor to file kidnapping charges. Instead Knievel was slapped with a charge of contributing to the delinquency of a minor. He was given a choice of either paying a five-hundred-dollar fine or spending a stretch in jail. Bobby's dad paid the fine, and the reckless young man walked free.

For the next few months Knievel had to become a gentleman in order to charm the Borks into letting him see their daughter again. He had to come out into the open and play the dating and courtship game honestly. After Linda graduated, and when her parents finally realized there was no way their daughter was going to go to college or forget the biker, the family gave in. On September 5, 1959, Bobby and Linda were married and started a life together. The bride and groom had little idea as to how challenging this adventure would really be.

As a high school dropout, Bobby had few job options. The mines didn't want him back, and working with his father didn't appeal to him much. Besides, he wasn't ready to live in an adult world. He still wanted to party, play games, and have fun. He figured there had to be a way to have a wife and the life he wanted. Thanks to athletic skills, a door did seem to open that promised all he wanted and more.

Since coming home from the service, Knievel had played on a local hockey team. He had shown enough promise on the Montana ice that a scout for the Eastern Professional Hockey League's Charlotte Clippers spotted him. The Carolina team offered Bobby a contract to play his favorite sport for money.

Knievel quickly became not only a fan favorite, but a team leader. Yet the applause wasn't enough. Bobby hated being away from Linda and Butte, and he quickly realized the National Hockey League was never going to see him play in Charlotte. With hard practices, a killer schedule, and long tedious bus rides between games, it was hardly the life for a man who didn't like to be confined. Not long into the season, with no hopes of making the NHL and the big paychecks that went with the top league, Bobby quit the Clippers.

One of the things Knievel had learned in his short stint with Charlotte was that the big money was not made by playing hockey, it was in owning the team. Coming home to Butte, Knievel started the Bombers, a semipro hockey team. Employing his gift of gab, he convinced local rink owners to let him use their facilities, other businesses to underwrite sponsorships, and many players to skate for almost nothing. As owner, coach, general manager, promoter, and player, Bobby not only lined up the opponents, but called all the shots. In his games with his teams, he also made sure there were enough fights and hard hits to keep fans coming back to see who might get injured or killed the next night.

Even with all his promotional skills, semipro hockey failed to generate much cash for the young man who was about to be a father. In order to fill the rink's seats and put some money in his pocket, Bobby knew that he was going to have to do something big. With the U.S. hosting the 1960 Winter Olympics in Squaw Valley, Utah, Knievel set his sights on trying to cash in on the Olympic fever that was sweeping the country.

While he knew the U.S. team was not going to come to Butte to play an exhibition, Bobby figured a foreign team might want to use his Bombers for a tune-up match. Though most of his friends told him what he was attempting was impossible, acting in his role as the team's general manager, the young man went to work. After several calls and a great deal of salesmanship, Knievel convinced the Czechoslovakian team to come to Montana and play his Bombers.

To get the Czechs, Knievel had promised to pay for their food and lodging during the days before and after the game. On paper this looked like a good deal. With a few house and concession sales, Bobby could see keeping a couple thousand dollars for himself. His plan would have worked too, if the Czechs' players, coaches, and team officials had numbered the usual twenty that accompanied most hockey teams. Knievel was shocked when he met more than forty representatives at the team plane. There were actually more government officials in the party than there were players and coaches. As Knievel the businessman and team owner counted heads, he knew that no matter how many seats and how much beer he sold, he was going to lose money on the deal. For one of the first times in his life, the master conman had been outconned.

The bad feelings caused by the Czechs taking advantage of Bobby's hospitality spilled over into the game. Fights broke out throughout the first and second periods. Usually Knievel was in the middle of them. Disgusted with what he felt were blatantly biased officials, the Czech coach threatened to pull his team from the ice if Bobby didn't allow him to officiate the remainder of the contest. Knowing he would have to return the ticket money if the opponents walked—and at this point he needed every penny he could find—Knievel gave in. With the foreigner in control, Bobby was hit with a game disqualification penalty and was booted out within moments of the last period beginning.

Disgusted, Knievel not only left the ice, he got dressed in his street clothes and left the building. Later, after the game ended and the Czech officials stopped by the box office to pick up their expense money, workers hired for the night discovered the game receipts had disappeared. They tracked down the Bombers' owner, but Bobby just shook his head and shrugged his shoulders. He did manage to explain that without the receipts, he couldn't pay the Czechs' expenses. He acted very sorry too. However, he didn't rush out to help find the crooks.

Over the next few weeks a huge battle between the Czech team and Knievel escalated into an international incident. With Bobby explaining that he certainly couldn't pay with money he didn't have, and with the Butte police unable to come up with any solid leads to recover the money, it seemed that the issue of money might end up in court. Finally, to keep the Cold War climate from heating up any more than it already had, the U.S. Olympic Committee helped make up the difference and paid the remaining bills for the Czech team.

When his son, Kelly was born, Bobby realized that he had to come up with a new way to support his growing family. He had discovered that being a sports mogul wasn't going to make him rich, so he began to look at other options. Though he would try everything from odd jobs to selling grave sites, it was his Sur-Kill Guide Service that seemed to offer the most promise of supplying regular income.

The area around Butte was filled with wildlife, both animal and human. Bobby was well acquainted with both. He had been hunting and fishing in the woods since his youth. He knew where the elk, deer, and bear lived and roamed. With this storehouse of knowledge, he figured that he would have no problem separating hunters from their cash by providing them with trophies they had long wished for. So Knievel boldly made a guarantee that no other guide service could or would match. If you signed up with him and paid his fee, he would guarantee you would get the kind of animal you wanted. If you didn't get the kill you wanted, then you didn't have to pay.

It didn't take long for word to get out that Knievel had a handle on bagging big game. Because of this reputation, he was soon hip deep in customers. Yet the good times had barely gotten started when the world caved in around him. The area filled with the prize animals was not free range, it was Yellowstone National Park. When the wardens got wind of where the guide was taking his customers, they placed Knievel in their sights. Soon, Bobby and his customers were spending as much time hiding from park rangers as they were shooting at elk. For most hunters, this was a risk they just didn't want to take. Sur-Kill may have taken off fast, but it died almost as quickly.

Desperate for money, Bobby dropped his hunter's garb and took a step toward being hunted. Calling himself a "private policeman," the strong and imposing young man began to pay door-to-door visits to Butte's businesses. He offered guaranteed robbery protection to each bar, store, and gas station owner he met. Knievel explained that with times so hard, many formerly respectable men were having to turn to crime to feed their families. To keep these men from breaking into businesses, he would begin night patrols of the businesses who subscribed to his services.

At first not very many clients signed up. However, after a while, when stores would be broken into and robbed within twenty-four hours of refusing to join Bobby's alliance, the private cop's client list grew. Amazingly, in the year or so he toured the Butte streets, no one had the guts to knock over any of his stores, while a rash of unprotected businesses were being hit time and time again.

Though he was making some money with his "security" operation, he still needed more. With few opportunities in the daylight hours, and with his private police work keeping him "busy" at night, Bobby had few avenues open to him. For survival, more than the rush of living on the edge, the new father became involved in real crime.

Knievel had very little stomach for armed robbery. Even though he had been in his share of barroom fights, he didn't want to be in a situation where he might hurt an innocent person who was either trying to do his job or be a hero. As a loner, Bobby also didn't want to become a part of an organized crime team. What was left to him were skills he could learn and then employ on his own. As he already had a bit of experience in nighttime burglaries, he opted to become a second-story man.

When pulling jobs where more than petty cash was at stake, there was a greater risk than Bobby was used to. Security guards and local police kept a close eye on the front and back doors of closed businesses whose safes contained fairly heathy sums of currency. If a door was ajar or appeared to have been forced, or a window was broken, it was a giveaway to those who made regular rounds that something was amiss and they would barge in with guns blazing. Also many of the stores had alarms that were connected to the windows and doors. Any person who attacked this kind of operation head-on was usually either stupid or much too bold. Knievel was neither. Yet he just couldn't ignore the possibilities offered behind those locked doors.

Bobby knew that the burglary of a business with no precautions and that wasn't regularly patrolled by guards or cops was not going to be worth his trouble. The small amount of money he took home probably wouldn't pay for the gas he used on that night. So the young husband and father had to figure a way to get at the money in the high security stores and go undetected at the same time. It seemed impossible to most people, but that only made it more inviting for Knievel.

Traveling from town to town throughout the states of Montana, Idaho, Washington, and Oregon, Knievel cased out stores and banks that shared walls and roofs with other businesses. Visiting the businesses during operating hours, he scoped out where the safes were kept and which companies had made it. He also noted if the safe could be seen from the windows in the front or back of the building. Once he found a target that seemed to be worth his investment in time, work, and risk, he finalized his plans.

Well after the residents of the town had gone to sleep, and just after the local policeman had made his regular check of doors and windows, Bobby would grab his bag of tools and climb onto the roof. As most buildings on a block were connected, he would often start by working his way up the lowest wall, then use the roof as an avenue to his target.

Once on top of the business he had chosen, Knievel would pull back roofing material and tar paper, then cut a hole in the roof. Using a rope, he would lower himself to the floor and find the safe. Using the tools he had carried on his back, secure in the knowledge that no one would guess a burglar was inside the building with the doors and windows secure and alarms silent, he would then casually and carefully go to work on the safe. When he had opened the vault and removed the cash, he would clean up his mess, climb back to the roof, put the cut-out section and roofing material back in place, and sneak back to his car. By the time anyone figured out that there had been a robbery, he would be more than a hundred miles away.

After the statute of limitations had run out on his illegal adventures and he had risen to the status of an American icon, Knievel told *Esquire,* "Man, I was taking some chances in that business. I was dropping through holes in the roof like every night in the week. I robbed so many safes in Oregon that one of the newspapers said it looked like somebody was dropping bombs through the roofs."

Besides working as a solo safecracker, Bobby would also join other con artists for sting operations, insurance scams, and card games. While he was engaged in the process, he enjoyed every moment of the high-risk hijinks. However, afterwards, when he considered the times he was within moments of being caught, he began to feel uneasy. In the past he and the police might have played games of chase with a squad car and a motorcycle, but there hadn't been any real harm involved. Even if he got caught, he didn't face any serious time in prison. Now, if his luck ran out, he knew he would be confined to a small, dark room for a long time. And if there was one thing he could not take, it was being trapped without an exit. Bobby had to be able to pick up and leave whenever he wanted to, or he would go crazy.

"The cops knew what I was doing," Knievel explained to *Sports Illustrated,* "but they couldn't prove it." Yet he was now wondering how long it would be before they were able to connect him with a bank job or a scam. And when they did, how long before the rest of his house of cards fell in on top of him.

By 1961, though most of his money was gotten though unlawful means, Bobby was providing well for his family. They even had a new Pontiac to drive around town. Yet when the Knievels did get out and look at the situation in Butte, it caused them to feel guilty about what they had. Many of the men who had made their living in the mines were now unemployed and their families were going hungry. The glory days of mining in Butte were a thing of the past. The cost of ore, the downturn in the economy, and the use of imported raw materials had struck a severe blow to the industry. Bobby could tell by the looks on the faces of the children that many of these kids were depressed and hopeless. Though he would often share a few dollars with those who had fallen on hard times, he knew that what he was giving them would only buy them a day or two of comfort and security. They needed more. Thanks to his days as a hunting guide, he knew where there was enough food to feed hundreds of unemployed miners and their families.

One of the reasons Bobby had led hunting expeditions on national park property was the abundance of wild game. Owing to government regulations that were nonsense at best, Yellowstone Park always had too many elk. The herds were so large that they were constantly over-grazing and destroying important wildlife. In order to keep the elk under control and the natural habitat in balance, park officials annually rounded up elk in huge numbers and slaughtered them. So while the government would not let citizens hunt and kill the Yellowstone elk, they were slaying the animals by the thousands and letting the meat, skin, and other useable parts of the animals go to waste.

Realizing what good could be accomplished with the meat, Bobby determined that for the sake of his friends he needed somehow to change this outlandish law. When he failed to get anyone at Yellowstone to listen to him, he decided to go to Washington and meet with President John F. Kennedy.

Bobby knew that just traveling there by car or plane would accomplish little in the way of media exposure and public relations. This was how everyone got to Washington. What he needed was a gimmick so that he would catch the imagination of those whose minds he had to change. The cause needed press and he had to figure a way to make sure the press was on side.

When Knievel left Butte, winter was just beginning. It was December and very cold. Carrying a suitcase and a set of elk antlers, rather than drive, he used his thumb to cross the country. As he rode from town to town and state to state, he explained the plight of the miners and the ridiculous park laws that were allowing animals to be wantonly killed and wasted at the same time people were hungry. Those who picked him up listened, so did the patrons of diners where he ate and the small-town newspaper reporters in the communities where Knievel held court. Even with support in America's midsection, it was still a bitter trip. Often Bobby spent hours in near-zero weather as cars and trucks passed him by. More than once the wind whipped up by speeding semis caused him to slide across the highway's icy shoulders and into snowbanks. Yet in spite of the fact he had no set appointments in the capital, he refused to give up.

In Chicago he made the news because his antlers had gotten caught in a revolving door at a downtown hotel. As the media honed in on the unusual man with the unusual story, Bobby told them why he was passing through the Windy City. Impressed by the Montanan's will and message, Richard Daley, the powerful political kingpin and mayor of Chicago invited Knievel to his office to tell him the story firsthand. Mayor Daley apparently warned his cronies in the capital that they were about to be hit by a mountain man on a mission.

On December 8, seven days and twenty-seven rides after leaving his home, Bobby arrived in Washington, D.C. Even though he had no appointment, he boldly tried to visit President Kennedy at the White House. When JFK couldn't see him, Knievel told his story to an aide, Mike Manatos. He also left the antlers at the White House as a gift for the nation's leader.

Rather than be satisfied with just a visit to the president's residence, Bobby then went to Capitol Hill. There he lobbied senators and representatives. At the meetings he carried a briefcase and wore cowboy boots and hat. Like a seasoned lobbyist he quoted figures, cited personal examples of the hardships of his friends, and pointed out the mess that had been made by edicts issued two thousand miles from the problem area. People came out to shake his hand because he seemed like a character from a Frank Capra movie. Those who met him discovered a passion and salesmanship that Capra's Mr. Smith never had in Washington.

Before returning to his rather colorful life in the West, Knievel took his briefcase to one of JFK's most powerful cabinet members and a fellow Westerner, Mo Udall. Udall listened, and as secretary of the Interior, he cited the reasons for the laws and regulations being written as they were. Then, as the two men said their good-byes and shook hands, Mo looked the Montanan in the eye and promised Bobby he would see what could be done. The next day the Department of Interior changed the slaughter law. The agency ruled the elk must be moved off park land so licensed hunters could hunt them as game. Before he could make it home, the wasteful slaughter had been stopped and many of Knievel's miner friends once again had a way to put meat on their tables.

The trip to Washington really was an adventure of a lifetime. Visiting the city had refreshed Bobby's patriotic zeal. Yet maybe the most important thing he learned was that the men who ran the most powerful government on earth were not much different than he was. They might have been better educated and generally wealthier, but no smarter. And they could be taken pretty easily too. Bobby had looked and sounded so much the part he played that not one of them had asked to look at his documentation. If he had been forced to open his briefcase, his expert status would have been immediately dismissed. The briefcase was empty. Yet no one asked, they just accepted him. If he could con the most powerful men in the world, then Bobby really believed he could be famous. He sensed that millions would listen to what he thought if he had a forum. Now he just had to find that outlet.

Back in Butte, Knievel returned to his life of crime. However, he was starting to have real doubts about his chances for a long life in this arena. First a friend who had tried to convince him to join in a bank robbery had been shot and killed. Then, Bobby had been working with another man on a con game when the man they were scamming figured it out. To keep the patsy quiet, Knievel had beaten him bloody. Using violence on a man who had really done nothing wrong began to gnaw at Bobby's gut. As he looked at his wife and son, he wondered just how much longer he could keep his charade alive.

One day, for reasons only he could guess, Knievel stopped his Pontiac on a bridge and tossed his burglary tools into a river. He was determined to go straight, but he was also just as determined not to do something ordinary. He wanted to be somebody.

5

Trying to End
the Evil Ways

Most people were surprised that Bobby and Linda Knievel's marriage had lasted. They had assumed the husband would quickly tire of being tied down and that the wife would grow sick of the uncertain life she was being forced to live. Yet neither of these forecasts were even close to accurate. Linda was devoted to Bobby, and as their family grew to include another son, Robbie, it was obvious to all who knew them that the couple's marriage was on solid ground.

It might well have been his wife's love that prompted Knievel to evaluate his own place in life. Four years into his marriage and almost twenty-five years into his life, he didn't have a great deal to be proud of. Though he was very intelligent, he was thought of first as a high school dropout. Though he had a great personality, most people looked at him as a con artist. Though he was a gifted athlete, he was usually remembered as the guy who spent most of his games in a penalty box. Though he was most often labeled a man between jobs, he had spent a great deal of his time secretly playing on the wrong side of the law. The labels that were hung on the man were not flattering.

"I did it and I got away with it [robbing businesses], but it's not the right way of life," Knievel told Gilbert Rogin of *Sports Illustrated.* "I love people. I want to be good to people. That's why I changed my whole way of life. I felt if I really loved my wife and children, I'd try to make a contribution to mankind and society as they should be contributed to."

While sincerely wanting to change, the problems that faced Bobby were the same ones that had plagued him for years. He was living in an area where there was not a great deal of employment opportunities, much less any that offered any real chance at upward movement to a high school dropout. To compound this problem was his own lack of really marketable experience. Being able to crack safes and rob banks just didn't read well on a resume.

One thing he could do better than almost any man in Butte was ride a motorcycle. If there was a way to make a living on a bike, then Bobby knew he could pay the bills and live in style. With moto-cross and other forms of cycle racing now beginning to grow, Knievel found a sponsor and jumped onto the circuit. In theory, it seemed like a surefire way to feed his family.

Bobby did well in moto-cross. When he failed to win, it was usually caused by a mechanical breakdown and just back luck. Few drivers could come close to matching his skill or courage. Yet, as Knievel soon found out, the gypsy life of a bike racer was hardly suited for a man with a wife and two children. Bobby's winnings barely covered his expenses and provided little to his household. Thus, with each new race and each new purse, the pressure mounted to get a better sponsorship package, win higher dollar prizes, and cut expenses. However, even when he won the big races, the money still wasn't big enough to do much more than plug one of the holes in his financial dike. Still, he kept plugging.

Just about the time he was growing into a regional racing hero, the wheels came off his biking career. Caught up in the middle of a brutal wreck, Bobby broke his collarbone and shoulder. Told he would be unable to race for months, he was now faced with the necessity of finding a new way to make a living. Again the prospects didn't look very bright.

While recovering from his injuries, Knievel noted an ad from the Combined Insurance Company of America. The company was looking for men in the area to sell insurance policies. Though he knew almost nothing about insurance and had no experience in legitimate sales,

Bobby applied for the job. His good looks, quick smile, and ability to appear more knowledgeable than he was won him the opportunity to work as a salesman. The rest was up to him.

Bobby's boss was W. Clement Stone. Knievel not only liked him, he listened to him. When Stone suggested the new salesman read a book that he and Napoleon Hill had written, Bobby got the book and immediately began to study it chapter by chapter. As he went through *Success Through a Positive Mental Attitude*, Bobby became turned on to not only selling insurance, but turned on to life in general. He also began to formulate a new concept for living. After reading the book Knievel believed that attitude, much more than any other factor, determined success.

A belief in a positive approach to life being the key to happiness and success had been around for centuries, but in 1962 it seemed to be almost a national posture. President John F. Kennedy had challenged people to "ask not what your country can do for you, ask what you can do for your country." He pushed attitude and service almost everywhere he went. The president's words, youth, and vigor had inspired many to get involved in public life, work in the Peace Corps, or devote themselves to higher causes. It was a moment in time when being a part of something greater meant more than being an individual. This infectious spirit even touched a young salesman in Montana.

As JFK was launching the race to the moon, Bobby was caught up in a race of his own. He decided he was going to be the greatest insurance salesman that Combined had ever had. In his mind, now consumed with the I-can-do-it spirit, there was no doubt that he would easily reach his goal.

There was an obvious zeal in young Knievel's work and an energy in his step as he began to seek out his initial sales contacts. His study of Combined's materials had given him a knowledge of insurance that was exceeded by almost no one. As he met with a prospective client, he had the answers before most of his contacts had the chance to ask the questions. It was almost as if he knew them better than they knew themselves, and most who met with him were left very impressed. It was obvious in his voice that he believed what he was saying, and it seemed equally obvious that the person who failed to purchase a policy from Knievel would spend the rest of life out of step with the world. Bobby could easily sell the notion that a man wouldn't be properly covered and that he and his family would suffer someday if he failed to do something now.

His supervisor and fellow workers were soon in awe of Bobby's ability to sell policies. Yet while others were slapping him on the back and telling him he how great he was, the new salesman was hardly satisfied. He wanted to sell more insurance in a day than most men sold in a month. Consumed by a passion to succeed in ways no one ever had, he pushed to extend himself even more. He ate and slept the insurance business.

Just like during his days of casing a business for a robbery, Bobby began to look for places and people who would offer him great sales opportunities. He questioned the logic in visiting with one person at a residence when he could talk to hundreds at a large business. In July, as he worked the roads that led from his home to what he hoped would be the end of the rainbow, he discovered a gold mine.

Visiting with both the employees and patients at the state mental hospital in Warm Springs, Knievel explained to them why they needed insurance coverage that they didn't now have. Like a preacher building on a sermon, Bobby charmed the crowd and brought them up to a fever pitch. Then, when he was given a chance to talk one-on-one with each person at Warm Springs, he explained why Combined had a policy that had been written especially for their individual situation. Both workers and patients saw themselves in everything he said. They found that they desperately needed what he had. He didn't even have to ask them to consider taking out a policy, they practically begged him to let them sign up. Before he left the mental institution, Knievel had sold 271 new policies.

The new kid on the insurance block was a hero at the home office. He had broken every sales record in company history. Bobby had taken his training and expanded it to include approaches not even the CEO had considered. W. Clement Stone believed he had just found the Babe Ruth of the insurance business.

Suddenly Bobby was taken off the road and taken out to eat by the company heads. While he was being wined and dined his story was trumpeted in press releases and he was spotlighted as a role model for every other salesman at the company. In a company-wide memo, he was even asked how he managed to sell so many policies so quickly.

"You ask me to tell you how I broke the records," Knievel told the newsletter. "Well, to tell you the truth it wasn't very hard. After I conceived in my own mind that I could do it, I enjoyed it. I had a lot of fun. All it takes is accepting the challenge."

Though only a few months into his new job, Bobby thought it was time for the company to really recognize his work and give him a new challenge. If he was going to continue to push as hard as he had so far, he wanted a guarantee of a better position with higher pay and more benefits. He had his mind set on being the youngest vice president not just in his company's history, but in the entire history of the insurance business in the United States. Yet rather than give their ace salesman any kind of guarantee, Combined simply told him to keep working and they would see what they could do for him later. *Later* was not a word Knievel liked to hear. It immediately transformed his positive attitude about insurance sales into a negative emotional response. He was insulted that the company would not reward him now.

There was no doubt that Combined did not want to lose Bobby, but they probably didn't believe that not offering him an immediate chance to earn the VP title would cause him to leave. About all they saw in the young man was confidence and great potential. If they had taken the time to look below those visible strengths, they would have seen the insecurities of a man from mining country.

To Knievel life was to be lived in the moment, and the future couldn't be banked on. When Combined didn't give the former miner what he needed instantly, then to him it seemed all his work was for naught. Not understanding this "cave-in" mentality caused the insurance company to lose their best man. Knievel would walk rather than patiently wait on his employer to decide when the time was right to move him up the corporate ladder. However, his days in sales were hardly wasted. He did take away something from the experience that would shape his life forever.

For the first time, Bobby had a deep thirst for knowledge. The high school dropout who once avoided homework now saw reading books as an avenue not only to success, but to a greater understanding of his own gifts. He was drawn both to history and stories that centered on success through practical living. Through reading, Bobby's attitude began to evolve from an immature, fun-loving hell-raiser to a more stable visionary. Even in bleak Butte he saw an opportunity at every corner. He also came to believe that he was very special.

More than the scores of works he studied, one book may have helped center and guide the father and husband more than any other. The words that so captured the young man had been written by Dr. Norman Vincent Peale in the minister's *The Power of Positive Thinking*. Peale's best-seller spoke of the great things that could be accomplished if a man was willing to constantly embrace a positive approach to living. To Bobby it seemed that if this book was right, a positive mental attitude won not only sporting contests, but battles in the business world too.

In a very real sense, Bobby had been practicing this positive approach for years. Though he had not embraced it in every facet of his life, he had used it when he was preparing for a track event like the pole vault. He had willed himself over the bar even before he had run down the ramp on his approach to the jump. He had even had that positive mental attitude when he had tried to beat the cops in his teenage games of cat and mouse. Now, with Peale's words ringing in his ears, Knievel really seized on this concept and started to look for ways he could use positive thinking in the business world.

In Butte few believed that Bobby would ever be more than a reckless biker. Though he knew he had changed, few in his hometown seemed willing to give him the chance to prove it. Deciding he needed to move in order to get a fresh start, Bobby took his family to Moses Lake, Washington. In this small town he became the area promoter of moto-cross racing and took over a local Honda motorcycle dealership.

As had been proven when he had worked for Combined, selling was in his blood. As he was a natural with motorcycles, the two elements of talent and experience should have come together in spectacular fashion at the Honda outlet. Yet while Bobby's attitude was right and he knew bikes, selling imports to Americans was not an easy job in 1963 and 1964. On top of this, selling Japanese motorcycles to conservative rural people was very tough.

World War II had ended less than twenty years before Bobby had become a Honda dealer. Though the kids had pretty much forgotten the battles in the Pacific, a lot of their fathers and mothers hadn't. The older generations still hung onto a great deal of bitterness and resentment based on their memories of the Japanese attacking Pearl Harbor and plunging the United States into a conflict that would cost America tens of thousands of young lives. So while the teens may have wanted a Honda to race around town, the grown-ups with the checkbooks were still harboring old resentments about buying things from Japan. It was far easier to sell a Harley or a Cushman than a Honda at that time.

The other problem confronting Bobby was the notion that anything from the Orient was cheaply made and wouldn't last. "Made in Japan" had been the sign of inferior workmanship and cheap goods for years. Convincing people that the Honda was a well-made motorcycle was tough. For most Americans at this time, if it was made in Japan, it must be junk.

Compounding all these normal sales problems was that in the past few months the national attitude had changed dramatically. John F. Kennedy, the president who had brought life and energy to the White House, had been shot. When JFK died in Dallas, so did a lot of Americans' faith and innocence. For many of the men who drank with Bobby in Moses Lake bars after work, the assassination of the president was just one of the signs that the country was losing its grip.

The civil rights movement, now in full swing, scared a lot people. Many feared race wars. Many who were now just barely making a living, feared that if blacks got equal rights, then they would lose their jobs to a man or woman of color. Many others were scared the country would change its whole value system by allowing a race of people equal rights. Though these fears were proven groundless and were based on ignorance, they were very common.

As if Americans didn't have enough to deal with, Vietnam was now beginning to build into something worse than Korea had ever been. As more and more American boys were shipped to Asia to fight against invading communists backed by Red China, millions began to worry that not only were we going to have thousands of our boys killed in a faraway jungle, but that World War III was just around the corner. Americans in Washington and around the country began to line up for and against this new "police action" in Asia, further dividing the country along the lines of not only race, but political beliefs too.

Though it hardly ranked with the murder of a president or a war in Asia, the fact that a British singing group was taking the nation by storm and stealing rock and roll from true Americans like Elvis Presley had people reeling too. To many the rise of the long-haired Beatles and Rolling Stones was another sign that the world was going straight to Hell.

Bobby was as concerned about these issues as anyone. A changing world was not only something he wasn't prepared for, but something that hurt business. If people didn't have faith in the future, then they wouldn't purchase things now. To stem what he saw as a growing movement of pessimism, as well as to fight off the often-negative image of his Japanese product, he came up with incentives to get people to come try out one of his Hondas.

Rebates and other dealer programs were a generation in the future; whatever Bobby did to sell his bikes would have to be his idea. If that meant giving away money or merchandise, then it would also have to come out of his pocket. He wasn't going to get any company support.

Knievel spent his spare hours swapping stories and drinking with friends in bars. More often than not, he didn't buy his own drinks. Since high school he had been challenging his friends to all kinds of athletics and games of chance to see who purchased the next round. Invariably, he would almost always win.

Arm wrestling was a contest that Bobby never lost. While he was in the army, his pole vaulting had built his arms and shoulders to the point where he was simply stronger than almost any man who would ever walk into a bar. The poor fool who believed he could beat Knievel in arm wrestling always found himself paying for the next batch of booze. The fact that he was an almost sure winner in this contest gave him an idea he took out of the bar and into the showroom.

At his Honda dealership Bobby began to challenge his customers to arm-wrestling contests. If they could beat him, the motorcycle dealer would knock one hundred dollars off the price of any model in stock. Though many tried, no one could pry the rebate out of Knievel's hands. Over time the winning offer rose to a free bike for the victor. Even though the offer brought in lumberjacks and farmers in droves, no one every drove out of Bobby's business without paying for what they were riding. However, after talking with the strong-armed winner, a few did pay for one of the new bikes.

Besides showing off his strength to get people to examine his wares, Knievel also raced from time to time on the American Motorcycle Association circuit. Because the purses were small, winning a race didn't do much for his pocketbook, but it did enhance his reputation as a shop owner who knew his business. Some of the race spectators ended up buying one of Bobby's bikes.

However, more than arm wrestling or racing, Bobby's best advertising came when he rode down the streets of Moses Lake. Seeing him on the city streets riding his Honda was a show that brought men and women out of homes and shops. Popping wheelies for blocks at a time, scaling steep hills without losing his balance and letting the wind blow through his hair as he rode at more than a mile a minute down the main drag made him not only a well-known figure, but an area hero to kids and those who wished they still were.

It was also no secret that everyone in Moses Lake was as awed by his gift of gab as they were his ability to ride a bike. Many of those who drank with him were glad he hadn't taken up the ministry. Bobby had so much charisma and charm, and so many people hung on everything he said, his buddies figured the whole state would have been dry if Knievel had taken up preaching. Yet while the man had reformed and was now a law-abiding citizen and solid family man, Bobby was not anywhere close to becoming a man of the cloth. He probably hadn't even been in a church since the time he had used one as a hiding place when he had kidnapped Linda in 1958.

In 1965, as poor sales were about to drive the motorcycle dealer out of business, Bobby was visiting Butte. One evening he stopped off at a bar for a few drinks at one of his favorite night spots. As the evening wore on his friends began to brag about all the tricks Mr.

Knievel could do with his cycle. Humbly nodding his head, the center of attention was enjoying listening to his admirers tell stories about his biking prowess. The tales went on for hours, with each one getting a little more unbelievable than the one that preceded it. At one point, an unimpressed and bored bar patron stepped forward with a ten-dollar bill and a challenge. Though no one jotted down the words as he spoke that night, witnesses now remember it like this.

"Okay, Knievel," the man said, firing the first volley, "it pretty much sounds like you can jump, climb, or ride through anything with that bike of yours."

Bobby just smiled and nodded while he studied the man. In the back of his mind he was anticipating a fight. He had been in enough bar brawls to know this was how most of them started. Yet tonight a fight was not in the offing.

The challenger continued. "I got ten bucks that says you can't ride your motorcycle over that little foreign car parked out in the street."

Led by the Moses Lake cycle dealer, the barroom crowd walked out the door and checked out the VW Bug parked in front of the business. As a couple dozen men watched, Bobby strolled around the car, shrugged his shoulders, mounted his bike, kicked the starter pedal, then reached into his pocket and pulled out ten dollars. Handing the money to the bartender, Knievel circled back down the block, turned, stopped, and froze, like he had done when he studied the bar before a pole vault, then suddenly and resolutely slapped the bike into gear. Half a block later, the rider jerked the front wheel off the ground, literally lifted his cycle halfway up the back of the car and gunned his engine. In the blink of an eye Bobby hit the top of the Bug and bounced down off the front side. Sliding his bike to a stop, he parked it and casually strolled back into the bar to claim his ten-dollar winnings. The loser, far from being mad, bought the next round and crowded in to hear Bobby and others tell of racing down mountains and evading cops. The celebration went on for hours.

Though it had not been planned and was only a spur-of-the-moment stunt witnessed by a few friends and bar patrons, jumping the VW quickly enhanced Bobby Knievel's status as a local legend.

By the next morning everybody in town was talking about it. The story was repeated so often that many of the details were replaced by bigger and more colorful renderings of the tale. By noon hundreds believed that Knievel had flown over the car, clearing the roof by more than ten feet. So many supposed eyewitnesses stepped forward to give their accounts of the stunt, that those who claimed to have seen the stunt would have filled a large rodeo arena. The question that had been haunting policemen for years was "What would Bobby do next?" Now that same question was a hot topic of conversation at every drinking establishment in town. Bobby himself couldn't believe how one little jump over a puny automobile had so stirred the emotions and imaginations of the people of Butte.

Back in Moses Lake, Bobby retold the barroom bet story a few times himself. The more he repeated it, the more people came by and wanted to hear it. His winning races had never really meant much to those who knew him. The fact that he had been a track star in the army hadn't wowed many folks either. Yet now, at a time when he was all but starving to death trying to sell motorcycles, everyone wanted to shake the hand of the guy who jumped over a VW. Almost everyone he now met seemed a sucker for a story about doing something crazy on a motorcycle. The more he considered what a man had to do to get noticed, the more Bobby became convinced that it was a crazy world filled with crazy people.

As the days of slow sales dragged by and Bobby became more worried about feeding his family and finding his unique place in life, a memory kept coming back to him. He was eight years old and watching Joey Chitwood's auto daredevil show. In the often-vacant showroom, Bobby rewatched that show again and again in his imagination. Then, it hit Knievel. Studying the new bikes around him, the store owner thought, If Chitwood could make good money traveling about the country thrilling people with his high-risk car act, then why couldn't I make money doing something like that with a motorcycle?

There was no scientific way for Knievel to test his theory, there were no models on which to base his belief that people would pay money to watch him jump over VW Bugs or trucks. However, a night in a bar and the way that story had taken on a life of its own indicated to Bobby that he might just be able to feed his family by doing things no one would dare do and few believed could be done. But could he do it and live?

6

Bobby Becomes Evel

For all practical purposes the Knievel Honda dealership had died. He just couldn't sell enough bikes to make ends meet. Bobby felt at least a part of the problem was the image of bikers. Most people thought of them as hoods. A part of the reason for this perception went back to Hollywood and the Marlon Brando movie *The Wild One*. Brando and his biker buddies had raped, pillaged, and terrorized a fictional California town. Even if it was just a movie, watching men on cycles become violent animals frightened many people. A large number assumed this behavior was typical of men who bought motorcycles. It was almost as if the motorcycle carried the disease that infected boys and made them terrors. Yet even though *The Wild One* seemed to embrace this concept, in truth Hollywood didn't create this image, it only built on it. Bobby was not only aware of this, he knew exactly where the bike had gotten its bad name.

It was the Hell's Angels, and other motorcycle gangs like them, who had blackened the reputations of almost all bikers. These men were so despised that most parents would have rather had their sons hang out with the Mafia than the Hell's Angels. In truth, for a period of time, organized crime and the biker gangs often worked together, so the mob and the Angels were on the very same road.

In the 1950s and 1960s, the Angels were a group of riders who represented blatant lawlessness. They were not unlike the guerrilla groups that terrorized many of the midwestern border states just after the Civil War. They were out of control and considered themselves not only above the law, but representing the final judgement on everything. They did whatever they could get away with, they constantly pushed the limits, they dressed in black, and they always rode bikes.

Bobby could understand why the public image of these biker groups had led to his having to close his business. Certainly he wouldn't want his sons to have anything to do with gangs like the Angels. Even when he was all but starving to death, he wouldn't even deal with anyone from a gang at his dealership. He wouldn't sell them a bike or fix one for them. In most cases he wouldn't even speak to them. Now that he blamed groups like the Hell's Angels for not being able to feed his family, Knievel's bitterness toward the group grew even stronger. Some years later this hostility would spill over into violence.

As he closed his shop for the final time, Bobby was being driven by two things, the need for cash and the need to launch an honest career that would continue to provide for his family for years to come. He could no longer afford to get into a business only to have to move on to something else a few months later. With a daughter, Tracey, now joining his two sons, there were four mouths to feed at home. He had to find something he could stick with, an occupation that would pay his bills and buy him a future.

To make a few quick dollars, Bobby opted to put on a motorcycle show for the people of Moses Lake. Promoting the event himself, Knievel rented the venue, wrote the press releases for the local paper, went bar to bar trumpeting what he was going to do, set up the show, sold tickets, and served as his own master of ceremonies the day of the event. Even with all his work, and even though he was by now well known in the area and his motorcycle exploits were the stuff of local legends, he could only interest a few hundred people in watching him risk his life. Still, those few hundred did offer him a chance at the best paycheck he had seen in some time.

To more than a few who showed up to watch Bobby Knievel's first professional stunt show, the brash young biker reminded them of legendary St. Louis Cardinals' pitcher Dizzy Dean. Like the Hall of Famer baseball player, Knievel was loud and funny. He could charm the ladies and still speak man-to-man with to the men. And like Old Diz, he was everywhere at once. Before he ever mounted his bike that day in Moses Lake, it seemed that he had personally visited with every man, woman, and child who had bought a ticket. In the process he had also convinced them that they were going to see one of the most spectacular stunts in the history of show business. People who had come out of curiosity, were genuinely excited by the time Knievel finished talking to them.

When showtime arrived, Bobby warmed the crowd up by doing a few wheelies, limited to only a few hundred feet due to the small size of the arena. He then turned off his motorcycle and spoke to the crowd. He asked each member of the audience to look behind him. There, in the middle of the arena, were two ramps placed more than twenty feet apart. In between the ramps was a very large box. After they had studied the box for a few moment, Knievel informed them that inside the box were more than 100 rattlesnakes. To assure the audience that he was not lying, he had several volunteers from the crowd come out of the stands and walk over to the box and look in. As the lid was opened, the witnesses were greeted by hissing and rattles. As they nervously peered into the crate they saw a mass of twisted, writhing, angry snakes, all looking for a way to escape through the one-inch boards that were between them and freedom. It was enough to give a grown man nightmares.

As the now pale and shaken witnesses climbed back to their seats, the audience began to whisper. What would happen if he missed? they wondered. If he landed short and hit the box, he would toss snakes in every direction. The crazy rider would probably be bitten a hundred times before he could get off the ground and run away. They just knew that he had to be insane to try this stunt. Yet none of them asked him to stop. None of them left to go home rather than watch this public suicide. They might have believed he was crazy and was going to kill himself, but they wanted to see it if he did.

After his audience had gotten used to the idea of Bobby jumping the box of poisonous vipers, he signaled for the final facet of his jump to be added to the mix. A man with two full-grown mountain lions appeared. As everyone watched, the man staked the two huge cats between the box and the take-off ramp.

Leaving the crowd to study the latest development, Bobby walked over to the animal trainer. He informed the man he wanted a lion on each side of the box. The man refused, explaining he believed that Bobby would fall short of the landing ramp and kill himself. The trainer didn't want to have one of his cats killed when the biker cashed on top of it, so he was going to keep both of them at the front of the jump. He also wanted to be paid at that moment because he didn't think he could stomach asking a widow for the cash later.

After the debate between the jumper and the owner of the cats ended, Bobby strolled back to the crowd to tell them about the new setup.

"We were supposed to have one lion at each end of the ramp," witnesses remember the biker explaining the situation, "but the cats' owner doesn't think I can make a jump that long. He figures I will kill myself trying. That is fine with him, but he says he can't afford to lose one of the cats too. I understand that. I also understand why he wanted to be paid in advance. After all, what man in his right mind could expect to make a jump like this?"

As he would do so often over the next few years, Knievel had used a possible negative and tragic turn of events to his advantage. The lion owner balking at the original setup just made the jump seem much more dangerous. As he spoke to them, the rider could see the fear and nervousness written on everyone's face. A few minutes before, most in the crowd might have been thinking he would crash and kill himself, but after this turn of events, they now seemed sure that he would. It was exactly the reaction Bobby had wanted. They had to think he was going to die in order to really appreciate the performance.

After spending a few more minutes talking to the audience and building up the stunt to further heighten the audience's fear factor, a confident Knievel hopped back on his bike, kicked up a huge spray of dust and exited the arena. Outside the crowd's view, he racked off his cycle's engine several times, then gassing it to the max, raced back into the view, rushing just in front of the ramp at more than sixty miles an hour. Thinking that he was going to jump, the audience had risen as one and taken a huge collective breath. They had been unaware the rider would need a few practice runs to fully judge his speed and the condition of the loose dirt floor. They didn't know that he was going to make them wait for several moments before letting them watch his "leap to death."

After a couple more practice runs, Bobby decided it was finally showtime. As he left the arena for the final time, he must have felt the doubts crowd into his mind. He had never practiced this jump. He didn't know if his homemade ramps would hold. He didn't even know how much speed it would take to clear the open distance between the two ramps. He had no figures, no formulas, and no tests to prove that his guess at takeoff speed and angle of lift would be too much or not enough. He had built this stunt on gut-level instincts and guesswork. Now he had to wonder if this would be his first and last jump.

Twisting his handgrip throttle, Bobby closed his eyes and pictured himself flying from ramp to ramp. As he concentrated on a positive outcome, he considered every foot of the trip he was about to make. He made mental notes of when to shift and how much to accelerate. He also tried to imagine how his body would respond to coming down from the air and hitting the plywood landing ramp.

As he went over the jump step by step, it must have been hard to keep his own doubts and fears under control. He had already informed the crowd of all the things that could go wrong. He had told them that he would never make the distance if he missed a gear, had a valve stick or his carburetor hesitate, or a tire go flat. Even though he hadn't told them what would happen if he failed to hit the center of the takeoff ramp, he was aware of what would happen if he missed by as little as a few inches. The takeoff angle would be totally wrong for landing. He would probably miss the landing ramp altogether. If he had waited any longer, he probably could have found a hundred more reasons why this was insane. However, he had promised he would make the jump, so there was no backing out or turning back.

Before doubts could wipe out his courage and any more fear could crowd his mind, Bobby gunned the engine and took off. This time his approach was smooth and flawless. There was no showboating, no spraying dirt or playing with the engine. As he approached the ramp, he was dead serious and concentrating fully on what he knew he had to do.

The crowd was now as one. On their feet, many standing in their seats, they silently watched Bobby speed into the arena and head for his homemade takeoff ramp. He hit the board square and drove up the incline at almost a mile a minute, then, in an instant, he was airborne.

As he left the ramp, it seemed that time stopped for a moment. No one could hear the bike, the snarling cougars, the rattling snakes, or the groaning of the old wooden grandstands. Everything was hushed, the wind seemed suddenly still, and Bobby and the bike were frozen in the air. Then, a millisecond later, the amazed patrons watched man and machine fly. He was over the lions and snakes and winging his way to the safety of the far ramp. The fans now thought the jump was a done deal. The rider knew better.

The instant he had taken off Bobby realized that he not had generated enough speed to make it as far as he needed to go. His back wheel was not going to hit the landing ramp. Still, in an attempt to lift the bike across the chasm with sheer willpower, the jumper pulled hard on the handlebars, trying to coax extra height from the bike. It was a futile effort. The back tire came down hard on the snake box at about the same moment the front tire hit the ramp.

Bobby should have been tossed like a rag doll over the motorcycle's handlebars. He should have flown from the bike and landed in the dirt arena surrounded by scores of angry snakes that his shortened landing had suddenly freed. Yet, rather than give up, Knievel hung on. Thanks to his tremendous upper body strength, he bounced the bike off the now shattering wooden crate and up onto the ramp. He then raced down the ramp, twisted to a spinning stop, placed his foot on the ground to hold the cycle upright, and lifted his arms triumphantly to the crowd.

At first too shocked to move, the audience finally realized that the stunt man had made it. Though there were scores of angry rattle-snakes slithering all over the arena, Knievel was safe. Cheering, screaming, and applauding, the fans raced to the edge of the fence to get near the crazy jumper. As he rode up to them, they reached out to Bobby like they would have a rock and roll singer or a movie star. At this moment in time, to almost all who had witnessed that first jump, this stunt man was the most important person in the world. After taking a victory lap, Knievel returned to his fans. Joining them in the grandstand, he signed autographs and told everyone how it felt to fly. Meanwhile, back in the arena, snake handlers tried to track down more than a hundred very hostile rattlers. Several of the snakes escaped; luckily, no one in the crowd was bitten.

Watching the adoration of those who caught his act in the small arena, Bobby felt he was on to something. He now fully believed he could make a motorcycle daredevil show into a big moneymaker. Yet he didn't want to do it alone. For starters there was simply too much risk in doing every stunt himself. Also, promoting, advertising, setting up and tearing down, servicing the bike, building the needed stunt equipment, and keeping it in good condition were simply too much work. He needed a hand-picked team with him, and he needed a sponsor to supply the bikes and advertising.

Trying to decide how to make his dream a reality was almost like determining which came first, the chicken or the egg. Without a sponsor and new bikes there could be no show. However, without riders who could do stunts, he probably couldn't interest a sponsor. Yet riders wouldn't quit their jobs and work for him without wanting to be paid, they couldn't be paid until they put on shows, and they couldn't put on shows without having the needed financing. Because he was broke, the situation seemed hopeless. Yet that didn't keep the ever-hopeful young man from making calls and visits trying to sell businesses on backing *Bobby Knievel and His Motorcycle Daredevils Thrill Show*.

In late 1965, Bob Blare, a distributor for Norton Motorcycles, stepped forward with an offer. He would give Knievel the needed bikes, but the deal came with a price. Blare wanted the daredevil to change the name of the show. He didn't want "Bobby Knievel and His Motorcycle Daredevils" on the marque, he wanted to resurrect Bobby's old Butte nickname, Evil.

Bobby had a problem with that. He didn't want to conjure up an image as a hood or as a Hell's Angels rider. He didn't want his own kids thinking of him as a bad guy either. Yet he understood why Blare thought the name made sense. By using Evil, the show had an aura that a name like Bobby simply couldn't provide. Besides, by tying Evil to Knievel, he would also have an easy name to remember. Bobby knew that name recognition and gimmicks were incredibly important in marketing and show business, yet even realizing this, he still felt uneasy about aligning himself with a name that conjured up images of black magic, history's demonic dictators, and the Devil himself.

As a beggar, Bobby didn't have a great deal of room to compromise. If this was what it took to put his show on the road, then he would have to do it. However, he did ask Blare to give him a little room to play. Knievel would drop Bobby and use the old nickname, but he wanted to change the *i* to an *e*. By using Evel rather than Evil, he thought he could still represent himself as a potential good-guy hero. Norton and Blare agreed and ordered the bikes "Evel" needed.

If he was going to make a living with his thrill show, then Bobby would be forced to emulate the airplane barnstormers of the twenties. He was going to have to become a modern-day gypsy. He and his band of men were going to have to roam from town to town, live as cheaply as they could, put on performance after performance, then move on to the next town. They would have to drive at night, sleep in their trucks and cars, and work like field hands. If they stuck it out, they might be rewarded with better-paying bookings in larger venues. They also might die before they could save a dollar or perform a single show in an arena that seated more than a few hundred people. He had to have team members willing to accept this lifestyle and the risks that went with it.

With the sponsorship in place, Bobby turned to finding the members of his troop. He began and ended his search with riders he had known during his days of racing. Uncovering a few men who were hungry enough to give up the circuit for show business, he began 1966 by organizing a performance routine.

When he wasn't designing and working out his show routines, Bobby was on the phone and writing letters. Every spare moment he searched for bookings. He didn't have a track record or a well-known name, so in an effort to sell his unproven act, he resorted to trying to sound big-time. Acting like a modern day P. T. Barnum, he tailored his spiel to whatever it was each venue needed. Finally, as weeks went by with little interest being generated and no up front money being offered, Bobby agreed to perform for no guarantee and a percentage of the gate.

This deal should have been seen by some bookers as a promotional opportunity too good to be true. After all, Evel Knievel was giving them an opportunity to book a show where men might kill themselves doing really stupid things. This surely beat concerts, beauty pageants, and clown shows. However, few could understand the real potential they were being offered. Most still passed.

The California Date Festival in Indio was the first date Knievel signed. In February, the exposition offered Bobby something Evel Knievel's Motorcycle Daredevils dearly needed: exposure.

Bobby pulled out all the stops for the event. In comparison to his first professional outing in Moses Lake, Indio represented a major leap forward. The show had to make the most of it. Emulating many of the routines Knievel had once seen Joey Chitwood's auto troop perform, the new show promised to be spectacular in both its variety and its thrill quotient.

Evel was clad in white leather with red and white trim. The outfit made him look like the biker version of Uncle Sam, and that was the point he was trying to get across. His name might have sounded like a son of Satan, but the performer wanted the people to know that he was a flag-waving patriot who loved his country and all-American clean living. During the performance he would speak out for the United States and against such things as the Hell's Angels and drug abuse. This combination of politics, patriotism, and preaching would soon evolve into as much a facet of each of his shows as the motorcycle stunts. These qualities would also pave the way for Knievel becoming a hero to a generation of American youths. For now, they served to set him apart from biker gangs and deadbeats.

Once he finished talking, slapped on his helmet, and mounted his bike, Knievel and his Daredevils were nonstop action. There was no doubt that this debut performance was unlike anything the crowd had ever witnessed. Besides the normal Knievel stunt of popping long wheelie runs, the biker hitched a kite up to a car and lifted himself into the air like a bird. As he rose to more than two-hundred feet off the ground, hanging onto the tiny bit of material and frame, the crowd strained to see the fearless man fly. While he soared he had their full attention, and when he finally came back to earth, his display of courage won a huge round of applause. Yet this was just an opening act.

After stunts of precision driving by the team and a unique display where Evel lay on the ground, braced a board over his body with his arms, and had his riders race up the board and do jumps off his body, it was time for the really big events.

Knievel's team lined up a series of a dozen plywood panels. Each board had been soaked in gasoline for a hour before the show, then braced and erected where it sat almost four feet off the ground. The boards were placed in a long row, each almost twenty feet from the next. When Evel gave the signal, the boards were lit. After a roaring blaze was leaping from each board, Knievel took off on his bike, hitting each of the fiery pieces of solid lumber with his shoulders and helmet. As the crowded silently stared, the rider struck one after the other at more than thirty miles an hour. Boom! Boom! Boom! With flames seemingly jumping off his body, Evel continued until all the boards had been smashed into at least two pieces and he and his bike were all that were left standing.

Most of the crowd thought the drive through fire signaled the end of the performance, but in truth, all that had preceeded this moment had just been a warm-up. In the middle of the arena the troop drove two full-sized pickup trucks and parked them tailgate to tailgate. Then two ramps were placed at the front of each of the vehicles. As the stunt was set up, Knievel visited with the audience. He explained that no one would attempt this jump because it was simply too dangerous.

Much like Moses Lake, his speech put each member of the crowd on the edge of their seats. As would be the case for almost all the jumps that followed, a poll would have probably revealed that half of the Indio fans wanted to see him wipe out, the other half was praying for him to make it.

Jumping on his bike, Knievel made his practice runs not only to add excitement to the stunt, but to check out the bike's mechanics. After assuring himself the cycle had been properly set up, he began his approach. Unlike at Moses Lake, this time his speed and lift were perfect. When he went into the air from the takeoff ramp, everyone could see that he would clear the trucks, now the only thing he had to do was land the bike.

It would have taken a slow-motion view to fully appreciate the pounding Evel took when he hit the far ramp. As the back wheel came down, his lower back compressed from the shock. Every muscle in his arms and legs strained just to hold on to the heavy Norton cycle and keep it up right. As sweat drenched his face, he landed the front wheel and roared down the incline and out onto the field. The crowd went crazy!

If Bobby had brought any souvenir caps or T-shirts, he would have sold out in minutes. Everyone wanted something from the man who could jump trucks. The Indio crowd hung around for hours just to get a chance to meet him and get his autograph. The adulation didn't stop there either. Word quickly spread up and down the West Coast and suddenly Knievel's phone was ringing. For a few days it appeared like the daredevil show really was going to be a gold mine.

Hemet, California, was the sight of the next show, but rain beat the troop to town. When the storms continued, the performance was canceled. With no guarantee or insurance, suddenly the bright times promised by the results of the Indio show now appeared bleak. Out of cash, Bobby bounced checks trying to pay for food and lodging. He prayed the businesses and authorities wouldn't find out until he had secured another date and made the money to cover the back checks.

The Daredevils' third and biggest booking yet was in Barstow, California. On the days before the performance, Knievel had polished the act. Dropping a few bits that hadn't worked, he added a new stunt he believed would wow the crowd even more than his jumping over the trucks.

The leg-split jump was as spectacular as it was dangerous. It was a timing stunt, and if the timing was off by even a split second, then death was a very real possibility. What made the stunt even more perilous was that there was no way to really practice it. As close as the troop could get to a simulation was for a rider to push a bike up to fifty miles per hour, then Bobby would jump and spread his legs as the cycle passed a few feet to his side. The other members of the team would try to find an angle and guess if their leader's leap was high enough and if he had been able to time his jump where he would be at the peak of his leap just as the bike passed under him. In practice it had looked great. Everyone knew it would work. Still, the closer it came to performing the stunt, the less confident each member of the troop grew.

There was a great deal of wind in Barstow, and it picked up as the show went on. The windy conditions made for a great parasail ride. Bobby managed to fly the kite to a height beyond three hundred feet. As always, the audience was fascinated with the man and his courage. The crowd's positive reaction echoed the response that followed for each new routine.

The rest of the early part of the show went just like it had an Indio. There wasn't even a minor hitch. The cycle team performed as if they had been programed by NASA. Each move was precise, each new facet of the act was a thing of balletlike grace and jet-engine power. Then, as the crowd listened intently, it was time for the big finale.

As before, the motorcycle jump over two pickups would end the show, but before that Evel was going to do the spread-eagle leap over a powerful Norton cycle.

As he got himself ready for the stunt, a dryness filled Bobby's mouth. Athletes call the sensation cotton mouth. It seems to plague people before any big event. Dry mouth now had the man the crowd knew as Evel. However, he didn't stop to get a drink. He knew the only thing that would give him relief was getting through the stunt.

As the rider began to rack off the bike's pipes, Knievel took his position, attempted to loosen the joints in his body, and prepared for the death-defying leap. For the man in the spotlight, this feeling of laying it all on the line was what had been been missing from high school and army track competition. During those days in the spotlight there had been no real glory in winning. Here, there was. This was a test of courage, guts, timing, skill, and fortitude. Yet in those earlier athletic competitions, losing didn't matter as much either. Now there was a real chance at something worse than disappointment if Bobby failed to finish on top.

Giving a wave to the cycle rider, Knievel crouched his body and readied for the jump. As the bike got closer, as the speed reached almost a mile a minute, Bobby focused on the Norton's front tire. As the bike picked up more speed and grew closer, the crowd rose to its feet as one. No one, including the man in the middle of the arena, dared to breathe. Pushing off the ground with the balls of his feet, employing every muscle in his body to gain lift and temporarily defeat the grip of gravity, Bobby reached for the sky and started to spread his legs. Even as he did, he knew he had waited too long. As the Norton flew toward him, he involuntarily stared death in the face. There was nowhere to run, no way to escape. It was too late for the rider to turn the bike and too late for Bobby to roll out of the way. He was going to be at least a foot from the top of his jump, a full foot short, when their paths met.

The speeding bike's handlebars hit Knievel in the groin. His body spun in the air like a dishrag, the momentum of the collision between man and machine tossed Bobby more than fifteen feet above the ground. After completing a sickening twisting spiral, he seemed to hang in the air for a moment, then, as if a lead weight had been tied to his limp body, he fell to the dirt.

When he hit the ground, every one of his team thought he was dead. As they rushed to him, he didn't move. So sure were they that Bobby had been killed, they called for a blanket to cover him up. Unable to respond to anyone's questions, Knievel thought he was either dying or paralyzed. Yet as the numbness began to wear off, replaced by excruciating pain, he not only knew he was alive, but that he was seriously injured. The shocked crowd said little as the medical personnel worked over the fallen biker. Most figured that if he was still alive, he would die on the way to the hospital.

The fall had pushed Bobby's ribs into his lungs. Breathing was difficult at best. His lower body had been severely bruised from his knees to his waist. He was lucky to still have a groin at all. He had never known such severe pain. Like the fans, he too thought he was close to dying.

A major facet of the Evel Knievel legend began that day with his incredible brush with death. As the doctors began working on his body, they initiated a routine that would become just another facet of the showman's performance in places like Las Vegas, Chicago, and London. Evel would tear himself apart, and the physicians would put him together so he could do it all over again.

Though he quickly vowed to toss the spread-eagle jump out of his show and concentrate on other stunts, the public's fascination with Knievel's act would be based on death as much as life from this moment on. After Barstow a large percentage of his crowds would buy tickets just to be there the time he didn't make it. He sold seats because of the desire to witness the final Evel stunt.

When he was released from the Barstow hospital, Bobby was so busted up he could barely move. He couldn't even walk without help. He should have rested for at least six months before attempting to ride a motorcycle, much less jump anything, but he didn't have that luxury. He owed the hospital for his care and owed scores of other businesses for everything from his leather suits to the trucks and cars that took him from one show to the next. With only two shows under his belt, he had to perform. Besides, if he waited he knew his mind would suffer. If he spent too much time away from the stunts, then he knew that he could develop a real paralysis, this one steeped in fear. He might never get back on a motorcycle without wondering if death was stalking him at every corner. If he allowed that to happen, he would probably never jump again.

Just days after leaving his hospital bed, Knievel returned to Barstow to finish the show he started a month before. This time there was an overflow crowd waiting. Most were probably there to watch him kill himself. A few were there to welcome back a hero.

Bobby was so weak and his body so fragile, he was unable to walk without aid. When it came time for him to perform, he had to be lifted onto his bike. His ribs pressing heavily into his chest, every word he spoke an effort, Knievel nevertheless promised to do what he had said he would do. With pain etched on his face, he popped a few wheelies and rode out of sight. When he roared back before the crowd, he raced toward a ramp and somehow jumped two pickup trucks.

His troop and friends watched in agony as the landing pushed his body down hard onto the bike. As his fragile ribs absorbed the pounding, the man the crowd only knew as Evel, managed to hold onto the handlebars. Sliding to a stop, he painfully lifted his hands above his head.

As the audience chanted his name, Evel Knievel knew he had not only won the respect of the crowd, but legitimized his name. He had also paid a price, came back to the scene of his defeat, and won. Even in the midst of incredible pain, he had never felt so much exhilaration. Maybe a man had to get this close to death to fully appreciate the joy of living!

7

Evel Alone

After the return trip to Barstow, Evel Knievel's Motorcycle Dare-devils fell apart. Because of his injuries, Bobby couldn't perform until he healed to the point of being able to walk on his own. As he was the focal point of the show, the group had little to offer without him. Impatient to work, tired of not making any money, seeing no real future in the act, the other riders left. What little money was left Knievel used to pay his riders for their work.

As he nursed his battered body, Bobby found himself in a deep hole. At times it seemed he owed everyone he had ever met. There were banks, mechanics, hotels, and hospitals all trying to squeeze money out of him. Private individuals were arguing that he owed them too. Without his daredevil show there didn't seem to be a way to pay his creditors either. Besides his motorcycle work, he didn't have any other options for paying jobs. Certainly no company was clamoring for him to join them in the regular business world either.

As Bobby began to feel better and stopped by old haunts to visit with friends in Butte, he was hit with a huge irony. Because he had come from a hospital bed to finish a near-fatal show, he was a hero in Barstow. The people of that California community had lionized him. Yet in the rest of world, he was just another bad debt. Even in his hometown he got little respect and no job offers. The Barstow fair ground arena where he almost lost his life would be his final booking and his last hurrah. He had finished the unfinished business there, now what could he do in the business world to pay off the debts he had incurred during his brief stay in the daredevil world of motorcycle stunts?

The one skill the young man knew well was burglary. Bobby didn't have to look at his uncertain financial position to understand that crime had paid much better than any job he had ever had in the legitimate world. It would have been easy for the pressures of debts and his failures in other business ventures to have driven him back to robbing stores and banks. It would have been understandable too. He loved his wife and kids and he didn't want to see them suffer because of his own lack of ability to pay the rent.

However, Bobby had vowed to stay clean. Even though he was financially ruined, he didn't want to soil himself or his family doing something unlawful. He realized his odds of surviving a motorcycle jump over a dozen cars were much better than having a long career as a burglar. Besides, even petty crime always led to other things that eventually robbed a man of his spirit, pride, and self-respect. He had seen this happen firsthand many times.

Bobby knew friends who had been caught doing "jobs" and ended up in prison. Their world was an eight-by-six cell they shared with another man. To these wards of the state, freedom was just a word or a dream they held in their hearts. It was not something they realized each time they woke up. Bobby might have been in debt, but at least he was free. He treasured this freedom more than he treasured all the money in the world.

Knievel also knew a man who had pulled one too many jobs and died in a hail of bullets in the middle of a city street. As he choked on his own blood, a few stolen dollars in his hand, no one rushed up to help him. Everyone thought he had it coming. His death was not seen as tragic, just the final outcome of a life gone wrong.

Finally, Bobby ran into a friend whose life on the wrong side of the legal tracks had caused him to trip out completely. While the law had never caught him, his own guilt had. A hopeless drug addict, the friend was a shell of the carefree man he had once been. He was always nervously checking his back, always running from imaginary demons, while at the same time trying to find another fix that would help him forget how scared he was of his own shadow. His breakdown was so complete, he was little more than a babbling idiot.

Yet more than just the negative images of his friends' sad lives affected him. Since Bobby had donned his red, white, and blue leathers, he had been caught up in what it meant to be an American. He still had a lot of rough edges. The biker still tended to fight when provoked and he wasn't going to turn the other cheek when insulted, but he also sincerely wanted to be a positive role model for his and other people's kids. He couldn't stand the thought of any youngster going to jail or getting killed just because they emulated him.

As he contemplated his future, words from the past came back to inspire him. He thought about *The Power of Positive Thinking* and the life of Teddy Roosevelt. He considered the men of history who had failed time and time again, but had fought back to win their biggest battles when everyone had written them off. In the face of a growing war with creditors, Bobby got back on the phone to try to slay his own personal dragon. His troop might have become history, but certainly his jumps over the trucks in Indio and Barstow must have built a foundation for him to go forward. After all, he had always done better on his own than as part of a team. Now it was time for the world to watch Evel Knievel fly!

When he first began looking for jump dates, he couldn't be picky. When he called a festival or fair, he just asked for a chance. When he offered to jump a few cars or trucks but they suggested a pit full of snakes, he would agree. For those first few appearances, as well as the one-man stunt show he performed before his jumps, he charged one hundred dollars. For this tiny fee he set up his ramps, unloaded his bikes and equipment, served as his own master of ceremonies, took a chance at killing himself, and then tore everything down. Loading his bikes and ramps onto his truck and trailer, he then pulled out and drove all night to the next venue that had promised him a chance.

As he often was injured on rough landings, many times his jump fee didn't cover his medical bills, much less food, gas, and lodging. An even larger expense was his phone calls. To secure dates he made scores of calls each week. In the 1960s long distance was still expensive. There were no special rates or plans and there was only one major national company. Yet, even as his time on the telephone ate up money he needed to fix a bike or buy himself a meal, there was no other way for him to sell himself.

In his early days as a lone rider, Bobby's main problem was that there were other motorcycle riders touring the country who were jumping a pit with a wild animal or pools of water. Most of these daredevils had a head start on Knievel. They were also better organized and usually being booked by a professional organization. Not having to worry about securing their own dates or venues, having their appearance fees set by bookers who knew the circuit very well, using a mechanic to fix their bikes, they only had to worry about their stunts. Those stunts usually weren't too difficult either.

Most of the circuit riders' tricks might have looked impressive to those who didn't ride bikes, but they were easy to perform and were relatively safe. These men were not going to take chances when they had another seventy shows to do over the season. So, rather than tax their bikes and find their own limits, they resorted to routines that were a rider's version of a magician's sleight of hand. They looked dangerous, but they really weren't.

To separate himself from the other motorcycle stuntmen, Bobby needed something beyond his nickname. What he finally saw as his special marketing niche was jumping cars and trucks. No one else would do it. It was too risky. He was the only rider who was ready to chance flying through the air from ramp to ramp to thrill a crowd. Knievel was the only rider ready to bet his life on his skill and courage.

As he sold his car-hopping show to bookers who had used other bikers in the past, he turned on the salesmanship he had once employed in the insurance business. Though he was rejected much more often than signed, Bobby managed to grab a prospective buyer's interest by painting a picture of a red, white, and blue motorcycle racing across an arena, leaping up a ramp, and then flying over four or five shiny new cars. It was something none of these men had ever seen.

When a promoter would tell him the jump was impossible, that he would be killed, Knievel responded something like this, "Yeah, that is what makes it such a crowd-pleasing stunt. Think of the tickets you could sell. Best of all, it is all profit. I am only going to charge you five hundred dollars. And if I die, you don't have to pay me anything!"

For a few months, as Evel established his name and act, the buyer would usually be able to negotiate the fee down, sometimes to as little as a fifth the quoted amount. Whatever the venue's booker ended up paying, even if it was the whole five hundred dollars, the buyer quickly discovered that Evel Knievel had been right—the crowds would pay to see a man either fly from ramp to ramp or kill himself trying.

Driven by a dream of being a motorcycle version of Elvis Presley, by 1966 Bobby Knievel had begun to evolve into pure Evel. Now jumping several times a week, he was quickly becoming a star in the world of fruit festivals, small-town rodeo circuits, and county fairs. With his bikes riding in the back of his El Camino and his ramps mounted on a trailer, this modern-day Lone Ranger rode into a town, put on his patriotic suits, and consistently knocked the crowd off its feet. In the process, he also paid off his debts and bought his family a mobile home in Butte. While he wasn't getting rich and he was a long way from the entertainment capitals of the world, at least he was not having to dodge creditors.

Knievel knew that in order to take his act to bigger venues, he needed to grow. Elvis might have been able to sing the same songs over and over again on his first few road trips in 1954–55, but by 1956 his audiences expected more. The King of Rock and Roll had to put on a hotter show, shake his hips a little harder, and sing a lot better. If Elvis hadn't been able to grow, he would have never had gotten a chance at the big time. Bobby realized that, like Elvis, his act had to grow and expand as well.

As buyers began to re-sign him for follow-up gigs in the same town and arena he had performed in a few months before, the pressure to do more fell hard on Knievel's shoulders. If he jumped the same number of cars or trucks he had in his earlier appearance, then the crowd wouldn't turn out. They had seen him clear three or four cars and he had made it look easy, so why pay to see him do it again? This attitude forced Bobby into having to add another vehicle on his encore trip. He also had to construct new ramps, ride a bike capable of more power and speed, and figure how much lift he needed to clear the added distance.

As the numbers of cars grew from three and four to six and seven, his wife, Linda, and the older kids, Kelly and Robbie, began asking him to stop touring. They really believed he would kill himself and they would be left alone without a husband and father. Yet even as she argued with him, Linda knew she couldn't stop him. The kids couldn't either. Bobby was now consumed with taking Evel Knievel to a level that would make him the greatest stuntman in the country. He was going to do whatever it took to get to that point, even if that meant jumping one hundred cars!

Though he now often brought a friend or two with him to help with his bikes and setting up the show, the road was still a lonely life. Pushing into backwater towns, performing in front of people who would have rather seen him die than land a solid jump, was not a pleasant way to make a living. And every car he added to his jump meant his body was going to take an even greater punishment than it had the month before.

Though he had not had another spectacular wipe-out like the one in Barstow with his Daredevils, his landings were beginning to affect his back. The longer he flew through the air, the harder the pressure when the back wheel hit the far ramp. When his spine took hit after hit, even a strong man like Knievel could feel the results for days. As he often jumped three or four times a week, the simple injuries caused by the stunts never fully healed.

That was the real reason his father, grandmother, and family friends joined with Linda and the kids in begging for him to quit. They wanted to see him live to celebrate his thirtieth birthday. Bobby did too, but he had no ambition to go back to a life where he was forced to work a nine-to-five job for someone else. If he was going live, he would rather live in pain or die in what he saw as public glory, rather than fade away into a "normal" world where there were no risks and no real rewards.

His family wanted to know when Bobby would stop increasing the jump distance. They wanted to know how far was too far. When they tried to pin him down, Knievel couldn't answer. He didn't know.

He only knew that he had to make one more car and that after he cleared that one, then he thought he could make the next one too. Only when he landed short would he be able to answer the question as to how far was too far.

Except for adding to the length of his jumps, his shows pretty much remained the same. He would ride out, pop a few impressive wheelies, stand on his seat while riding the bike fifty miles an hour, perform a few standard motorcycle turns and spins, then address the crowd. Decked out in his red, white, and blue, when he spoke he sounded like a cross between an evangelist and politician. He would talk about the duty of all people to support America, the honor of living in the greatest nation on the earth, and the pleasure it gave him to bring entertainment to the fine people who were citizens of this nation. He would speak about how much he loved the flag and how principles and values had made this country what it was. He would quote great American heroes and then give history lessons. Each night, in each city, he would tell kids to honor their parents, study hard in school, and never get involved with drugs of any kind. When he finished his speech, the crowd would cheer. They might not have known much about him before he addressed them, but after his spoke, Evel Knievel had become John Wayne in a motorcycle jumpsuit.

However, as his jumps grew longer and the nightly stunts became more outrageous, even other daredevils thought him less like the Duke and more like an escapee from a psychiatric ward. Bobby didn't care what people were saying or thinking about him—besides even he thought he was a bit crazy—because his crowds were growing by leaps and bounds and so were the paychecks for his shows. It seemed the more chances Evel took with his own life, the more people were willing to pay for the opportunity to see him die. As the number of cars grew to eight and then nine, he began to believe that he had made it. He really was going to earn a living risking his life while riding a motorcycle.

Though he wouldn't have quit for anything, even Bobby had to realize that as the jumps lengthened so did the workload. He had spent most of his life running from hard labor, now he was working longer hours and doing more taxing work than he had in the mines.

The risks were far greater too. Yet it was his life, and even though his body was screaming at him to slow down, the soon-to-be twenty-eight-year-old man was enjoying the spotlight too much to give it up.

Only a few days after he jumped nine, the cars placed between the ramps numbered ten. The vehicles that made up Evel's shows weren't new cars or foreign models either. They were full-sized American cars. Most had been manufactured in the 1950s, during the days of sedans as long and wide as many people's dining rooms. Yet while jumping VWs might have been easier, the stuntman couldn't complain. In those early days, when there was no television coverage and a gig in a town the size of Yakima was a big deal, no car dealer was going to risk having one of his nice cars damaged if the jumper fell short. So the cars that lined the jump site had either been borrowed from members of the audience who in turn had received free or discount tickets, or were full-sized family clunkers picked up from local junkyards. In truth, what Knievel was jumping didn't matter to his fans, only that he had promised to leap more than one hundred feet in the air and somehow stick a landing.

By the fall of that year, Bobby was the king of the small fair circuit. No longer a warm-up act, in less than a year, Evel had become the show closer. He had accomplished this status all on his own too. He hadn't used bookers or promoters; he was the sum total of his entire team. So he was the only one to blame when he booked a show at a fairgrounds in Missoula, Montana, that would challenge even his own limits of ability and courage.

As always, he unloaded his equipment, checked out his bikes, and then after the cars were pulled in side by side, so close together their doors almost touched, Knievel borrowed a forklift and unloaded his ramps. By now the show was so big it was no longer a one-man operation. It took Bobby and a team of locals to pull the ramps off the trailer and place them in the proper position on the ground. Only after the ramps and cars were lined up did Knievel began to pace off his route to the ramps and calculate the speed and lift it was going to take to clear the thirteen cars.

After surveying the scene only once, Bobby realized the jump was just too long. With the limited distance he had for a takeoff and the power and weight of his Triumph motorcycle, he was not going to be able to clear the last vehicle, a van. Yet he had promised the promoter he would jump thirteen cars, so he wasn't about to renegotiate now. Rather than try to readjust the jump, he tried to figure a way to hit the ramp faster and get more power from his takeoff. As the crowd began to arrive, the stuntman still was no closer to finding a way to make the distance he needed to fly. With showtime less than an hour away and with no rain in sight, it was time to get ready to meet his fans.

When Bobby Knievel donned his patriotic leathers with the E.K. sewn in the middle of the chest, he became Evel Knievel in much the same way Clark Kent became Superman when he slipped into his costume. Both the real man and the cartoon character had a very different aura in costume than when they were dressed in street clothes.

When Bobby put on his red, white, and blue jumpsuit, he seemed to have almost mystical powers. He looked bold, brave, and heroic. He appeared much bigger than his six-foot frame, and as his blond hair glistened in the stadium lights and his smile electrified the arena, he made men proud to be men and women swoon at the thought of this man.

Evel worked his way through his usual prejump banter with ease; the crowd never guessed he was uneasy about the task he faced. But those who knew him detected a bit more emotion in his tone than usual. For the first time this year, he sounded as if he believed the impossible stunt he was describing to the crowd was really impossible. The positive attitude that always willed him from ramp to ramp was not evident tonight.

A normal man would have backed out of the jump. A normal person would have made some excuse. Evel could have complained about an injury or a problem with his bike. The crowd might have been upset, but the excuse would have held up. Yet he couldn't do that. For months he had told the kids who came to see him jump how important it was to be honest and do what you said you were going to do. Now he had made a promise and he would keep that promise. Tonight, no matter the outcome, even if the final result was death, Evel Knievel was going to stand by his word.

Those who saw Evel just before he began his run could clearly see the worried look on his face. His confidence was not there. He appeared to be a man who knew he was going to die. As he studied his approach for the last time, as he tried to visualize a successful leap and landing, he also prayed for a miracle. He needed God to send a big wind to lift him over the last few feet. He also must have thought about his family back home. He must have wondered what their lives would be like without him. Finally, and with very little warning, he resolved it was judgement time. Twisting the throttle, the man on the bike began accelerating for glory or disaster.

The takeoff was perfect, but even then Evel knew he didn't have enough lift. Pulling hard on the handlebars and standing and leaning back on the pedals, he tried to raise the cycle with pure strength. He couldn't do it. He flew easily over twelve cars, more cars than any man in the history of jumping had ever done, but he didn't clear the unlucky thirteenth vehicle, the plain-Jane cargo van. He hit it hard, the weight of the bike and rider all but pushing through the van's roof. At almost the same instant, Knievel's front wheel hit the ramp. If he hadn't stretched the bike that far, if his lead tire hadn't found the edge of the ramp, he would have probably slid under the ramp and been beheaded by it. Yet by his will alone he had gained enough distance to cheat death for at least a moment.

When the front wheel caught the ramp, Evel was tossed from the bike, over the landing ramp, and onto the asphalt. He rolled more than fifty feet across the hard pavement, every inch of his body hitting the surface. Knocked unconscious, his left arm broken in half and flopping like a propeller as he rolled to a stop, more than a thousand fans watched what they thought was man dying in front of their eyes. Even when the announcer stated Knievel would be all right, no one believed him. Most left to go their cars speaking in hushed tones. They had come to see an entertainment extravaganza, instead they had watched what they had concluded was a funeral.

Rushed to the hospital, immediately surrounded by medical personnel, Evel was wheeled into the emergency room where doctors quickly discovered that his smashed arm was the least of his troubles. Almost all of his ribs were broken, he had bruised internal organs, sustained a traumatic head injury, and had numerous other assorted other cuts, scrapes, and bruises. In an effort to save his life, the team simply stopped the bleeding, administered transfusions, and stabilized his vital signs. When his system began to respond, they placed him in ICU and had nurses monitor him around the clock. Though he would be talking to his family within hours, it would be almost two weeks before he even gained enough strength to go into surgery and have his arm set. A long nasty scar on that limb would forever remind him of just how close he had come to death.

Linda and his two oldest children were now forcefully begging him to quit. As he listened to his wife's pleas, his own injuries were crying out for him to stop too. Even this macho motorcycle man must have wondered how much more his body could take and bounce back another time. Yet even though his family, his logic, and his bones cried for him to end this daredevil madness, to acknowledge that the bike and the man had reached their limits, the special quality and driving dream that had turned Bobby into Evel Knievel couldn't quit. He would not walk away from a defeat. He could not end the quest for fame and fortune when he was so close to moving from an obscure bit player to the big time. Besides, the wreck and hospital stay had been a public relations bonanza. Now a host of venues wanted him, some of them in big cities, and the money they were offering blew away anything he had received up until then. He not only wanted to jump again, he knew he would jump for a long time and make a lot of money doing it.

Bobby Knievel had always loved living on the edge. He had felt it for the first time while jumping his bicycle over burning bushes and open ditches as a child. He had experienced it during his days as a pole vaulter, rodeo rider, ski jumper, gambler, and even as a bank robber. But nothing he had done had given him the rush that willing a motorcycle to fly for more than a hundred feet from one small ramp to another in front of thousands of quivering and excited spectators gave him. It was like no other high on earth.

The emotions that now controlled Evel Knievel's thirst for adventure were like those of a fighter pilot who longed to flirt with death in an aerial dogfight, an astronaut who wanted to be blasted into space just one more time, or a soldier who yearned to jump out of one more plane and fight his way to victory one more time. In each case the thrill of the moment had become a rush, and without experiencing those events time and time again, life seemed boring. Even in the midst of incredible pain, the rush called out to him. As he lay in his hospital bed, Bobby not only heard that call, he was already mentally preparing for his next jump and all the glory that would come with it.

8

Evel Bounces Back

Even as Bobby Knievel was recovering from his horrific crash in Montana, the phone was ringing. Up and down the West Coast event chairmen and bookers wanted to know when Evel would be well enough to work their venues. In a very real way, he had become someone by almost killing himself trying a jump he knew in his gut he couldn't make. He had been rewarded for keeping his work ethic and trying something he knew he couldn't do. Now any chance that Linda had to talk her husband out of climbing back on his motorcycle and trying more jumps was over. With each new phone call Bobby Knievel was disappearing and Evel was taking his place. And Evel was impressed by the money people were now offering for his services.

This opportunity, the one to work for paychecks that totaled in the thousands of dollars, was what he had dreamed about since first envisioning his own cycle stunt shows. As he signed new performing contracts and resumed jumping, he was able to not only purchase the things his family needed, but a lot of items Linda and the kids thought they would never have. Bobby believed that it was time for the Knievels to begin to live in a first-class manner and the only way to do that was to embrace Evel full time.

Finding himself in demand meant not only more money, but more dangerous jumps. Those who had watched or the tens of thousands who had heard about his Missoula crash were not going to be satisfied seeing Evel go back to jumping over *just* ten cars. The growing legion of Knievel fans wanted to see the stuntman clear thirteen and then more. One by one the number of cars would add up, and with each new vehicle there was added risk.

With so much more than just his life at stake now, Bobby began to think about each jump very carefully. He wanted to know the setup before he got the venue. He wanted to know how much room he had to take off, what the surface was like, and what kind of space he would have to land on and stop the bike. He also wanted to make sure there were medical personal standing by just in case he didn't make it. Most important, he wanted to be guaranteed that if he was going to risk his neck, the money was on hand to pay for that risk.

He was still working some fairly small communities, but now he was also appearing in cites like Seattle and Los Angeles too. In a matter of just months Evel Knievel's reach grew beyond what even he could have believed possible. He was not only jumping longer distances, he was doing so in front of thousands of people who knew who he was before they showed up at the venue. In 1966 a big crowd numbered just over a thousand. Those customers were often there to watch another event that came just before or after his jump. He was simply an added attraction for a car race, rodeo, or fair. Now, he was the main event, and the crowds that were coming just to see him topped any that had showed up for the package shows he had once been a part of.

The money Evel was generating allowed the master showman to beef up not only his bikes and wardrobe, but even the way he arrived at a venue. Buying a used Rolls Royce, Evel now made his initial appearance before the audience from the backseat of the luxury car. That English sedan also replaced the trucks and El Camino Evel had once used for towing his cycles and equipment. Soon a semi and flatbed trailer joined the British car, as did a small team of trusted friends who not only helped Knievel set up his shows and keep his bikes in top shape, but who also kept him company on the road.

Before the end of the 1967, Bobby would earn more than $100,000. Yet the increased earning didn't come without a huge toll on the man. Even though he was firmly sticking almost all his jumps, even with all the added precautions, the jumps couldn't all be perfect. As he was fond of telling the crowds, "This is something that can't be practiced and can't be perfected." Even with complex formulas figuring horsepower, speed, and angles of ramps, the element of human mistake and mechanical failure still meant that death was haunting his every appearance.

After successfully clearing thirteen cars, then fourteen and fifteen, to keep the fans coming back for more, the stuntman stuck another car in the mix. In Graham, Washington, Evel attempted to break his old world record and set a new one—sixteen cars. As it turned out, all he did was match his former mark.

Though the approach and takeoff looked perfect, he apparently didn't generate the speed he needed. Though he would later wonder if the chain had stuck or the bike had simply sucked a valve, it was not something he could fix in the air. He was doomed to crash for the first time in months. Coming down hard on a panel van that was the last vehicle, being separated from his bike, then tumbling down the ramp and into the arena was brutal for the fans and especially the jumper. Yet even though he rolled across the track, just missing being hit by his own motorcycle, Knievel ended up with "only" a serious concussion. After a few days in the hospital, he was ready to jump again.

As he had once done in Barstow, a month later Knievel returned to Graham to finish his uncompleted show. This time Bobby spent many hours working out the parameters of the jump. Understanding what had gone wrong the first time usually allowed him to correct the problem the next. Yet as he stared again at the sixteen vehicles, as he judged his take over distance and ramp angle, he felt a bit of the same uncertainty he had just four weeks before. No matter what he did to restructure the stunt, it just didn't seem like he could get enough speed to provide the lift he needed to make it over sixteen cars.

As he watched the crowd come in, a bystander asked the rider if he was scared. His answer must have surprised all those around him. It was blunt, straightforward, and incredibly direct.

"The day I am not scared, that is the day I need to quit."

Those close to him knew that the macho man spoke of fear as if it was a foe that kept him alive and gave his life meaning. It was fear that made him more careful. Fear pushed him to look at all the possibilities. It was fear that also constantly showed him that he was just a mortal human being. Fear constantly reminded him he was flesh and blood and he had bones that were easily broken. With each new ache and pain, fear tried to resurface and cloud his mind with new doubts and deeper burdens.

Yet while fear brought him doubts, caused him pain, and kept him humble, it was also a motivating factor in his doing what he did. Evel thrived on the rush that came from defeating his own fear. There was nothing like the feeling of sticking a landing, because it meant that he had not only done something no one else had the courage or skill to do, but that he had looked his own fear in the face and then beaten it again. Since childhood facing and defeating fear defined him; it always had and he felt it always would.

On his encore trip to Graham, Evel climbed easily on his bike, waved to the crowd, and pushed his fears out of his mind. He was going to do what he had promised, he was going to jump sixteen cars.

"You never know the sensation of going through the air when you make it," Knievel told Gilbert Rogin of *Sports Illustrated,* "but you sure know it when you miss."

It was the latter that haunted the rider that night in Graham. In front of thousands who were watching him leap through the sky toward a distant ramp, Evel realized he was going to come up short a second time in a month. Standing on his bike, pulling the front wheel up hard, he prayed and then he, like the fans, watched helplessly. Though it would take Knievel less than two seconds to fall short of the mark he needed to hit, the scene that played out in front of him seemed to take place in stop action. Everything slowed down and each millisecond of life took on meaning, each reflection of light on a piece of chrome, even the spinning spokes on his front wheel were elements of life to hang onto. And even though he was unable to do any more than he had already done to stop the coming crash, his eyes and brain kept taking in everything until the moment of impact when he was forced to grit his teeth and wait for whatever life or death had to offer.

When asked about what it was like to crash, Bobby often described the experience in ways that made it sound almost as if he, like the fans who had paid to see him perform, had observed the event rather than being in the middle of it. With car roofs disappearing under him, with flash bulbs from cameras going off all around the arena, with his hands fiercely fighting to pull another few inches out of his jump, he took the whole scene in as if it would be the last things he ever saw. Then, as the bike began to fall from the air, as gravity reclaimed him, as the far ramp began to rush toward him and as he prepared to have his body go from eighty miles an hour to zero in a matter of a few feet, Evel always breathed, "Let me make it. Let me wake up . . ."

On that night in Graham, when Evel's bike hit the van, he couldn't hold on anymore. Even his strong will was unable to help create a miracle. With his hands flying off the handlebars, his body following behind his hands, the stuntman was now at the mercy of the earth. The path his body now took would ultimately tell if the man lived or died. A foot to the left and his head would be smashed, a foot to the right and he might lose an arm or leg. If his chest took the first shattering blow, then his ribs might push into his heart or lungs. Worst of all, there was nothing he could do to determine where he would go or how he would end up.

On that night Evel broke his left wrist, right knee, and two ribs. Those who witnessed the fall were shocked it hadn't been worse. For that matter, so was Knievel. Just like a month before in that same arena, or a year before in Missoula, he should have died, but he didn't. The fact that he limped out of the hospital just a few days later seemed to indicate to many he was the toughest man in the world. Just like Superman, Evel Knievel seemed invincible.

Bobby should have waited for the injuries to heal, but he couldn't. He had dates booked and good money just ahead for the taking. Within a couple of weeks he had removed the casts himself and was in his Rolls headed for more shows. Though in constant pain, he tried to forget about it. When he couldn't, he just accepted it and pushed on in spite of it. Though he often took a belt of whiskey when the hurting grew intense, he would not fall to the temptation of drugs offered by those he met at the venues. He was much more scared of what acid could do to his body than he was of crashing after a two-hundred-foot jump.

In Los Angeles Knievel did more than just perform. His wrecks, much more than his successful stunts had made him a curiosity. Joey Bishop's late-night television talk show on ABC wanted Evel as a guest. This was a chance he had been looking for and one he wouldn't have had had he given into the pain and doctors' orders to stay home and heal.

While gaining national exposure for the first time, as he talked with the show's host, one of the members of the famed Rat Pack, Evel came across as witty, intelligent, and honest. After they ran some footage of his most sensational makes and misses, Bishop openly began to question his sanity. "Why would anyone do this?" he wanted to know. Yet Evel's charms not only convinced Joey that he knew what he was doing, before the show had concluded, the stuntman had even convinced a few viewers he was safer on his bike flying through the air than they was riding home in L.A. traffic.

Evel's Los Angeles leap at the Ascot Raceway seemed to prove the point too. Several fans missed the show because of wrecks on an L.A. freeway, but with sixteen cars between his ramps, Knievel made his commute seem like child's play. As easy as it had appeared, few could have guessed just how many different things Evel had to think about before and during the exercise in terror.

The jumps were now so big there was no room for even a tiny mistake. When he had been jumping three or four cars it was just a matter of having enough speed and being able to keep the bike in position to stick his landing. If the cycle hit the takeoff ramp at a slight angle, because the jump was short, Knievel could still correct the problem and find the far ramp safely. Now, if he missed his takeoff point by just a few inches left or right, this fraction of a foot played out over more than a hundred feet in the air to become several feet, and he might miss the ramp altogether. If he missed the far ramp, he would die. Now each mile per hour, each shift of the gear, and even the most seemingly insignificant shift in takeoff angle were all vital in every jump. Each had to be perfect.

"The big thing about jumping over cars on a motorcycle is to hit the takeoff ramp just right," he told reporters in Los Angeles. "I don't want the bike's front wheel to hit the ramp too hard. That might throw me over the handlebars. I have to hang on tight. And then I fly through the air and hope for a safe landing."

The safe landing in Los Angeles, combined with his body's ability to heal so quickly from major injuries, must have begun to cause Knievel to feel almost immortal. In one year he had absorbed more punishment than a hundred normal people experienced in their combined lifetimes, and he was still not only walking around, but jumping hundreds of feet on a motorcycle several times a week. He seemed to be not only the emerging King of the Stuntmen, but to have authority over the Grim Reaper too.

Due to Evel's success and the money and publicity it had generated, other motorcycle daredevils who had once played it safe with impressive but simple stunts were now trying to jump cars. A past member of Knievel's Daredevils had even cleared ten vehicles. Yet unlike Bobby, when these men crashed, they didn't bounce back as quickly. Rather than grow stronger with each disaster and hospital stay, they grew more fearful. They usually quit, a couple who didn't, paid with injuries that forced them off bikes forever. However, it seemed like nothing could derail Evel.

Now with his bigger shows, bigger crowds, more elaborate costumes and his first national exposure, Knievel was experiencing the beginnings of hero worship. Famous people wanted to drink with him, they wanted him to tell them stories and explain what it was like to fly through the air. Movie actors such as George Hamilton and John Derek began to call him a friend. In the blink of an eye he had become a celebrity, and because most believed he would get killed very soon, the rush to understand and know the man became even more frantic.

Though Bobby Knievel had always been considered a lady's man, Evel was a lady-killer. Along with Hollywood's male stars, women flocked to the thrill-seeker's side. They not only wanted to be around him, they wanted him. These beautiful ladies would do anything to spend the night with a man who faced death in the arena. As he fell victim to temptation, a few women got their wish.

Yet the group that seemed most enamored of Evel was kids. Boys of all ages and ethnic backgrounds wanted to shake his hand, spend time with the man and get his autograph. Unlike most men in the spotlight, Knievel not only didn't mind being hounded by these boys, he encouraged it.

Evel must have seemed like the devil himself to those who tried to negotiate contracts with him. In these business meetings he could be ungiving and brutally honest. With friends in a bar he was a wonderful guy, but he could often be profane and irreverent too. With women he was a man often consumed by playing the roll of a modern-day Casanova. He made no effort to show love or compassion to the ladies who came on to him. Even if he enjoyed their pleasures, he made it clear he only loved one woman, his wife, Linda. In that way he seemed cold to many women who were willing to give him all they had.

Yet with kids Knievel was gentle, compassionate, warm, and giving. He took the time to visit with them, and he tried to give them solid advice as well. If he found out they came from a broken home or were in a hellish situation, he shared with them how his own life had not been ideal. He constantly told the kids they were important and unique. He preached that in American any person could rise from nothing and be something very special. Even in the hours before a death-defying leap, he allowed many of these adoring youngsters to help him set up his ramps, play with his motorcycle, share a game of catch, and give them autographs and souvenirs. Almost always he presented them with free passes to his show. Afterwards, he often sought them out again to say good-bye and good luck.

Evel's themes when he spoke with children one-on-one or as members of one of his crowds always revolved around getting an education, respecting adults, and staying away from drugs. It was ironic that of those three, the last one, the one that offered the sweetest temptation for his generation, was the only one Knievel had ever succeeded at. He considered narcotics the most insidious force in the country. In his mind they were the devil's blackest tool. Drugs didn't just affect you for a few moments, they didn't stop calling out to you until they owned all of you—your judgement, your money, and your soul.

To his credit, even as he grew more popular, he continued to use his spotlight to preach to the kids who followed him. Surrounded by a culture that was begging teens and young adults to tune out and then trip out, Knievel tried to do his best to refocus the young people he saw to a cleaner and safer life.

"Don't compare me with freaks," he told his critics. "I don't smoke dope. I get my highs on terror and victory."

Though many writers didn't pay any attention to Knievel's words, kids ate it up. But even though they appreciated the biker's message, parents were concerned about what he was teaching their children by example. The kids who idolized Knievel were saying no to drugs, but they were also building ramps in the backyard and using their bikes like Knievel used his cycle. Many parents were paying far too many trips to hospital emergency rooms because of hero worship.

Evel packed up and left Los Angeles and his first bid at national attention, only to have to jump sixteen more cars in Seattle three days later. Again, he made it look easy. In Washington he not only cleared the cars, but almost jumped past his ramp. Even he couldn't believe how far he had flown. Yet jumping too far was almost as bad as missing short. In Seattle he had too much takeoff speed, resulting in too much lift. Because he went so far, his landing had to be improvised. Coming down much harder and further down the ramp than normal, his spine, which always compressed upon impact, couldn't take the pressure. It cracked and shot pain up and down Knievel's back and legs. Yet, in the face of anguish the likes of which he had never know, he held onto the bike and safely guided it to a stop. He even took a few moments to thank the crowd before going to the hospital.

As he recovered, Evel used some of his money for enjoyment. A gambler in the arena, he flew to Nevada to gamble in Vegas. Relishing the challenge of beating professional card sharks at their own game, the crafty Knievel usually won as much as he lost. While in the gambling mecca he did more than spend his nights in the casinos, he spent his days looking around town.

Las Vegas was the capital of risks. It was a place built by people who loved to play for high stakes. Everything in the city was on the table. While life in Vegas was celebrated twenty-four hours a day through very adult games played with millions of dollars, life itself was also cheap. If you were out of money, you were as good as dead. Only the ones with money got a chance to play, the other players were dismissed and shipped back home when they busted out.

Knievel understood this Las Vegas mentality because he had lived it his whole life. He was always measuring the risk versus the possible outcome. He performed each night for all or nothing. Here in the city that never slept were people who understood why he did what he did and didn't think he was crazy. Most considered him extremely smart. He was conning suckers in a game that they were too cowardly to attempt. Evel was taking their money just for the privilege of watching him take a chance with his life. In Vegas this seemed like a good bet with a good chance of a high return.

However, Evel knew that with other stuntmen now jumping cars and with his own body wearing down so quickly, he was going to have to make a spectacular move to continue to ensure his place at the top. Though, in the world of daredevils, he was considered the real thing on the West Coast, Knievel still wasn't a household name in mainstream Vegas or Los Angeles. And while he was making solid money, he still was not making the really big bucks the rock stars and movie actors pulled down. And they weren't risking their lives like he was. They had the promise of much longer careers than he did. His stay in the spotlight might end the next time he jumped. For that matter, so might his life.

As he thought about his future and thought about what he was paid to do what he did, Evel realized that to make more money he needed more exposure. That made perfect sense, but to gain more exposure he was going to have take even greater risks. That was frightening. What more did he have to lose than his life?

Though few would ever compare the two men, as Knievel enjoyed the pleasures of Las Vegas he must have felt he was a great deal like Charles Lindbergh. The pilot who made the first solo flight across the Atlantic didn't get the nickname "Lucky" by *trying* to do what no man had ever done, he won that name by *doing* it. Others had attempted the flight and had died. In truth, other than their immediate families, few people mourned these dead aerial daredevils. Most of the world's people really didn't see the need to fly from America to Europe. Ships were much safer and had made the trip for years. So in a majority of minds, Lindbergh was risking his life for the prize money and nothing more. Before he tested his courage and the endurance of his plane, *Spirit of St. Louis,* before he landed on the other side of the sea after more than a day of straight flying with no help, he had been just another fool and gambler. A pretty good pilot with stupid dreams. Yet when he made it, Lucky Lindy became a hero.

Lindbergh had the Atlantic to jump. It defined him and made him one of the world's best-known celebrities. Leaping rows of cars might continue to make Knievel a living for a while, but this stunt alone was not going to make his famous. He had to find something else that would turn the world's eyes on him. He had to find his Atlantic. Ironically, it was only a few blocks from where he played cards in Vegas.

9

Caesar's Hails Evel

Since beginning his career as a stuntman, one of Evel Knievel's favorite sayings had always been "Fly through the air and live in the sunlight." At first glance those nine words appear to say and mean very little. Yet the stuntman knew that sentence summed up every option for his career. As long as he flew, he was a star. The further he flew, the greater his chance of becoming a superstar. The opportunity of having fame and fortune made the risks seem reasonable, and if you were going to risk it all to earn fame and fortune and live in the sunshine, then why not take your chances in the gambling capital of the world.

Evel had made what was becoming one of many return trips to Las Vegas to watch Dick Tiger fight a middleweight title fight. It was on this visit the stuntman studied in detail the incredible fountains outside the city's newest and grandest attraction, Caesar's Palace. Hundreds of visitors came by the casino everyday to take a picture of the man-made water extravaganza. Yet where the tourists only saw beautiful sprays of water and a tremendous photo opportunity, Knievel saw a gold mine and an opportunity to make himself into a nationally recognized celebrity.

Most individuals would have never thought about even trying to jump the fountains in a car, plane, or motorcycle. The distance and height were simply too great. Evel thrived on doing not only what others said couldn't be done, but what no one else would even think about doing. He was motivated to live his dream by pursuing what would be most people's nightmares. Yet who in their right mind would let him do something like jump the fountains? Even in Las Vegas, where millions of dollars changed hands on pro sporting events every day, betting on a man's life was seen as poor taste. However, while dreaming of jumping at Caesar's, Evel still had other, if less spectacular, bookings to fulfill.

Knievel's last big jump of 1967 was in San Francisco. It was another near miss. A foot peg had broken on his Triumph when he stood up to lift the front of the bike off the takeoff ramp. Already airborne, Evel had to use his body lean to correct his balance and then land the bike one-footed. Proving what most already knew, that Knievel was a motorcycle acrobat like no other, he managed to stick the landing so perfectly that many in the crowd were unaware he had been in any trouble at all. Yet even this kind of performance, even jumping sixteen full-sized cars with a broken cycle was not landing him on national television. Without exposure from the TV networks, Evel was never going to get to take his act to the world and reap the benefits that came with this kind of exposure.

In the daredevil's imaginative mind, a jump over the fountains at Caesar's might just accomplish what leaping over Chevelot Impalas and Ford Galaxies couldn't. In a Vegas setting, with thousands looking on and a major casino pushing the event, Knievel finally might get the big break he needed to go from regional phenomenon to national icon. If he could live through such a stunt.

Not long after going solo as a stuntman, Evel had recognized he rarely got anywhere on his own. He needed a team to put together the big shows and contracts. Seeking out names who would not only understand him, but place his interest even above their own, Knievel organized his stunt work into a legitimate business. Under the banner of Evel Knievel Enterprises, he finally allowed others to get on the phone and negotiate his bookings and deals.

The president of his new team was H. Carl Forbes. Sophisticated and well versed in business and entertainment law, Forbes would often serve as the point man for E.K.E. He would make the initial calls, sell the act, and explain why Knievel's jumps were a bonanza for everyone who used them.

If Forbes failed to close the deal on his own, he called in Vice-President Mike Rosenstein. To all who had the opportunity to talk with him on the phone, Rosenstein came across as a hard-driving lawyer who could go blow for blow with even the toughest booker. He understood the way businessmen thought and knew how to squeeze the most money out of every deal. He was a shark who protected Evel at every corner.

The team closer was the secretary/treasurer Carl Goldberg. Goldberg made sure everything was in order, defined how and when Evel would be paid, and what each venue needed to guarantee the star in order for him to work that date. Goldberg dotted all the i's and crossed the t's.

This team of businessmen stood in stark contrast to Knievel himself. Evel was a high school dropout who was plain-speaking and direct. Each of these easterners was well educated, well spoken, and often evasive. However bizarre, this business marriage helped move Knievel from working for a few hundred dollars a jump to making more than ten thousand dollars for a few seconds' worth of flying through the air on a cycle.

In order to convince Jay Sarno, the CEO of Caesar's Palace, into bankrolling Evel's dream of jumping the casino's fountains, Forbes, Rosenstein, and Goldberg went to work. Using letters of introduction, newspaper clippings, and telephone calls, the trio sold Sarno on the fact that their man was the biggest attraction since Elvis. The team presented Knievel as the one person who could put the new casino and its fountains on the national map. With a single jump, they explained in each of their unique ways, Evel could make Caesar's Palace and its fountains the most recognized name and landmark in Vegas. Even with three men working his phones, Sarno was not impressed with Knievel's team or his vision. He couldn't see that a stuntman jumping his fountains would accomplish anything other than getting the biker killed. While this act may have appealed to many state fairs, having someone die in his parking lot was not the kind of promotional concept that interested Sarno.

Yet even as Forbes, Rosenstein, and Goldberg slowed their assault and regrouped to form a new plan, a second wave of Evel troopers moved in. Representatives from ABC-TV, *Sports Illustrated*, and a number of other national periodicals had been informed of the possible jump by Knievel's business trio. Sarno began receiving several calls a day from all over the United States asking if a crazy motorcycle rider was really going to jump his fountains. It seemed that while many of the organizations couldn't remember how to spell or pronounce the stuntman's last name or how many cars he had jumped a few months before in L.A., if this guy was going to try to leap over the fountains at Caesars, they wanted to be there covering this huge sporting event.

The more men who called Sarno, the more intrigued he became with the idea of a stuntman jumping his ornate fountains. He couldn't go out the building's front door without considering a parking lot filled with people, press from all over the world staying in his hotel, and a man on a motorcycle flying over his beautiful fountains. When the CEO got wind that a movie production company wanted to film the stunt and use it in a movie, Sarno began to get stars in his eyes. However, because he had initially been so unimpressed with Knievel and had tossed all the information he had received from Forbes, Rosenstein, and Goldberg in the trash, he didn't know how to get ahold of the stuntman's team to put together a deal. Sarno was saved when one of them called him.

"Jay," the call began, "Evel is going to be in town on some business this week and wants to visit with you. He is really busy, but he could stop by about 1:00 P.M. tomorrow if you would have a few moments free."

As if being contacted by God Himself, Sarno couldn't clear his calender fast enough. By now he would have moved heaven and earth to meet the stuntman. After all, Knievel was the man who was going to put his casino on the map. Not only had he received that word from Forbes, Rosenstein, and Goldberg, but from ABC and *Sports Illustrated* too!

When Evel walked into his offices the next day, the CEO met him at his secretary's desk. After enthusiastically shaking his hand, Sarno sat Knievel down and informed him how much he was looking forward to having Evel fly over his fountains. Though it had taken a team of businessmen and the growing interest of the national media weeks to convince the casino manager of the potential of this special event, he was now ready to make the deal and all but allow Knievel to set his own price and pick his own date. By the time the stuntman left his office, the deal had been closed and the jump date had been set for January 1, 1968.

Jay Sarno was one of the top businessmen in Las Vegas. He had earned his position because he was a hard deal maker who couldn't be fooled. After signing Knievel he felt as if he was really on top of his game. He may have lost Elvis to the MGM Grand, but he had the next best thing. He probably figured that every other booker in Las Vegas would be green with envy. Little did Sarno realize he had been bluffed into the deal by a team of one.

Using different accents and vocal inflections, Evel had talked many times on the phone with Sarno. The trio of Forbes, Rosenstein, and Goldberg didn't exist. They never had. Knievel had placed those fictional men on his letterhead because he thought Jewish names made him seem more legitimate in the business world. He then used those names coupled to different accents and personalities when he called his contacts. While it was always Evel on the phone, the promoters and bookers thought they were talking to either Forbes, Rosenstein, or Goldberg. Contact from the business team seemed to indicate to the various venues that Knievel was an established fixture in the big-time world of entertainment. The fictional trio thus made a host of real deals. Yet in Sarno's case the ruse had just begun with Evel Knievel Enterprises and the operation's officers.

All the producers, writers, and media moguls from companies such as *Sports Illustrated,* the *New York Times,* and ABC Sports who called Caesar's and asked about the jump had their offices in Butte, Montana, too. Knievel had impersonated these men as well. So the rash of telephone calls and interest in the New Year's Day jump had really all been the work of the jumper. As he usually did, Evel had taken things into his own hands to make sure his dream of earning a place in the national spotlight would be assured. To his drinking buddies in

Butte, this con was better than any the stuntman had pulled when he was really working the wrong side of the law.

Those who knew Knievel well knew he could not function in a team atmosphere. He was an individual and proud of it. Yet very few people outside Butte knew the stuntman at all, so he was able to pull this scam time and time again. The one in Vegas didn't stop with the booking either. When he got his deal with Caesar's Palace, the national media began to get calls from the same team as had Jay Sarno. Because Sarno had signed up, the forces in the media were now interested too. *SI* guaranteed they would send a writer to cover it. So did the wire services. It turned out the casino would get almost all the media coverage Knievel had promised. No one had ever played a hand any better at any high stakes poker game than Evel had played this one. But signing a contract now meant he would actually have make the jump.

As the Vegas publicity machine ground out the news of the big event, Evel wondered if he could really make it happen. The stunt at Caesar's was like nothing Knievel had ever done. The twin fountains and the pools the water cascaded into covered almost a half a block. Not only did Evel have to contend with a distance of more than 150 feet, but with height as well. The fountains tossed water into the air more than four times as high at the cars the stuntman usually leaped. Because of the unique manner in which the two fountains had been built, Knievel was also going to have to contend with trees and unique angles for takeoff and landing.

Knievel was fond of saying, "You can't practice what I do. You can't master it either." And while those sentiments were true—he couldn't line up sixteen cars and jump them at a practice facility until he felt he had it right—at least he did have a feeling as to what it was like to jump fifteen cars before he tried sixteen. He also knew the potential of his bike, he could be confident in the way the ramps had been set up, and he was aware of how much distance he needed for takeoff and landing to cover the span. For almost every jump, he had at least a rough idea as to how to make it work. Though he was using a couple of years of experience jumping long distances, he was still shooting in the dark.

The fountains were so different from anything he had ever tried, it was like starting all over again. As the weeks flew by, as Christmas passed and New Year's loomed just ahead, Evel was as concerned as he had ever been before a stunt. He worked out the details over and over again and still wasn't sure if he had it right. As the stuntman studied the way to make his jump a success, the national press jumped on board to follow him each step of the way. About all he lacked to make his plan complete was a national television network crew.

Evel had hoped that ABC would film the jump. He had lobbied hard for them to come to town and make the event a part of *Wide World of Sports*. He argued that whether he was successful, his test of machine, will, and courage would fit perfectly into a series that began each week with John McKay saying, "the thrill of victory, the agony of defeat." If Evel made it over the fountains his image could be featured in each show's opening to represent victory. If Knievel missed, then the marriage of his crash and "agony" would be perfect. Yet while ABC passed, they did offer him a carrot. If he were to have an independent film crew capture the jump and it proved as spectacular as he promised, they might use it later.

Though it went against his business philosophy, Evel decided to use his own money to film the Caesar's leap. Contacting John Derek, who had now given up acting for producing, Knievel made a deal for John's crew to capture the event. Even though Derek would be calling the production shots and using his own equipment, Evel himself would be the sole owner of the film. As this was strictly a work-for-hire situation, to keep his costs low the producer used his wife, *Big Valley* star Linda Evans, as one of his camera operators. It turned out that Evans would capture one of the most storied pieces of film in sport's history—the landing.

The biggest challenge for the New Year's jump would rest on the motorcycle. Evel literally had to rebuild it to fit the special needs brought on by the fountain's challenge. Taking the Triumph that he normally used for car jumps, Knievel began by modifying the bike's rear suspension and front forks. Because of the height and distance required to clear the fountains, the bike would take a tremendous pounding when it came down out of the air onto the far ramp. With a standard setup, Evel figured he would bounce off the bike upon impact. With the modifications he made, he hoped the bike would cushion more of the landing. If it did, then he might be able to hang on.

Speed and power were also an issue. Evel didn't have a great deal of takeoff room, but he needed to hit at least ninety miles an hour when he approached the ramp. To get the quick acceleration and power he had to have, the stuntman broke the engine down and rebuilt it with new cams, pistons, and valve springs. Even though he continued to tinker with the bike's engine up to the jump, Knievel was not nearly as concerned with the takeoff as he was the landing. He believed that he could make the jump, he just wondered if he could hold onto the bike as it fell back to Earth on the far ramp. He was well aware that the question most bothering him could not be answered until he jumped.

During the final days leading up to what was turning into a huge event even by Vegas's standards, Evel fulfilled a few interview requests, gambled a bit in the casino, and spent some time with family and friends. He also visited the jump site several times to readjust his thinking and his ramps. By New Year's Eve he was ready to put on his leathers and clear the pools, and he was confident he was going to stick the jump and hang onto the bike when he landed.

A bright sun shown down on Caesar's Palace on January 1, 1968. In the parking lot and around the fountain area more than ten thousand people arrived early to see a man on a motorcycle leap across a distance that almost equaled the length of the Wright brothers' first airplane flight. Many had come out of curiosity, others because they had seen Evel jump before and were now fans, but most turned out because they had grown fascinated by the man himself. They had seen him interviewed on local television and read about him in the newspapers. What he said struck a chord with these common people. Each of them had always wanted to try something crazy but never had been able to work up the courage to do it. As Knievel jumped, they knew a part of them would jump with him. They were getting the thrills they had missed in their own lives by watching him.

"It doesn't matter if you get killed," Evel had told reporters, "as long as you are doing something you believe."

Those who read the quotes couldn't relate to a "belief" in jumping over a pair of fountains or a long line of cars; what mattered to them was Evel actually believed in something. At this point in time, when the United States was enduring war protests, free love, and heavy drug use, when the American dream itself seemed to be a myth to middle class and poor people, belief in anything seemed a rare commodity. A man who spoke proudly of his country and wore red, white, and blue became an icon worth hanging onto. At a time when many politicians ran from the label, Knievel was a patriot. He was a hero in a day when few wanted to assume that mantel. So even if what he said sounded crazy, he was man enough to say it. He was like Gary Cooper's Will Kane in *High Noon*; he rode into town to do something no one else would dare to do. When the time he came, he would have the courage to do it all too.

Even though he was quickly becoming a folk hero, Evel was also a mystery to the media. Writers didn't really know what to make of him. They couldn't get a handle on who he was. He was wild and crazy, but at the same time a person who preached virtue and values. He was proud of his family, but he was often seen in the company of beautiful women who were not his wife. He did crazy daredevil stunts, but didn't like to ride in cars without seat belts and preferred to be driven rather than drive on busy highways. To those raised outside Butte, Montana, nothing really fit or made sense in the man's choices and lifestyle. He was an original in a world intent on putting everyone into a niche.

On the morning of the jump, Knievel walked down from his hotel room, stopped in the casino and placed a bet on the roulette wheel. He wagered on red, the wheel stopped on black.

As he walked passed the bar he stopped and ordered a shot of Wild Turkey. He quickly drained the whiskey, then headed to the door leading to the fountain plaza. Once there he was joined by several members of the Caesar's staff, as well as two scantily clad showgirls. Taking a woman on each arm, Evel walked out into the sunlight to thunderous applause from the thousands who had gathered to see him either make history or die. As the sunlight sparked in his blue eyes, the wind whipped his carefully combed hair, and thousands reached out to him, it must have seemed like a beautiful day to live. However, most in the crowd were thinking it was a beautiful day to die.

After addressing his audience and performing a few wheelies and other stunts, Evel took a last look at the jump site. A strong wind had him rethinking his arrangement of the jump itself. Should he alter where he hit the takeoff ramp? Should he try to gain a little more speed? Would the wind push him away from the far ramp and if it did, could he make up for that factor by adjusting his body and bike while he was in the air? The longer he thought about the distance and height needed, the more he noticed and considered the wind, the more questions popped into his mind. He knew that at this point the last thing he needed was to consider all the bad things that might happen; he had to think positive. He had to picture himself making the jump and sticking the landing. He had to think about the reaction of the crowd as they rushed toward him when he was successful. He had to jump.

Nodding his head, Evel looked over at a friend and said something like, "Nothing gets done if you wait till you feel right." He knew he was prepared, he had figured this jump as closely and carefully as any he had ever taken. If he hit it right, he would probably land on ABC-TV and become famous. If he missed, the brick and concrete wall beyond the landing ramp would probably make fame a moot point altogether.

After warming up his modified jump cycle with a few practice approaches, Knievel took the bike slowly and gently coasted up the take-off ramp. Stopping at the top, the rider silently surveyed the fountains and the large pools for a final time. In the distance he could see the landing ramp. In between he saw nothing but death and danger, concrete and water, and everywhere there were people shading their eyes and staring at him. The thousands who had come to see the stunt proved this was the stuff daredevil fans loved, but it was also a daredevil killer. This jump was unforgiving. One mistake and there was nothing between him and his maker but a short prayer. Was it worth it? At this point even Evel didn't know.

With three huge stars stitched to his chest and stripes down his sides and his arms, his red, white, and blue leather suit jumped out in the beautiful sunlight. With his gloved fingers squeezing the handlebars and his helmet in place, there was nothing to do but jump. It was the moment when his throat was always tight and his body tense. Yet as he studied the fountains from a distance, he suddenly wasn't worried. As he rode back to his takeoff point, Knievel knew he could make it.

Twisting the throttle, Evel easily took the bike through the gears as it approached the ramp. Having been stripped of its mufflers, the Triumph screamed so loudly that many in the crowd covered their ears, but no one turned his eyes away from the rider and bike. As he hit the ramp and literally jumped up the boards, Knievel's stomach suddenly dropped. Something had gone wrong, the cycle was not generating enough power. He had felt his speed peak and then go down. He should have been accelerating through the takeoff. He wasn't.

With Caesar's Palace's huge sign advertising *Fiddler on the Roof* serving as a backdrop, as he left the ramp, Evel stood on his bike and tried to will the Triumph across the fountains. While he was in the air the jump was a thing of beauty. Bike and rider were straight and true, gliding like a hawk, soaring more than twenty feet above the fountains and almost luminous pools. Hidden from the cheering spectators were Knievel's eyes. If the fans could have seen inside his helmet and under his visor they would have known what Evel had known at takeoff, something was terribly wrong.

Though he easily cleared the fountains, his bike's sudden power drain at takeoff had cost him a chance at sticking a perfect landing. He was no more than six inches short. Knievel's front tire hit the ramp hard, while the back wheel barely caught it at all. The impact generated by the short landing tossed Evel off his seat. If he had been able to hang onto his handlebars he might have kept the bike upright and somehow stuck with his ride down the landing ramp. However, even his strong hands couldn't hold onto a bike that had come out of the air and landed so hard. As the handlebars were ripped from his hands, Knievel was thrown head over heels beside the cycle. No words will ever do justice as to the stuntman's journey over one-hundred and fifty feet of concrete.

Those who dared watch the macabre scene felt as if they were viewing an execution. Rolling like a limp rag while still bouncing like a ball, his arms and legs flying in every direction, Evel was being torn apart. Bike and rider side by side, each racing down a parking lot for a brick and concrete wall that signaled sure death. The few who did pray that day must have prayed that Evel would expire before he felt the sudden crushing impact of that unforgiving wall.

In this smashup, Evel didn't pass out. Though he was disoriented, he felt the driving force of every bite the cement took out of his body. Even he must have believed that death was just a few feet away.

Like a demon, the Triumph motorcycle seemingly stayed upright and beside him just to taunt the rider. Many felt the bike would crush Evel before he had a chance to hit the wall. Yet the separated team never came in contact. When the bike finally hit and rolled over the four-foot wall, its engine was still screaming, and the rider continued to follow. When Knievel, his leathers skinned and scarred by his journey, smashed into the same wall, he was too seriously injured even to scream.

An old friend from Butte, Boots Curtis, a part of his team for this jump, was one of the first to reach him. Probably fading into shock, but still conscious, Evel pleaded with Boots to straighten his leg. As Curtis pulled the leg back to where it seemed to line up, Knievel's gut started to burn. He could barely speak above a whisper. As paramedics raced to where he had finally come to rest, the modern-day gladiator was all but dead. His blood pressure was falling, his breathing was shallow, and his body was mangled. Only his helmet had prevented him from dying in the parking lot. Now, as he was loaded aboard a Cadillac ambulance, it appeared that he was living one of his own assessments of his life.

"We have little choice about our lives," he had told many friends, "so our only real choice is about our death. Mine will be glorious."

Few of those who had come to Caesar's would have agreed that this scene was anything close to glorious, but it was certainly spectacular. As Jay Sarno saw his worse-case scenario come true, the stuntman was being taken to the hospital. As ten thousand shocked spectators quietly went home, it looked like gambling on this jump for a future shot at fame and fortune had cost Evel Knievel everything, including his life.

10

Evel Cheats Death

"A man can fall many times, but he is never a failure until he fails to get up."

Evel had shared that bit of wisdom with friends and fans on many occasions. He believed it with all his heart. Yet after the fall at Caesar's Palace it appeared the stuntman would not get up ever again. The event that was supposed to put him on the map seemed to have cost him any chance at ever leaving a Las Vegas hospital alive.

Initially it was blood clots that almost killed him in the operating room. These clots were creating trauma situations like few of the surgeons had ever encountered. The clots seemed to be everywhere. As they fought to get them under control, the doctors and nurses fully expected their patient's heart to stop. Yet it didn't, or in the case of this man, it wouldn't.

Once the doctors had taken care of the clotting, they were faced with a long list of other problems. The fall had crushed Knievel's pelvis and one femur; both ankles, one hip, and his right wrist had been broken; he had numerous cuts and abrasions, and massive head trauma. The fact that he hadn't died in the crash was a miracle in itself. Now the questions were where to begin, whether his body could stand the stress of surgery, and how long would he live even if they were able to halt the bleeding, the clotting problems, and restore some kind of normal bodily functions. For hours the medical team worked on a man who looked as though he had been hit by a mine.

As the doctors opened up Knievel, they came face-to-face with a host of other surgeons' work. It seemed that everywhere they cut into Evel's body, they found screws, plates, and other signs of previous injuries. He was a testament to the miracles of modern medicine, yet at no time in the past had so many different injuries hit the man all at once.

Though he had been conscious on the ride to the hospital, Evel did not wake up after surgery. As he was closely monitored in intensive care, the biker remained still, not just for hours, but for days. With his family and friends waiting close by, Knievel silently struggled for life. Pale and drawn, he looked nothing like the boisterous man who had come within six inches of the most incredible stunt in the history of Las Vegas.

For more than two weeks Evel remained in a coma. Out of touch with the world, he had no idea that the newspapers in Las Vegas were closely monitoring his condition. He also couldn't know that the hospital was being bombarded with calls, letters, cards, and flowers. Thousands were praying for him too. He would have enjoyed the attention so much, it seemed a shame that he was missing the outpouring of adulation and love he had dreamed of for years.

As the days passed, the doctors worried that he might never wake up. If and when he did regain consciousness, the medical staff also cautioned the family he might have some brain damage. They didn't think he would ever walk again either. The medical team assured his family that if he lived, Evel's life after Las Vegas would be far different. He would have to settle down, give up his career, and probably remain homebound. He would never again be the daredevil he had been before he missed his landing.

At this point his family hardly cared about motorcycles or fame. Linda just wanted her husband back. She wanted him to be healthy. She wanted him to be a father to his children and a man who could still enjoy the simple things in life. If she had to go to work to support them, she would. If he never spent another day in the spotlight, it didn't make any difference to her. She wasn't asking for a miracle, she was just begging God to let her have her Bobby back. The good Lord would give her a great deal more than she expected.

When Evel finally came out of the fog, he showed no signs of brain damage. He returned to full alertness much more quickly than most patients who have been in a coma for just a few moments. Within hours he was complaining about the food and the care. He also wanted to know when he could be released. However, as he met with his doctors and came to understand fully just how close he had come to dying and just how many serious injuries he had sustained, even the cocksure Knievel must have questioned if he would ever perform again.

The fact that Knievel had been told he would never walk without crutches or ride a motorcycle again must have seemed like an incredible irony. As the stuntman began to check his mail and messages and catch up with the news of his near demise in the papers and via television reports, he discovered the crash had made him famous. Even though John Derek, as promised, had not shown his film of the Caesar's stunt to anyone, news of the horrific crash in Vegas had made its way from coast to coast and border to border. Gilbert Rogin, a writer for *Sports Illustrated,* now wanted an exclusive interview so he could tell Evel's story to the whole sports world. Now that everyone finally wanted to see Knievel and seemed willing to wait in line and pay any price he named for his work, he couldn't perform. It must have seemed like a crushing blow to Evel to know he couldn't cash in on his newfound fame. Of course, he really didn't believe the doctors for more than a few seconds, and he had no personal doubts that he would fill huge arenas with fans willing to pay to see him jump his cycle over cars, trucks, tractors, or maybe even fountains.

For six weeks the stuntman lived at the hospital, and for the last month of that stay he drove almost everyone on the staff mad. He constantly kept them running in circles. He wanted better food, more opinions, more optimistic news about his future, better-looking nurses, more room for his guests, and a private phone line so he could give round-the-clock interviews and make new deals. When he was finally released, it was not so much that he was physically ready to go home, as it was the staff simply didn't want to put up with the constant circus that revolved around him.

In truth, Knievel was simply stir crazy. He had never been able to stand being cooped up. He had to have freedom to come and go as he pleased. Being in the same place with very little to do was too boring. There were worlds to conquer and dreams to live, and he couldn't get to any of them from his hospital bed. The stuntman was also ready to visit with friends, have a few drinks, and eat real food whenever he wanted.

Gilbert Rogin caught up with Evel in Los Angeles. Once in town, Knievel used his celebrity status to visit the best clubs and restaurants, as well as see some old friends. One of those he looked up was John Derek.

Evel felt he owed Derek a great deal. With the stuntman hovering in limbo between life and death, John could have sold the film from the jump and made a small fortune. No one would have blamed him for the mercenary act either. Everyone wanted to see it, and the money they were offering would have tempted many who claimed to have great moral principles. Yet the producer resisted the temptation and kept his deal with Knievel. Evel would not only profit from his friend's honesty, but would also come to value Derek as a true gentleman and genuine friend. It was a compliment that the stuntman rarely gave, except for a few men he had known since childhood.

John Derek's film, including the mind-numbing seconds that Linda Evans caught of Evel rolling helplessly across the Caesar's Palace parking lot, would be sold to ABC. The network paid a great deal more for the rights than they would have if they had filmed it themselves. Yet with Evel on the mend, *Wide World of Sports* was ready to show the graphic evidence of the man's courage to the world. Here was the agony of defeat spelled out in infinite detail. Besides the network, *Sports Illustrated* also rushed to document not only Knievel's fall, but the story of his life too.

Along with *Wide World of Sports*, Rogin's February *SI* article did a great deal to put the rider on the map. After watching the film of the jump and reading the feature, people were talking about him everywhere. As it turned out, it was not clearing the fountains that had turned the eyes of a nation to Evel, it was simply surviving the crash that made him a marketing success. He was one of the first Americans to find fame for not doing it the right way.

Too crippled to jump in the near future, looking at half a year off from his stunt work, Knievel realized he was going to have to come up with a big hook to keep the media and fans' focus on him. This gimmick had to be something bigger and more dramatic than the Caesar's jump. It had to be something that would keep all of America talking about the crazy motorcycle rider from Butte. The origin of the proposed stunt that would keep Evel in the spotlight had been hatched a long time before his fall into sudden fame.

He had not yet considered jumping the fountains in Vegas when a drinking partner of Knievel's had pointed to a picture on a bar wall and said, "Why don't you jump that!" Taking it as a dare, Evel studied the photo for a few seconds, shrugged his shoulders, and said, "Why not!" The framed image in the Montana bar had been of the Grand Canyon.

When he decided to jump the canyon, he had probably had a few too many drinks. He also really didn't know much about the canyon itself. He had never even seen it. He had been told and really believed it was only six hundred feet across. Yet when he visited the Grand Canyon for the first time, he found himself staring across a deep chasm that was more than a mile across. This stunt would be a leap that no one except Superman himself would try. Of course there were times when Knievel believed he was the Man of Steel. So, even seeing the great distance between the canyon's walls did nothing to convince him to back out of his boast. He had told his friend he would jump the Grand Canyon, and therefore he had to. It was as simple as that in his mind.

Many in the news media figured Evel was using the canyon jump idea to generate some press and to keep his name in front of bookers and promoters while he recovered. Yet even if it was just farcical nonsense, the mere image of a man on a motorcycle flying more than a mile through the air was crazy enough to get people's interest, so the scribes wrote about the world's most fantastic stunt anyway. When they visited Knievel, they began to get the idea that he wasn't trying to pull a collective public's leg.

A recovering Evel explained to the media that he would have to have a ramp that was 735 feet long and rose more than two hundred feet in order to accomplish the stunt. He figured that he could modify a Triumph 650 cc motorcycle and equip the vehicle with a streamlined body, thus cutting down on the wind resistance and giving him a chance to glide for a long distance after the engine gave up. The bike's body would have two wings to help the bike stay upright and stable. The wings also seemed like a good idea as Knievel was planning on mounting two jet engines that would deliver more than two thousand horsepower to the back of the cycle.

Evel further explained that the bike he had planned would take him from zero to three hundred miles per hour in four seconds. He would be strapped to the machine, his hands tied to the handlebars, and he would wear a space suit for protection. A parachute would deploy when he had cleared the mile-wide gorge.

"If the center of thrust and the center of gravity," he explained, "and the center of lift coincide at the center point, and if the thrust is set in the right position, and if the right amount of thrust is being applied to the back of the motorcycle, this machine will be stable."

There were far too many "ifs" to make even the craziest man want to take such a risk, but Evel seemed confident. He also pointed out that while the national news media might have just heard about his desire to jump the Grand Canyon, he had spoken about the dream jump more than a year before on *The Joey Bishop Show*. So this was not some yarn to create press now, it was an old dream that he now wanted to make a reality.

The image of a man tied to what amounted to little more than a V2 rocket sporting wheels and handlebars seemed much more appropriate for a *Looney Toons* cartoon than it did real life. It seemed to be something that Wile E. Coyote would have ordered from Acme. Yet that didn't stop Evel from continuing to paint the picture of himself, his rocket cycle, and the Grand Canyon in greater detail. Yet, to make the jump appear legitimate he also put his plans in motion by contacting the owners of the possible takeoff and landing sights—the United States government and the Navajo Indians.

Robert E. Vaughan, a deputy assistant secretary of the Department of Interior wrote to Knievel, "Obviously, we would have no objection to your making the jump outside of the park. Your self-confidence . . .

is only mildly reassuring to those of us who have read about your plans. But you have our best wishes for success in your undertaking."

The ruling body of the Navajo nation was less enthusiastic. Even when Evel offered to employ members of the tribe in the construction of the ramp and other needed facilities, they balked. When he proposed posting a $100,000 bond, they turned him down. The Navajos simply weren't interested in being sucked into what seemed like a joke or publicity stunt.

In Washington, the higher-ups in the government agreed with the Native Americans. Mo Udall, Secretary of the Interior, cut Knievel off with no comment. Local senators and representatives also refused to get involved. No one wanted the man to kill himself trying to jump over a national landmark. Still, Knievel refused to give up. Through the media he took his case to the people. He also had his trucks and cars painted with signs promoting the Grand Canyon jump. If this was a free country, he declared, then he should have the right to live his dream. Besides, he argued, the government and the Navajos could make a lot of money from tickets, concessions, and other fallout from the many people who would come to see his leap to either fame or death.

As he spoke to the press and fans about radio teams, pounds of thrust, and what it would be like to crash to the bottom of the canyon and die, Evel created a building firestorm of interest in himself. More and more people wanted to know who this crazy man was. As he talked about spending more than a million dollars just to try to jump the canyon, he defined himself as a man who would spend whatever it took to make his dreams come true. In a country where few ever had the guts to give up just a little to live their very small dreams, this man was willing to risk it all to reach his.

Those who responded most deeply to Evel's words and goals were kids. They gravitated toward him like they would a superhero. In their mind he couldn't be outdared and he was scared of nothing. In spite of his injuries, he appeared to be having fun too. He hung around with famous movie stars, drove a nice car, didn't have to work a regular job, and dressed in really cool suits. In a world populated by adults in suits who didn't stand out or seem to stand for much of anything, Knievel was different. He was an antihero who still seemed to represent America in a positive fashion.

The adults who were fascinated by Evel were probably sucked in by his seeming lack of regard for death and his thirst for fun and adventure. Most middle-aged Americans found the new modern age predictable and boring. They didn't live on the edge or take many chances. Their days were the same and they figured that the real fun had ended when they left high school or college. They had never been the best at anything and no one cared if they had dreams. Be responsible and follow the leader seemed to be what the world told them each day. The other central message they heard was "Don't make waves!"

Bobby had become Evel to escape this kind of existence. He didn't mind scraping by as long as he did it in style. Rather than give in to a humdrum life, he was constantly looking for another mountain to claim as his own.

"I would crawl to Florida to be the first man to set foot on the moon," he was fond of saying. "But I wouldn't give anything to be the second man there. I want to be first. I want to be the first man to jump the Grand Canyon on a motorcycle or die trying."

Even as he added more and more names to his canyon team, some even affiliated with NASA, the media considered the Grand Canyon jump just a ploy. No matter how much the man claimed he was serious, the press saw this as a gimmick to set this man apart from all the other stuntmen. Yet the more he spoke of the canyon jump, the more Knievel became convinced that this was his destiny. This would not only be a first, but it would be something that no one would ever try to do but him.

Though it had almost killed him, Evel had been the first man to try to jump the fountains at Caesar's. Even as he was recovering from a multitude of injuries, he was more than happy to point out that he *did* clear the fountains, he just failed to stick the landing.

The latter did not cancel out the former in his mind. He admitted that he had paid a huge price in the jump. He had almost died. And maybe the press and the public were becoming so fascinated with

Evel because he didn't really succeed. They loved him because he *almost* made it.

As early 1968 raced by and more and more people discovered Evel Knievel, these new fans, including the millions of kids who were now calling Knievel their hero, seemed to embrace him not for his successful efforts, but for his failures. They loved to hear him talk about about the times he hadn't made it over a long line of cars or the fountains in Las Vegas. They also loved to watch these catastrophic episodes on their television set in slow motion. Many seemed to memorize the way Evel's body rolled and broke as he crashed.

It didn't take long for Knievel to pick up on the fact that people seemed to lionize him more for what he had survived than what he had accomplished. As the legend of his living through accidents that would have killed any other man grew, someone in the media wrote that Evel had "broken every bone in his body at least once." While the stuntman hadn't ever made that statement himself, he was more than happy to allow the public to believe it. This fictional fact made him even more remarkable in the eyes of his fans. He wasn't Superman, because he broke, but he always got up too. He always lived to try the impossible one more time.

Even Evel couldn't talk forever about the Grand Canyon, Caesar's Palace, or other jumps that almost killed him. He also couldn't spend the rest of his life recovering from the injuries that almost killed him in Las Vegas. He was becoming famous, but he wasn't making any money with his fame. He had bills to pay. So as soon as he could limp from his home to his car, he set in motion his return to the spotlight.

11

Evel Returns

There is a old saying, "You can't keep a good man down." In spite of doctors' warnings and his family's pleading, Evel Knievel refused to be kept down for long. When he wasn't performing, he was just Bobby Knievel from Butte. When he was on a bike with thousands of men, women, and children watching his every move, he was Evel the star.

In the months following his release from the hospital, Evel was in a wheelchair but on the move. He traveled, he kept his name in the newspapers, and made deals for future work. Like a gypsy, he simply couldn't be in one place too long without feeling a need to move on and see what the next town or bar or nightclub or casino had to offer.

His old friends in Butte enjoyed the new media star more than ever. His new stories about meeting stars and the lavish parties he attended were an interesting peek at how things worked in Tinsel Town. And Knievel, whom they still called Bobby, was as fun-loving and boisterous as he had been before he landed on *Wide World of Sports*. Yet as they listened to his stories about jumping the Grand Canyon, as they relived the Vegas crash with him, as they watched the crippled man limp in great pain, each step a herculean task in itself, they wondered how much longer Bobby would live before Evel killed him. In the past his crazy stunts had been largely driven by a need to make enough money to get by, now they were driven more by a need for enough money to buy anything he wanted. His friends were concerned that by living it up, he would die far too soon.

Though everyone tried to convince him either to quit stunt work altogether or at least wait a year for his body to heal before entering the arena again, Knievel would have none of it. Even before he got out of his wheelchair, he was putting together bookings. Though after Vegas he should have been scared to death, he seemed to be looking forward to jumping any and everything with his cycle. He wasn't even ruling out a return to Caesar's. If the money was right, he would be glad to try to clear the fountains again.

Jay Sarno didn't have the stomach for another stunt at his casino, so Knievel's first jump was across the desert in Scottsdale, Arizona. It had only been six months since his near-fatal fall in Las Vegas. Everyone but Evel knew it was far too soon.

The large crowd which had turned out to see the return of the King of the Stuntmen was excited. Though many of them had not heard of Knievel before his crash at Caesar's, thanks to *Sports Illustrated* and ABC-TV his image and his legend were fast becoming a part of folklore. Just surviving made him a hero. They couldn't wait to see in person what they had witnessed on their televisions.

As the outdoor stands filled up, the crowds began to talk about the performer. One of the most often repeated statements concerned Evel having broken every bone in his body. In the six months since Caesar's, this was the highly fictionalized fact that had been interjected in almost every magazine and newspaper story filed about the stuntman. It was great copy, and few in the Knievel camp were going to deny it.

The Scottsdale crowd represented the beginning of a new type of Evel Knievel fan. They had been hooked by the jumps he had missed. They had come to love the man who bounced off his motorcycle and rolled across the concrete, smashing bones as he went. Most of these fans were here because he had crashed so spectacularly, not because he held the world's record for jumping cars. How many of the thousands who had gathered that summer day were rooting for a crash on that day was unknown, but in the back of everyone's mind was the thought of seeing Evel being thrown from his bike and rolling helplessly across the pavement. Most didn't want him to die, but if he did, they wanted to say they were there and saw his "glorious death" in person. And if he only smashed up a little, it would be "fun" news to share with their friends and family.

The Knievel who appeared in Scottsdale was a much different man from the one who had jumped in Vegas. He now walked with a limp, due to the fact that the Vegas mishap had left his left leg a full inch shorter than his right. Though he greeted his fans with a cane, out of the public's eye he was still using crutches. He still had scores of pins, screws, and plates holding him together. Even he didn't know how many bones were not completely healed. Yet even in the face of great pain, the money he was being offered to get back in the saddle was far too appealing to turn down. Some bookers were dangling jump contracts for $20,000 at him. With no more than fifty jumps a year, Evel realized that by Butte standards, he could become rich almost overnight.

His hair now showing a few gray highlights, frail or not, in his white leathers Evel was a sight to behold. With his easy smile and jaunty style, the stuntman defined the image of cool. To the thousands who came to see him that day, he must have seemed bigger than life. Most couldn't fathom a man who looked so eager to tempt death again.

Much more than in the past, Knievel projected an aura that set him apart from average men. A great part of this had to be attitude. Always cocky, since surviving Vegas he was beginning to think of himself as invincible. Because of the many pins and plates in his body, he often joked about being a "man of steel." Yet there seemed to be a double meaning to this phrase. Death didn't appear to haunt him now. If he crashed, he fully believed he would get up. Thus the "Color Me Lucky" that was painted on his bike's gas tank was more than just a red, white, and blue design; it represented an attitude. Like the Souix Indians who rode off to war convinced they could not be killed because of dancing the Ghost Dance, Knievel seemed just as sure that he was not going to die in the arena. If the fall in Vegas didn't kill him, nothing could.

As he addressed his Arizona fans, Evel spoke of leaping the Grand Canyon. He painted a picture so vividly, he pleaded his case so fluently, that his need to leap over the gorge seemed almost spiritual. Hundreds of middle-class, conservative men and women even roared out against the United States government for blocking the proposed stunt. They were ready to rally to his cause when he begged them to write or call their congressman. By the time he finished speaking, many believed he was actually being denied his rights as a citizen just because he couldn't convince the park service to allow him a chance to kill himself.

On that night it was obvious Evel enjoyed being back with his fans. He obviously loved the spotlight and relished every one of the cheers that came his way. As fans screamed out, "We love you, Evel," he shook his head and grinned. He had spent three decades trying to find a way to be the center of attention, and now he had made it. He was a star. Among those who performed daredevils stunts for a living, he was Elvis on his way up. Caesar's had given him his first big hit. It had been number one with a bullet. Now every performance that followed could drive him closer to being a real superstar and having all the perks that went with that title.

Beside the crowd being so enthusiastic and loud, the jump in Scottsdale had a different look and feel about it from his jump of a year before. No longer were the cars that had been lined up for him to jump old junkers, they were shiny new Mustangs. Even if he landed in the middle of one of them, the local Ford dealer figured he could recoup his money by simply being affiliated with the Knievel jump. The staff and management didn't treat Evel like he was heading up a freak show either. They bent over backwards to show him how much they appreciated his being at their venue. This was a first-class gig, not a preliminary act for demolition derby. On this night, unlike any night before, everything was perfect; the way he was being treated, the crowd's response, and the setting. Everything was perfect that is except for the jumper.

Evel wasn't as ready as he should have been. He was still a long way from being in top shape. His athleticism and strength, two things that had saved him when he had had problems with jumps in the past, were significantly diminished. At this moment in time, he was simply not ready to perform. The mind was able, but the flesh was weak.

As he sat on his bike, he must have realized that. He must have known he was risking far more than he should have. He had to have realized if there was the tiniest error in mechanics or judgement, he would be unable to correct for it. Yet because he had promised he would jump the fifteen new Fords, he ignored all the inner voices and set about getting himself ready for the task at hand.

Before his crash in Vegas he had jumped sixteen full-sized cars with very little trouble. If he had been in peak health, the distance created by the rather smallish Mustangs probably wouldn't have bothered him. Yet because he was still recovering from the fall that had placed him in the national eye, the line of pony cars seemed longer and more intimidating than they should have. Even after a few practice runs and easing up the ramp for a final look at the jump, the stunt seemed too much too soon. Yet he went anyway.

Evel's approach seemed perfect, so did the leap from the ramp, but the jump was a bit short, the landing was rough and the rider couldn't hold onto the bike. Rolling across the ground, he finally skidded to a rocky halt feeling the same kind of pain he had in Vegas. After an ambulance ride to a local hospital, Knievel discovered he had broken his right leg and foot. Again he was on his back and out of commission. Hundreds of thousands of dollars and scores of cities were begging him to perform, and he was at the mercy of doctors.

While recovering, Knievel booked future dates and continued to talk about jumping the Grand Canyon. Yet, while at home in Butte, he also spent many hours painting. Unlike when he was a child, he was now taking the craft very seriously.

It was comforting to his family to see the stuntman applying himself in safer areas than stunt work. Linda prayed her husband would find a way to make the money and gain the fame he needed from his artwork. She badly wanted him to give up jumping. While his art, inspired from either his own motorcycle feats or Western history, was impressing friends and fans, Knievel knew that without the fame generated by his jumping, his canvases would never have much sales potential. He couldn't give up stunt work to paint, but the more famous he was, the more his paintings would be worth. If he quit jumping, no one would care enough about him to buy one of his works of art.

Besides painting, when he healed up enough to move around, Knievel was enjoying spending time with his boys. He took them hunting and fishing and began to teach them how to ride motorcycles. Beginning with minibikes, the stuntman worked with Kelly and Robbie on first how to handle the two-wheelers, then later how to pop wheelies and do easy stunts. Though it gave his wife nightmares, the father even talked about having his sons join him in his shows. Evel thought that a family show would be just the ticket to bring more families to his jumps. Yet there would be time for those dreams later, after only a few weeks' rest, he was anxious to get out of Butte and back on the road.

As soon as he took off the cast, about four weeks before he should have, Evel went back to work. Making money hand over fist, his rhythm seemingly back, Knievel jumped in front of thousands and was probably clearing as much as $25,000 a week. The way he was now spending money, he had to have been making cash in huge chunks. The showman was buying boats and cars like candy, building a new home just off the Butte Country Club's golf course and dressing like a king. He never went anywhere without custom suits and boots and always had a large wad of bills in his pocket. To his fans, Knievel appeared to be in the same financial league as Presley or Sinatra. This image meant that more and more of the jet-setters of the era were trying to get Evel on their guest list.

When he wasn't on tour, Knievel was now living the life of a star. He was staying in lavish suites at the best hotels, he was constantly in the company of movies stars and models, and women were hanging all over him.

Young, beautiful, and willing to satisfy all his needs, the starlets and bunnies who clung to Evel may have been drawn by his good looks, fame or fortune, but in truth they also fell for the aura of danger. Knievel represented something that few of them had ever known. Like a real-life James Bond, he lived on the edge all the time. He never knew if the next moment would be his last. This mystique made him more appealing than a hot rock star or actor. The woman who spent the night with Evel might lay claim to having been the last person to be with him when he was alive. This appealed to many who hovered around him.

Not all the woman who tried to attach themselves to Knievel were empty-headed bimbos. Many were intelligent and driven. They gravitated to the stuntman in an attempt to understand what made him tick. They were fascinated by someone who was so confident about his own life, he tempted death just to relish living. He was like no one they had ever known: a loner who relished the company of people, an outlaw who also had a unique value system. At discos and clubs, Knievel was the center of attention. It didn't make any difference who walked into the room, he was the king.

When he got out of Butte, Evel usually partied hard. When he was away from his family, he let down his guard completely. Not only did he "date," he also gambled and drank. It seemed to be his way of releasing the pressures of his profession. During this time, few, including his own family, judged him for this lifestyle. During the era of free love and "doing your own thing," Knievel's passions were much like those exhibited by other heroes like Joe Namath or Micky Mantle.

At one of the party spots along the trail, Lake Tahoe, Evel not only lived it up with his fans and friends, but he performed as well. This jump, though not any different from the ones he had been making for several months, would halt his partying ways and almost end his career. Unable to hold the landing, the jumper would fall hard. The crushing landing would break his hip again. Though no one who witnessed the stunt gone wrong believed he was going to die this time, everyone who ran with him on the circuit could see that this injury, on top of the torture he had been through earlier in the year, could end his career as a stuntman.

When they opened Evel up in the operating room, the team of surgeons were amazed at the number of procedures that had already been done in the man's hip and thigh area. The doctors quickly discovered they didn't have much solid bone left to work with. Taking a steel plate, the physicians screwed his smashed hip to his pelvis. Neither bone seemed strong enough to support the other. Closing him up, the doctors had him wheeled to a room for what they believed would be a month or more of hospital recovery. Yet over the doctors' objections, it would be only a matter of days before the jumper had checked himself out of the hospital.

Evel was about the only person who took the Tahoe fall in stride. He would come back, he reasoned, he might have to make a few adjustments, but he would jump very soon. Again, as his body began to regain some of its strength, he painted and talked about jumping the Grand Canyon. He also had a skycycle built.

The skycycle that Evel had constructed was more a show piece than an actual motorcycle. With a couple of jet engines capable of producing more than fourteen thousand pounds of thrust bolted to the side of the fairly normal looking cycle, the X-l looked more like a Hollywood prop from a 1940 science fiction serial than it did a real bike. In reality it was just that. Yet this red, white, and blue wonder more than met Knievel's promotional needs.

At motorcycle shows and venues where he was scheduled to perform, the X-1 wowed fans who knew little about motorcycles but hung on every word their hero uttered. While Evel never claimed this would be the bike that would jump the canyon, just having visual proof of such a vehicle made his talk about the Grand Canyon seem more real. Even his doubters had to take a second look. After all, if he had spent the money to make up this prototype, then maybe he was going to make good on his planned stunt.

Besides the skycycle, the promotion for the Grand Canyon jump was now everywhere. The custom trucks hauling Knievel's bikes and ramps from town to town had the proposed jump written all over on them. So did many of the advertising posters used to promote Evel's shows. In bars or with newspaper writers, the stuntman constantly spoke of the impossible jump. Though his stories about why he was not being allowed to jump, as well as the cost of such an effort, often changed, his seeming commitment to make the jump did not. If Uncle Sam would let him, he was willing to mount the jet cycle on July 4, 1970, and take off into the wild blue yonder. The fact that the government would never go for the plan made the promotion even more successful. Not only was the actual stunt impossible, so was fighting the United States government.

Though he was fast becoming a big star, what kept the stuntman from being pictured as insane was his fight with the government. Rather than being pictured as a man with a death wish, Evel was seen as the little guy taking on the forces of a nation. Frank Capra couldn't have scripted it any better. In an era when big government was seen as poking its nose into too many people's business and not doing very well at home or abroad, Knievel was the lone wolf with enough courage to take it on. It was indeed a strange and ironic picture.

When he was well enough to get out of his house, Evel again took to the road. He now seemed to be unable to stay in any one stop very long. With several boats and cars at his disposal, with friends in every city ready to party with him, Knievel was determined not only to live life at full throttle, but to spend every dime he had. Even as the most successful financial year of his life came to an end, he had little in the bank to show for it. The money he had earned had gone to buy any and everything he had always wanted. If he didn't look ahead to tomorrow, who could blame him. Most figured he wouldn't see that many tomorrows anyway.

"I'd rather live rich than die rich," he often told his drinking buddies. The way he was spending cash, he seemed intent on living up to that motto. However, as long as he could recover from each of his crashes, there appeared to be an endless list of venues ready to keep his cash flow coming.

12

Evel Arrives in Style

When Hollywood offered Evel Knievel a $25,000 advance to film a movie about his life, he knew he had really arrived. The movie, set to star George Hamilton, would be a low-budget flick, but just having the picture start production at all was a sure sign the stuntman's legend was quickly growing. If the powers in the motion picture business thought he was bankable, then he had emerged as the national motorcycle icon. Even though most of the Hell's Angels were probably choking on the fact the the man in the red, white, and blue suit had replaced their image in the minds of most Americans, Knievel found that this was a very nice position to be in. He was bound and determined to enjoy every moment of his new status. Yet the only way to cash in on his growing fame was to perform. He couldn't take advantage of his famous image sitting on his rear. Though he would do the stunt work in his film, and many shots of his past hits and misses would be included in the final cut, his priority could not be the movie about his life, it had to be getting well and jumping. He knew that unless he was working, he wouldn't be feeding his family or his own expensive tastes.

Though still suffering from a staph infection, a problem that would plague him off and on throughout his performing career, Evel pulled himself off his crutches long enough to book dates across the West. He also began to build on a concept he had first conceived when he was forming Evel Knievel and his Motorcycle Daredevils. Then he didn't have the power to use it, now he did.

Knievel the businessman was no longer satisfied simply to have companies give him a bike or truck and let him use it for free. He decided it was time to become a product endorser. He not only wanted free use of products, he wanted to be paid to use them. Evel realized that any motorcycle company should be more than pleased to have him riding its bikes. Not only that, it should pay him for making the company famous. When Triumph didn't pony up enough of the perks he asked for, the stuntman began making calls. He quickly discovered a lot of bike manufacturers who would not have given him the time of day two years ago were now interested in him.

The first contract he wanted to develop was a bike deal. The winner in this auction was American Eagle motorcycles. His new contract not only gave him the bikes he needed for his stunts, but provided him with endorsement revenue as well. Yet this was just the beginning of the marketing of Evel. Over the next four years he would take the American Eagle deal and build on it to include dozens of companies and scores of different products. With American Eagle he was laying the foundation for a business empire. Besides Knievel, no one could have begun to understand just how much money this facet of his company would soon be producing. Within three years Evel products would make the money the performer earned jumping cars seem like petty cash. And his paychecks for jumping were now nothing to sneeze at either. Though he was still in great pain, his future looked bright.

Even before the release of *Evel Knievel,* Evel the performer was seen as a real draw. He had more live box office appeal than most of the rock stars of the day. This drawing power was especially true on the West Coast. His act was so hot that many venues didn't just want Knievel for only one night. In places like Los Angeles, his contracts now demanded three and four shows spread over several nights. Remarkably, even though at each venue he did the same show on consecutive nights, many fans bought tickets to every performance. He had evolved into a superstar and had become what he had long wished for, Elvis on Wheels.

The torturous scheduling required of the star did have its down side. No longer was Evel able to have a few days to recuperate from the huge toll his body took with each jump. Even though he rarely fell, just the shock of so many landings was tearing up his body. Though he didn't complain, his inability to fight off staph infections and other nagging injuries certainly pointed out the problem to others. Many were sincerely worried he might become so weak that some night he would kill himself on what should be a very easy jump. Yet he wouldn't stop. As a matter of fact, he even demanded a tougher schedule. He had to make his fortune while the public was hungry for him. He knew that in America no one stayed on top for long.

With money rolling in, Evel continued his buying sprees. He purchased rings, specially made boots, new performance leathers, luxury cars, thirty-foot boats, and even an airplane. He often arrived for his outdoor performances via a rented helicopter. He put his name in huge letters on his trucks, his plane, and even his wardrobe. This huge Evel Knievel logo was not so much a statement of his ego as it was his sense of what it took to promote the product he was selling. Barnum and Bailey had nothing on his promotional skills; he saw every angle and exploited each of them whenever he could.

If Evel was out in public, he saw it as a chance to enhance his image. The clothes he wore, the cars he rode, even what he drank, were all a part of building in the public's mind an image of a man of confidence and power. Yet when the spotlight hit him, the star transformed himself into a common man. He even somehow got this blue-collar image across as he waved his bejeweled fingers at a group of fans. He knew how to play both sides of the fence and did it well.

Rather than pull back from the public as he became more famous, Knievel got more involved with his fans. He bought people he didn't know drinks. He purchased bikes for kids he met before his shows. He even grabbed boys from the ghettos and barrios and used them as a part of his act. He would introduce these kids during this show and let them stand with him as he spoke of the importance of values. Remarkably, when he came back to the city for another show a few months later, he could not only pick these boys out of a crowd, but remember their names as well.

It would be unfair to say that Evel was exploiting the kids to enhance his own image. He probably sought out young boys because he was getting to spend so few hours with his own children. He was on the road almost all the time. Back in Butte they were growing up without him. Though the way he enjoyed the nightlife didn't indicate his family meant that much to him, those who knew him well often spoke of the sorrow the man felt by not getting to be with Linda and the kids more. The kids he met on the road allowed him to be a buddy and father, something he missed and needed.

The times when a very softhearted Evel bought a bike for a child or spent time talking of homework with a boy skipping school would have probably been missed altogether if the press wasn't constantly seeking him out for stories. There always seemed to be a reporter walking beside him. Evel understood what these men and women wrote about would pave the way for more opportunities to make money, so he didn't take them for granted. He freely allowed the media access to this world, letting them see the way his jumps were set up and even giving them an insight into his own fears and concerns.

Knowing the press always needed new angles for stories, Evel constantly looked for new things to talk about. One of his best publicity moves came when he hired famed defense attorney Melvin Belli to fight a legal battle to obtain government clearance to jump the Grand Canyon. Would the lawyer make any real difference in landing the biker a chance to fly over the giant gorge? Probably not, but once again it seemed to prove that the stuntman was deadly serious about taking on the Grand Canyon. As long as he appeared serious, fans got excited about the jump and all other things Evel.

In the past Knievel had spoken of the canyon effort as almost a solo project. Now, when he showed the press and fans a model of his new X-2 skycycle, he talked about Doug Malewicki. Malewicki was a rocket engineer who had stepped in to oversee the mechanical end of the canyon jump. The craft Doug had designed look like a missile with a cockpit, three fins and two motorcycle wheels. Though a full-scale working cycle had not been built, the model appeared like it might be able to take the biker a mile or more though the air. Some in the press even thought Knievel now had a chance. But they questioned whether this was a motorcycle or whether Evel was simply being shot out of a cannon like the age-old circus act. Knievel assured everyone it took an engineer to design and build the X-2, and a professional bike rider to make this effort fly. The canyon jump would be no stunt or trick, it was simply an example of what a man with a dream could accomplish when he surrounded himself with men of talent and vision.

Besides scientists like Malewicki, a lot of the Knievel team were just trusted old friends like Ray Gunn. Ray had taken over the setup work that Evel used to do all by himself. Gunn helped build the ramps and make sure the cars were positioned as they should be. If necessary he fought with the promoters. He argued for changes and he took charge of any problems with a venue. With as many as four jumps a week, Knievel now had to have men like Ray setting things up. The star just didn't have the time to do everything for himself anymore.

The jumps were now as varied as the locations where Evel was booked. There was no standard setup, no redefined records on the line and no carved-in-stone parameters. In Los Angeles he jumped only ten cars, but he had to do it every night for almost a week. Each performance fans packed the seats just to watch Knievel fly and listen to him talk. With each new show he became even bigger than life. Yet the next crowd might be seeing him on a dirt track and watching from a wooden grandstand as he tried to fly over fifteen cars. So the new and old, indoor and outdoor, and long versus short all blended together into a pattern of change. Everyone on the team seemed to be constantly adjusting.

While his outdoor jumps remained much the same as they always had, Evel's inside jumps were a whole new ball game. In small arenas, not only were there new challenges created by the lack of space, but there had to be new ramps. Many times the stuntman had to ride down a ramp setup that looked like it was meant for ski jumping. Getting the speed necessary to push over ten cars inside required skill and courage that few men possessed. Stopping his bike before hitting walls that were only yards from his landing ramp was something that only he could or would do. Yet as long as he was being paid big money, there were few shows or venues that Evel was going to avoid. One of the thing bookers loved about Knievel was that his team would figure out a way to make each new challenge workable.

Wide World of Sports was now regularly showing up for Evel's big shows. A record-setting jump meant good ratings for the ABC series. It also meant more money in the pocket of the star. He was a natural for television. One of his jumps could easily be translated into an hour-long-show. Though he was only airborne for two seconds, millions would turn in just to see film of past jumps and crashes, as well as having announcers like Frank Gifford provide commentary on each facet of the jump they were about to see.

ABC also loved the man because Evel was made for television. He could sell himself on camera like few athletes from any era. His vocal inflection captured the problems and dangers of each jump. In his red, white, and blue all-American leathers, using his soft-spoken manner to speak about about love of country and God and his obvious skill and courage, he was easy to admire and like. Viewers might have tuned in to watch him crash, but after listening to him, they usually found themselves rooting for Knievel to land safely on the other side of the long line of cars. They also counted the days until they got to see him again. He was unique and common at the same time. He had more courage than any man they had ever seen interviewed, but he still came across like he could be their neighbor too.

Evel was smart enough to know that each new fan he converted via television or at live shows meant more money in his pocket for his next show. Of course the money didn't stay there long. Knievel used it to purchase things like a custom truck, a ten-carat diamond ring, and even an antique cane. This walking stick had once belonged to the mayor of Philadelphia. Sporting a solid gold head, the cane was almost a hundred years old and even had secret compartments to store small quantities of liquor. Along with all this custom suits and cars, the cane fit the Knievel image of living like a king. He was now being treated like royalty too. Everyone wanted to be around him.

Steve McQueen had joined John Derek, George Hamilton, and a host of other movie stars in the Knievel camp. Race car driver A. J. Foyt had not only become a friend, but made the biker a part

142

of his pit crew for the Indianapolis 500. When he was at the world's most famous racing event, the fans often ignored Indy's biggest drivers just to meet the stuntman. It seemed the moment Knievel appeared in the public's eye, most others faded out of sight. Perhaps only Elvis could pull the spotlight away from the stuntman, and that might have happened only because Evel would have insisted that Presley was the bigger star.

However there was a facet of this newfound fame that created problems. Evel was often challenged on the streets and bars by men who thought they could prove their manhood in a fight with the star. In the past Knievel had never walked away from a fight. Butte bar patrons had a legion of Bobby Knievel fight stories. He had taken on the toughest men in one of America's toughest towns and won more than he had lost, but that was in the past. He now had a career to protect. He couldn't afford to ruin his image as a hero by beating up every drunk who wanted a piece of him. To ensure he was protected from the crazies who felt a need to challenge him, Evel now rarely went anywhere without a bodyguard.

Boots Curtis, another old friend, was the man most often at his side. Curtis had always been there for Knievel. Even before Evel was a star and needed some protection, Boots had been there just to talk and keep him company. Curtis was the first person to reach the stunt-man after the Vegas crash and had continued to rush to Evel each time he had crashed since then. The husky, middle-aged man would have walked through fire for his boss, and Knievel appreciated that kind of loyalty. By this time, he needed it as well.

Though he had long considered himself a loner and had hated playing team sports since his youth, the four or five men who now made up his team gave Evel a sense of security. They not only pro-tected him, but they reminded him of the hard days when he was poor and headed nowhere. They looked at him the same way now as they had before he had money. They hadn't changed and they didn't mind that he had become the star and people still didn't know or care who they were. Only with this small group of men, a few friends at home in Butte, and his family, could he still be Bobby Knievel. From time to time, the star needed to be just Bobby.

Though he was now jumping so often and the setups were so perfect that each jump seemed almost routine, there were still moments when things got out of hand. In San Francisco, just as he was making his final approach, a man jumped out of the stands and tried to throw himself in front of Evel's bike. Only his skill as a driver kept Knievel from running the man over. The individual later told his doctors he had wanted to commit suicide. He had thought about jumping off the Golden Gate Bridge, but decided he could generate more press by having Evel hit him. This unusual situation really spooked the usually unflappable stuntman. Several days later he was still visibly upset when discussing the near tragedy.

If anything seemed to have changed about Evel since he gained stardom it was his lust for not just living, but for life. In the past he had faced death with little fear. He looked upon death as just a part of life. Now it seemed he was not as anxious to face life's final curtain. He was much more careful. He often talked about his fear of leaving a successful show and being hit by a drunk on the street. He also now admitted he didn't want to die in a fatal jump. He had matured into a daredevil who wished to embrace fully the joy of life and live for a long time.

Still, in spite of his growing appreciation for living, Evel kept tempting death by jumping. Now, as he hit fifteen perfect landings for every shaky one, he also appeared to be growing bored. He had never liked routine, and even though he was traveling to scores of different cities and making millions of dollars, his life seemed to be in a rut. He performed, he golfed, and he partied. He lived on the road and spent very little time at home with his family. The stars and celebrities he met, the thousands of fans, and even the venues began to look the same. It was all too easy and too routine for a man who had always lived for challenges.

Originally titled *Call Me Lucky*, the George Hamilton feature film would be released simply as *Evel Knievel* in 1971. Filmed in and around Butte for only $600,000, the movie would gross more than $20 million in the United States alone. Entertaining, the film was a mix of fact and legend and many of the scenes may have taken great poetic license with the subject's life story. Yet the portrait that was painted by the film served to take Knievel's name and fame world-wide.

Hamilton captured Evel's swagger and attitude. He also caught the humorous outlook that Knievel often employed in his life. Yet the film couldn't really show the real price the stuntman paid for fame. It couldn't portray the pain and suffering that went with the fame and fortune.

While *Evel Knievel* gave a glimpse of a man's life, it was also a forum for his dreams. The film's final shot had Hamilton on the edge of the Grand Canyon talking about his goal of jumping this majestic national treasure. If Evel himself had never spoken to the press about the canyon jump, if he had never built an X-1 rocket cycle, if he had never approached the United States government to gain the right to make the jump, the movie still would have painted him into a corner. Now millions around the world knew that Knievel had bragged he was going to jump the Grand Canyon. So while nineteen cars was impressive, the crowds wanted more, so much more from the stuntman.

However, even as he continued to talk about this big jump, Evel knew that he was never going to take on the Grand Canyon. The government wasn't going to let it happen. So what would he do if he couldn't live up to his promise to fly over the Colorado River? What could he do to prove he intended to keep his word, as well as keep the career momentum at the fever pitch it now enjoyed?

The answer would come from out the air, but the Evel dream would still be a long time coming.

Though he never became a huge television or motion picture star, Evel's presence guaranteed solid ratings for series like "The Bionic Woman" and acceptable box office in movies such as "Viva Knievel." Even today, television biographies on Knievel earn top ratings and claim viewers from a wide range of demographic groups.

Fotos International / Archive Photos

Though he successfully leaped a huge pile of more than fifty wrecked and stacked autos, Evel failed to pin this landing at the L.A. Coliseum. When his parachute did not slow his landing, the stuntman literally jumped out of the stadium, only to be stopped by a chain link fence. Unlike many other jumps, he made it through this rough landing uninjured.

Earl Wilson / Archive Photos

A good looking man whose charm and charisma were legendary, Evel was lionized by millions of youthful fans, while also being an object of affection for countless women.

Evel Knievel never shortchanged the kids who sought him out. He often signed autographs for hours. He also gave away hundreds of tickets to his shows to children who were too poor to purchase their own. Though he often walked on the wild side in his private life, when he was with children, Evel's focus turned to being an all-American role model.

Archive Photos

When Evel talked about the technology behind the sky-cycle, it was easy for fans to believe that the machine would clear the Snake River Canyon. Yet, in truth, the project was a largely underfunded piece of guesswork and even Knievel doubted he could live through the stunt.

Express News / Archive Photos

At the peak of his days as a practicing stuntman, Evel reflected the confidence of a man who could meet any challenge and win every contest on his own terms.

Fotos International / Archive Photos

By the late 1990s, Evel showed the wear and tear of a life lived on the edge. His liver failing, a transplant was the only hope to give Knievel a chance to make the leap into the next century.

Reuters / Blake Sell / Archive Photos

When Evel was king, his toys, clothing, bikes, and posters were the hottest items on the market. In his own arena, Knievel had become larger than life, much like his heroes Elvis Presley and John Wayne.

Mike Powers and Mark Fraser

13

Evel as an Icon

By 1971, even as the motion picture *Evel Knievel* was still trumpeting the stuntman's desire to jump it, Evel knew the Grand Canyon was out of the picture. He could have staged a jump north of the park, on private land, and jumped a gorge that was two-hundred feet wide, but the government was simply not going to allow him to use their property to jump the widest part of the tourist mecca. With jumping the famous canyon impossible because of events beyond his control, Evel could have passed on a spectacular rocket-powered jump into fame and concentrated on normal stunt work, but he didn't. In part he wanted the big leap to keep his fans interested in his career, but more than that he wanted to jump the canyon just to keep his word. So rather than give up when the government closed the door, he began to search for another special stunt that would please his fans and allow him to feel he was a man of his word.

Friends and fans had lots of suggestions for a one-of-a-kind motorcycle leap. Some thought that jumping the mighty Mississippi would be a terrific crowd pleaser. Others believed jumping from skyscraper to skyscraper in New York would generate a great deal of interest and publicity. A few pointed to the Astrodome, at the time considered the "Eighth Wonder of the Modern World." If Evel jumped over the Dome, he would turn the world on its ear. Yet these possibilities and a few hundred others didn't grab Knievel. He wanted something as grand as his proposed canyon jump, yet he was at a loss as to where to find it.

Because of the heavy demands his career had now placed on him, Evel was spending more and more time flying from appearance to appearance. On a trip back to Butte from a performance tour, the stuntman happened to look out the window of his plane. He was very close to the city of Twin Falls, Idaho. Beneath him, deep and wide, was the magnificent and awesome Snake River Canyon. It might not have been as famous as the Grand Canyon, but it offered just as imposing an obstacle. As he took in the majesty of this natural wonder, a canyon jump seemed once again possible. When he discovered the land around the canyon was all privately owned, Knievel really got excited. After touring the area and seeing the width of the canyon up close, Evel knew he had struck gold. What fueled his fire was finding a piece of property where the Snake River had spent more than a million years eating away a huge chunk of land, leaving a one-thousand-foot-deep gorge that was a mile across. In his mind it was the perfect jump site. And this time there was no government agency to get in his way.

The land Evel wanted was barren and used for grazing livestock. The property above the canyon has little real value to those who didn't love it for its raw beauty. So when the stuntman offered a rancher $35,000 to lease three-hundred acres, it didn't take long for the deal to be struck. Both parties thought they had hit a home run.

For Knievel, having the land and a canyon he now controlled gave him a new marketing hook and a chance to generate the kind of publicity he felt his career needed. Yet more important, as he had his trucks repainted with a new site and date for a jump, it also allowed him to say to the media and all the doubters, "I told you so." By putting up his own money and fixing a date of Labor Day, 1972, for the stunt, Evel had firmly established that he was going to jump a mile. Now he could thumb his nose at all who doubted the worth of his promise. Yet as he would soon discover, even when he had control of the site, things were not completely in his hands. This event was going to take a lot longer to come together than even Knievel could have guessed.

Before he could leap a mile, there was a lot of work to be done at the site, as well as scores of already-scheduled jumps over much more mundane fare such as cars, trucks, and vans. Even while dreaming about his big jump, he had to take his regular show on the road. On January 8, 1971, just three years after the crash at Vegas put him on the national map, Evel was ready to light up the world's largest indoor stadium, the Astrodome. His climb to the top had been meteoric and now he really was one of the best-known celebrities in the world.

When he arrived to find an overflow crowd waiting for him at the Dome, Knievel was thrilled. When he was informed his two nights of shows were complete sell-outs and he would hold the record for the greatest number of tickets sold for back-to-back events at the facility, he was both humbled and honored. More than 100,000 people had bought tickets just to see him clear fourteen new Ford cars. When he first performed at Moses Lake less than a decade before, he would have given his right arm to draw just one thousand paying customers.

After his usual speech and a number of impressive cycle stunts, Evel readied himself to rocket his cycle between the two Confederate flags that had been placed at the top of the takeoff ramp. As he juiced his bike and raced toward the line of cars, the state-of-the-art scoreboard hailed him as "King of the Stuntmen." After he easily sailed over the rows of Mustangs, Torinos, and LTDs, who was going to argue? He was the best at what he did and there could be no debate.

In show business and athletics, there is an old saying that the "best could not rest." So to continue to be called the best, Evel knew he had to break one of his own records from time to time. His fans expected it. While there was always risk when jumping a motorcycle over cars, the "normal" jumps offered minimal problems. However, when you added another car to that mix, then new calculations had to be made and unknown risks had to be accepted.

In February, Evel returned to California. At the fairgrounds in Ontario, just outside of Los Angeles, Knievel pushed his own limits and jumped nineteen cars. That leap not only set a world's record, but put him so far in front of all the other motorcycle thrill seekers he was literally in a league by himself. Flying more than fifty yards in the air on a motorcycle was something no one else would even dare to chance. Yet for Knievel it was a normal facet of his show.

After the Ontario jump Evel accepted congratulations and praise, but in reality passed the stunt off as pretty commonplace. He then began to talk about his future leap over the Snake River. That was the world's record that he wanted much more than nineteen cars. That jump would be one for the ages!

Now generating as much income in a single event as he had for all of 1967, Evel was jumping far more than he needed to or should have. Yet with so many offering so much for his services, he simply couldn't say no.

In May in Yakima, Washington, Evel was signed to leap thirteen huge Pepsi delivery trucks. He probably wouldn't have agreed to attempt the leap, except as a favor to the local bottlers who were close friends of his. Besides the size of the trucks, the jump offered a number of other problems. To get the speed he needed, he was going to have to start on pavement, cut across on grass and then come back onto pavement. Anytime the surface changed under the bike, the handling was unpredictable. It was also much harder to judge speed. When the surface changed twice in a matter of seconds, it really placed the rider at a disadvantage.

Evel would later say he knew he wasn't going to be able to hit the jump. Conditions just weren't right. Yet he wouldn't back out. He was determined to try to please his friends and his fans even though he felt the odds of his making it were very long. His crew knew that when a stubborn Knievel made his decision, there was no talking him out of it.

In spite of having to go from pavement to grass to pavement, the American Eagle 750 roared down the takeoff area and onto the ramp smoothy, but when the thousand pounds of cycle flew through the air, it was obvious to Knievel and his crew that he didn't have enough speed. Evel cleared the trucks, but the lack of speed had caused the bike to come down front wheel first. As it wildly bounced down the far ramp, Knievel somehow held on. Still, with each bounce down the ramp there was more distance between his body and the Eagle's seat. Finally, at the base of the ramp, he was tossed completely off the cycle, hitting the concrete at eighty miles an hour. For fifty feet he skidded along the pavement, before finally coming to rest on his side. He was in great pain and badly hurt, but he didn't have any premonitions of imminent death. As usual, his diagnosis was correct: he would live. When he arrived at the hospital the doctors informed Evel he was lucky, he had only smashed his collarbone and broken an arm. As the physicians examined the compound fracture, with bone sticking through the muscle and skin, they matter-of-factly discussed how many screws and pins would be needed this time. The injuries had now become as routine as the show itself. Two days later, Evel was back at home discussing his next jump.

Though most men would have been flat on their backs for weeks, Knievel limited recovery to a matter of days in order to get back on the tour circuit. Yet even he knew he wasn't ready. In Carson City, Nevada, his confidence had bottomed out, and evidently so had the promoter. This time the cars he was to jump were not new Detroit models, but mainly old junkers, relics from a wrecking yard. In reality, in his current physical condition so was the stuntman. Yet he didn't complain and the fans never guessed. In their eyes he was a dynamic figure on top of his game and at the peak of existence.

Even while he spoke to the thousands who had come to see him, he realized that he was too weak to really push himself to the levels he needed for success. When his concluded his speech, he gave his rings to a friend and told him what to do with them if he didn't make it. He then informed the promoter that if he died, the fans should get their money back. On this night the promoter got to keep his money, but barely. Evel landed well short of his landing ramp, crushing a van's roof with his cycle. Bouncing off the bike, the stuntman broke a hip on landing. Knievel knew he was lucky to have cheated death again, so he had no problem taking the busted hip in stride. Within weeks he was ready to jump again. It seemed that nothing but death would now hold him down for long.

Again, as they had many times in the past, his family was urgently trying to get him to at least cut back, if not retire. Knievel would have none of it. When he wasn't jumping, he was nervous and anxious. He hated recovery and his temper often showed as he waited for his bones to heal enough to get back on the road. When he was in pain he was demanding and could be rude. Some even called him vile and mean. He was such a bad patient that nurses and doctors, as well as his wife and children, couldn't wait for him to get well enough to get out of their hair and off their backs. Yet they all knew that he would soon come back, beat up and angry again. They were tired of the injuries and the frustration exhibited while Knievel was pieced back together.

On July 4, in Seattle, Evel tried to fly over nineteen cars. He didn't equal his world record this time. The result of the horrific landing was two spinal fractures. Most men would have been down for a year, but the "King of the Stuntmen" missed only two weeks' worth of shows. His grinding schedule of jumps kept coming and so did the falls.

A month later Evel smashed his upper back at a thirteen-car jump at Pocono, Pennsylvania. On this trip he had brought his family along with him. Before the jump he had taken photographs of his sons jumping off small ramps. This must have been terrifying for Linda Knievel: her worst nightmare was coming true before he eyes. Her boys were getting hooked on the spotlight and danger just like their dad. However, Linda was aware she couldn't shield the boys from their father's work, and certainly she couldn't deny that the incredible life they were living was due to the money their dad was making by risking his life. Still, how she wished her husband could direct Kelly and Robbie in a different direction.

Later in the year, Evel arrived in the Big Apple for the first time. He had been scheduled to jump at Madison Square Garden. This was a far cry from Butte, and the New York media was fascinated by the stuntman in the cowboy hat. This Western wild man seemed bigger than life to the button-down collar world of Wall Street. It was as if John Wayne had come to town and kicked the mayor out of city hall. On every street corner and in every bar, the talk was of Evel Knievel.

To make his first major appearance in the financial capital of the world, Knievel hadn't flown, he had ridden to town in a sixty-foot custom-made Kenworth cab-over-truck that served as his office, home, game room, and entertainment lounge. Complete with every state-of-the-art gadget known to man, the shiny red truck and trailer were a rolling billboard for Evel's planned jump over the Snake River. It was also living proof as to just how much people were paying to see the man jump cars and trucks.

The custom Kenworth was often compared to the buses country music stars built for their road tours. Yet this description was almost an insult to Evel's truck. If a fan had been lucky enough to tour both vehicles, he would easily have seen that Conway Twitty had a motorhome and Knievel had a rolling palace. The stuntman's truck featured a dark wood-paneled bar fully stocked with scores of different kinds of liquor as well as Olympia beer on tap. Everywhere he walked Evel's feet were cushioned by thick-piled zebra-patterned wool carpet. Huge closets were filled with more than one hundred changes of clothes and shoes. At his disposal he had a color television, stereo, and various lighting modes. Visitors sat in black leather chairs around hand-carved tables. This truck was grander than even the private Pullman cars once used by the railroad barons. Like the man himself, it was one-of-a-kind and bigger than life.

Yet if there was one facet of the moving palace that stuck in most visitors' minds, it wasn't the breathtaking luxury, it was a small framed quote from the revered American poet Robert Frost. "The people I want to hear about are the people who take risks." This truck, as well as all the cars, planes, boats, homes, jewelry, clothing, and numerous other perks, were the result of the risks Evel was taking. As he was more than glad to point out, it beat the heck out of taking the same kind of life-or-death chances working in Butte's copper mines. It paid a lot better too!

By the time Evel arrived in New York, his American Eagle bikes had been replaced with Harley-Davidson motorcycles. The most famous American bike producer had cut an even sweeter deal with Evel than American Eagle. That rich deal was why Knievel now had a Harley #1 logo on every one of his jumping outfits. Before his stunts, he always told each member of every crowd how proud he was to be riding the best motorcycles in the world, Harley 750s.

Besides the motorcycle firm, Washington's Olympia beer had also jumped on Knievel's bandwagon. The beer producer paid a hefty price to have its logo on Evel's truck and an Olympia sign at all his performances. Without Evel the company had little means of taking itself nationwide, but with him, Olympia could push itself anywhere.

Evel's jump in Madison Square Garden, as well as the rest of the touring year, went well. He continued to make more and more money and he kept spending it too. Most important, he kept talking about his jump at Snake River. And every time he spoke, more sponsors came forward to initiate negotiations for new endorsements.

On March 3, 1972, at San Francisco's Cow Palace, fifteen-thousand fans had bought tickets to watch him make a dangerous indoor jump. Most of those in attendance were family groups. It was now a strange demographic fact that mom, dad, and the kids were the principle buyers for shows that placed Evel's life on the line each time he performed.

As he was getting ready for his jump in front of the excited mass of humanity, a Hell's Angel got up and pushed his way through the middle of the crowd. When he got Evel's attention, he lifted his right hand and shot Knievel the finger.

Someone heard Evel mutter, "I always wanted to punch one of those guys." Riding his motorcycle up to the grandstand, the stuntman jumped off the bike and nailed the Angel. At that moment four or five of the biker's buddies jumped on Knievel and all hell broke loose. As scores of San Francisco policemen rushed to the scene, the crowd, including many moms and dads, came to Knievel's rescue. These normal, God-fearing middle-class people jumped between the stuntman and the black-leather-clad villains. Soon the Hell's Angels had disappeared under a sea of flying fists. It would take the combined force of every cop and security guard on duty to pull the fans off the bikers. Two of the Angels were so badly beaten they were transported to the hospital in ambulances. For days both of the men remained in the intensive care unit.

As order was restored, Evel's friends begged him not to jump. Besides the near riot, there was simply not enough room to land and guide the bike between two concrete pillars just beyond the landing ramp. Besides, his crew argued, the bike didn't sound right either.

Evel shrugged his shoulders, got on the cycle, kicked the starter, and said, "What do you want me to do, give them their money back?"

In front of thousands of standing and screaming fans, he readied himself to ride for the people who had come to his aid when he needed them most.

The moment before Evel jumped at the Cow Palace was filled with fear and excitement. Everyone knew it was incredibly dangerous, most realized that the fight and near riot had taken its toll on Knievel's physical and mental condition. Yet as he raced up the ramp and flew through the air, the jump was perfect. But his crew had been right, there wasn't room to land the cycle. As he hit the ramp and tried to slow the bike, Evel lost control. He was thrown over the handlebars, then the one thousand-pound Harley landed on top of him. Skidding along the ground at more than a mile a minute, the rider flew down a tunnel, just missing the two concrete pillars. He would still strike a wall of concrete before he stopped. With most of the fall hidden from the crowd, few knew just how badly the rider had been hurt. It was only when his fans read the paper the next day that they realized Evel's injuries had required back surgery to repair bones he had never before broken. However, even as badly as he was hurt, probably coming as close to death as he had at Caesar's in Vegas, Knievel was out and performing well before the two beaten Hell's Angels members were out of the hospital and back on their bikes.

After healing he managed several perfect jumps and landings. Then a few months after the incident in the Cow Palace, while jumping at the Michigan Fairgrounds in Detroit, Evel cleared thirteen cars but slammed into a concrete wall. Everyone thought he had been seriously injured again. As an emergency medical team raced to his side, Knievel got up bruised, but unfazed. He then walked back to thank the crowd for coming out to see him.

It would be an early-summer event in Atlanta that taught Evel a bitter lesson he would never forget. At a practice run the day before the Georgia jump, the stuntman fell and was injured. This time even he knew he wasn't in the kind of physical shape it would take to clear the length of the jump. After doing a long routine of impressive motorcycle stunts, he explained his situation to the thousands who had gathered. He told them he couldn't jump. For the first time in his life, he was booed. Knievel was shocked at how quickly people turned on him, hurling obscenities and threatening to come out of the stands after him. What probably hurt the worst was having little boys call him a coward.

Many in the crowd that night thought the old Evel would have jumped. The Evel who was hungry and barely making ends meet would have challenged the odds and his own health to earn a paycheck. For that reason some suddenly started saying the money and fame had made the stuntman go soft and had robbed him of the desire to face death in the arena. Knievel realized that the night he failed to jump in Atlanta he tarnished his image of the gladiator of the modern age. In many people's eyes he had wimped out.

In truth Knievel probably hadn't suddenly become soft, just a bit wiser. He may have had several pounds of steel screws, pins and plates holding his body together, but the last few crashes had convinced him he wasn't the Man of Steel. He did have his physical limits, and the Grim Reaper would find him if he decided to challenge those limits too many more times. If he was going to make a jump now, he was going to have to be in top form. Otherwise he might never get the chance to fly over the Snake River Canyon.

For several months Evel had been telling interviewers and fans about his Labor Day jump at Snake River. Yet as the year quickly rolled by, he realized he just wasn't going to be ready. He needed a new rocket cycle, as well as crew to design and build it. He also needed a media team that could help him make the most out of this one-of-a-kind event. Sensing there was a huge market for both a live gate and worldwide television, Knievel put the Snake River jump off for at least a year. While he was still promising to jump, the thirty-four-year-old stuntman was adopting an attitude similar to the one he had displayed in Atlanta, he would wait until conditions were perfect.

Needing rest and rehabilitation, physically and mentally beaten, Evel returned to Butte late in the summer of 1972. Tired of the road, exhausted from injuries and a hard schedule of jumps, the Montana native thought some quality time with family would help him recenter his life, as well as focus him on the dates he had booked later in the year. Besides, even though his jet-setting life had seen him party with the world's most beautiful women and hang out with the movers and shakers of Hollywood, he missed his wife and kids. He also had a longing for the slower pace of life he could find on the streets of his hometown.

In Butte, Evel once again became just Bobby. He drank with old friends, played golf, enjoyed his new large home on the sixteenth fairway of the country club, and got reacquainted with his wife and children. As he visited his old haunts, he became starkly aware that many of the people he knew were having a very hard time just making ends meet. If anything, the economy was worse than it had been when he was trying to make a living in the area. Though it was not reported, and certainly Knievel wouldn't talk about it with the media, the stuntman's caring spirit kicked in as he very quietly purchased food and clothing for destitute families and new bikes for young kids who had few toys and no bicycles at all. Like Santa Claus, Bobby usually gave his gifts when no one was looking and then later acted as though he knew nothing about the charitable act. Yet most in Butte knew how the sack of groceries or the fancy kid's bike had ended up on a family's doorstep.

Even though he could still be a hard-driving man who demanded a great deal of his wife and family, Evel seemed to be developing a more spiritual side too. Still it was true that when he was injured and in pain he often lashed out. Sometimes, in front of guests, he also tried to establish himself as lord of his manor by ordering his wife around. However, Knievel also now talked a great deal about God. He often said he believed that the man in the sky was watching out for him. That he "felt His hand on me when I jumped."

Evel's spiritual views hadn't come through church attendance or the guidance of a minister. He didn't have much regard for most evangelists, stating they were worse than many con men, but he did admire and respect common men and women with a faith that they quietly used each day. Linda was like that. She prayed, studied, and lived in the manner she believed God wanted her to. She was a loving mother and a forgiving wife. Considering the wild life Knievel had lived when he was away from home, another woman would have left him years before. Yet Linda overlooked her husband's many falls from grace and his seeming rush to meet death. She accepted what he gave her and was grateful for it. As he had told many of his friends, Linda's love was unlike any the man had ever known. He was really proud that she was his wife and the mother of his children. Knievel also now fully appreciated Linda's family too.

In spite of the rocky ground he had found himself on when he had first gotten to know Linda's father, Evel was now accepted and liked by John Bork. When Evel was in town, the two men often spent time together. John was a good man who had devoted himself to being a wonderful grandfather. Evel considered this a great gift for his children. Evel's schedule kept him on the road so much, and Bork's time spent with Kelly, Robbie, and Tracey meant a great deal to the children and their father.

While he was at home this time, Evel was pleased to have an opportunity to join his father-in-law on a duck-hunting outing. The two men decided to make the trip a male-bonding experience by taking Robbie and Kelly along too. What should have been a chance for Knievel to get out of the pressures of the spotlight and genuinely enjoy his family in a bucolic setting, turned into the greatest tragedy of his life.

Foul weather plagued the outing. As heavy rains poured down from a rapidly developing summer thunderstorm, the quartet was caught floating on a suddenly angry, swollen river in a ten-foot-rubber raft. As the craft was tossed up and down in the white, swirling water, Evel must have realized the irony now confronting him. He and his father-in-law were fighting for not only their lives, but the lives of two small boys. Danger was all around them. With each crashing wall of water and each new whirlpool, the family was dragged closer to death than any of them, including the stuntman, had ever known.

In an instant almost too quick to see with the naked eye, Kelly and Robbie were tossed out of the boat and into the river. Surrounded by rocks and debris, the boys were struggling just to keep their heads above the water. Sensing he could do nothing for his children from the raft, Knievel jumped into the raging river to try to save his boys. In an act far more heroic than any jump he had ever attempted, Evel fought through the flooded waters, grabbed his children, and dragged them through the rushing current to the shore. After he got his sons safely on the shore, Knievel looked back to the water. As he breathed heavily, he searched the stream for John. All he saw was a capsized raft caught up in the undertow. His father-in-law was nowhere to be seen. Quickly glancing down both sides of the bank, Knievel again came up empty. John was not there. Unlike the three of them, he had not made it to safety on the shore. Plunging back into the swirling water, fighting the current, shouting for John at the top of his voice, Knievel continued to struggle up and down the flooded waterway until he was completely worn out. Yet the river wouldn't give up John Bork until the life had been completely drained from him. In spite of his son-in-law's efforts, the man drowned.

It haunted Evel that something as harmless as a hunting trip, an excursion that he had successfully completed countless times before, had cost the Knievel family more than any of Evel's jumps ever had. It seemed so stupid and pointless. This was no way to die. It shouldn't have happened.

In the past the "ifs" in Knievel's life had concerned motorcycle parts and functions. "I would have made the jump *if* the chain hadn't broken or the valve hadn't gotten stuck." But this time the "ifs" were much more personal and much harder to answer.

What if they had paid closer attention to the weather? What if they had noted the rising water sooner? What if, what if, what if . . . When one watches a friend and family member die in an accident the way that John Bork had died, it causes one to believe that when one's number is up, it is up. It is as simple as that. So many around Evel said that it was best to live life large now, because, no matter what you do or who you are, tomorrow might be your day to die.

Over time it would be easy to rationalize John Bork's death by saying, "He died doing something he loved." Using that logic, if Evel died doing a stunt in front of thousands of people, then his death would be easier to understand and accept too. Yet, as Bobby now looked at his family, especially his children, he realized that he wanted to live for them a great deal more than he wanted to die in the arena. For that reason, his earlier decision not to jump in Atlanta was not only justified, but necessary.

Some thought John's death might cause Evel to retire. He seemed to have the resources to do so. He owned a nice home, scores of cars and motorcycles, clothes, jewelry, and everything he and his family could ever want. Yet appearances were deceiving, in truth Knievel was running his financial tank on empty. He had to work and jump just to keep paying the bills he had run up living the lavish lifestyle that made him look well fixed. If he quit stunt work, then he would have to sell almost everything he had and go back to a much more modest life. He wasn't about to step backward. So he stepped back on his bike.

Evel's next important and really dangerous jump came in front of a huge crowd and a national television audience in Los Angeles on February 18, 1973. Knievel had arrived in L.A. early, and the city had opened its arms to the celebrity biker. He was wheeled around town in a Maserati sports car and wined and dine by city officials. Movie stars sought him out; he was invited to premieres and given special medals and awards. As he made numerous personal appearances, he wore an $8,000 mink coat and so many rings and jewelry that Zsa Zsa Gabor and Liz Taylor would have been green with envy. He acted like he owned the town, and in truth, he did. Hollywood, Beverly Hills, and the rest of Los Angeles appeared to be his for the taking. It seemed if he asked for anything, he got it.

It rained the day of the jump, but by the time the fans began to arrive, the weather had become sunny and bright. Yet things were not as picture-postcard perfect as they appeared.

Jumping over fifty smashed and stacked cars at the famed L.A. Coliseum represented a huge challenge. In order to gain the speed needed for takeoff, Evel had been forced to build a ramp that began at the top of the far end of the structure. The ramp was so steep that most experienced bikers couldn't have controlled a slow ride down it, much less hit the speed and balance needed to explode off the end of the ramp and over the fifty cars. As the rain had made the ramp's surface slick, the jump now seemed incredibly dangerous.

One of Evel's initial problems was just getting his Harley to the top of the takeoff ramp. The steep climb would have been a challenge even for the most experienced biker. The stuntman had to put so much power into the climb that he was in danger of having the cycle's front wheel leave the surface, thus tossing the bike and rider into a roll. When he finally made it to the top, he had to have men positioned on each side of the takeoff point just to catch the Harley before it either rolled backwards down the ramp or went flying off the other side. Just getting into position to try this jump was a stunt most men would have never attempted. Yet this was easy compared to what he had to do next—fly over fifty cars and then stop the bike before he flew out the other end of the stadium.

In a practice run Evel's bike slipped on the two-hundred-foot-long landing ramp and the rider was lucky to escape with just a broken finger. Then more rain came. Even though the camera crews from ABC were in place and the stands were filling with paying customers, the promoter, auto-racing's renowned J. C. Agajanian, begged Evel not to jump. Agajanian told the stuntman that he would take the blame for the cancellation. So the rider had a ticket out with no possible fingers that could be pointed his way.

Yet Evel had learned a lesson from the crowd reaction in Atlanta. He knew he now had to jump even though it was too wet. Besides, how many times did he get a chance to perform in a place as historic as the Coliseum? It had been built for the 1932 Olympics. Countless legendary athletes had performed there then and in many contests of skill since. For the stuntman this was a chance to join the immortals of sports. It was an opportunity Evel was not going to be denied, even if it meant meeting his maker.

After his customary visit with the crowd, "The King of the Stunt-men," "The World's Greatest Daredevil," and "The Last of Gladia-tors," wowed the television audience and his live fans with his long, almost-straight-up run up the takeoff ramp. Then he slowly turned the bike to face the mind-numbing jump stretched out more than fifty feet below him. Racing down the wet ramp, shifting through three gear changes to gain the needed takeoff speed, hitting more than one hundred miles per hour when his wheel left the ramp, Evel soared gracefully through the air, over the mass of twisted auto wreckage and onto the waiting landing ramp. Hitting a button, he released a para-chute that opened, but failed to slow him down. Holding onto the Harley, downshifting and braking in an attempt to slow down, the rider fought a desperate battle to stop in the two hundred feet that he had been given. He couldn't make it. The last section of the landing ramp led up into the far end of the stadium. The uphill ramp had been designed to give Knievel a chance to let gravity help stop the bike. It didn't. Beyond the ramp, Evel rode his motorcycle through the far end of the Coliseum and out of the facility, leaping a walkway and crashing into a chain link fence. Thus the best show might have been the one the fans never saw.

Lying on the concrete, Evel carefully moved his body, then stood up. He felt fine. All that really hurt was the finger he had broken the previous day. With a gasping crowd waiting, the red-white-and-blue suited stuntman walked back into the Coliseum a conquering hero, greeted by a standing ovation and thundering cheers. It seemed his luck was changing.

Two months later, in Portland, a huge audience and ABC-TV once again came together to watch Evel jump. This time he was trying to clear seventeen vans and trucks. It was a jump that even he didn't think he could make. Beginning his approach in the tunnel beneath Portland Memorial Coliseum, Evel roared out toward a standard take-off ramp and an anything-but-standard row of vehicles. Because they were larger and wider than cars, this jump would demand more of him and his bike than any car jump he had ever attempted. Before taking off he had even told members of the television crew he wasn't going to make it. He didn't seem to feel he had the necessary room to gain the needed speed to clear the length to the landing ramp.

With flash bulbs popping like strobes, Evel raced into the stadium, made a slight right turn past some lighting equipment, then accelerated toward the ramp. As he hit the wood it didn't seem he had enough speed. Rising in has seat, standing to steady his bike and lift his front wheel, Knievel rode through the air like a gliding hawk. It was poetry in motion. As he headed toward the landing ramp, everything stopped except the flashes of light from the fan's cameras and the steady course of bike and man through the air. Would he make it? That was the question on thousands of lips.

Evel brought the bike down just eighteen inches beyond the last van, his back tire coming down perfectly on the ramp. The rider then eased the forward wheel gently to the wooden surface. The jump was as perfect as any he had ever made. The crowd rose to their feet and saluted the man who was just a motorcycle hero but an American icon.

Talking to the television audience Evel admitted that even he didn't think he would make the distance. Then he added, "We sold this place out tonight and I would have just as soon missed the jump as have them boo me out of here." Then, in a show of honesty that must have stunned his many fans, he added, "I am almost to the end of my road. I am going to jump in Los Angeles, San Francisco, Tulsa, Kansas City, and Canada, and then we are going to the canyon, Sunday, September 8. I will see you there."

Though it was now scheduled for two years later than he had planned, with the Snake River Canyon jump Evel appeared to be saying farewell. Through his own words it seemed that he was going to use that stunt to put a final cap on his career. Some thought Knievel was pushing the thought of the canyon as his final jump and the dates booked before that jump as his final performances just to drum up tickets sales and interest. However, there were now others who were reading something far more frightening into Evel's words. They thought he was saying he would die at the canyon. If that was what he meant, then it would truly fit Knievel's own philosophy of life.

Evel was fond of quoting Teddy Roosevelt. "Far better it is to take a chance to win glorious victory and triumph even though checkered by failure, than to take rank with those poor spirits who know no victory nor defeat because they live in the grey twilight and have tried neither."

Knievel had tried and he had failed more often that he cared to recall. Somehow, through his own failures, he had become a household name and money-making machine. Now the time was coming to risk his life for financial rewards and glory that he might not be around to enjoy. Would he have the guts to back his long-promised canyon jump or would he disappoint his fans like he had in Atlanta? No one, probably not even Evel, knew if his lust for life had now grown beyond his thirst for tempting death.

14

Evel on Tour

When Evel Knievel tried to jump the twin fountains at Caesar's Palace he was virtually unknown. By 1973, he was a national icon and one of the country's most recognized celebrities. A year later, as he prepared to make the two most important jumps on his 1974 "dance card," he was better known than any player in the NBA and most who made their living in the NFL and Major League Baseball. The name Evel Knievel ranked with Elvis Presley, Frank Sinatra, and John Wayne.

The incredible growth in Evel's career had come with a price, mostly broken bones and little time at home. It had also presented him with a huge dilemma. He simply couldn't manage every facet of his business by himself anymore. Five years before he had done it all. To appear legitimate back then, he had used the names of imaginary business associates on his letterhead, but in truth Knievel had run the whole show. Now he needed help to market his bigger-than-life image. The job was simply too large for one man to handle.

Scores of promotional experts and marketing companies approached the stuntman with offers for representation. After shifting through stacks of offers, Evel cast his lot with Marvin Glass & Associates. The Chicago firm not only took over a large chunk of marketing Evel, but they also relieved the stuntman of some logistical nightmares. For a few months he found himself with enough time to golf, party, and make a few jumps. For a man who had been working as much as twenty hours a day trying to manage a hundred different things at once, it was a needed vacation from the rigors of the business world. This move also gave Knievel's wife a chance to kick back a little. Linda had become the manager of more and more of Evel's day-to-day business and she too needed a break.

Anson Isaacson, a managing partner of Glass & Associates, quickly told everyone, including *Business Week* magazine, that Evel was going to be huge. "He will probably wind up being a folk hero," Isaacson explained. Anson may have been attempting to inflate the aura of Knievel in order to gain endorsements, but as it turned out, the promoter wasn't far from wrong either. Even though only America's kids had caught on to the fact, Evel was already a hero to millions. Thanks to Glass & Associates it wouldn't take the business community long to catch up.

Beginning with an Ideal Toy contract that just covered a battery-operated twelve-inch-tall Evel Knievel rider and motorcycle jump toy, Glass sold Knievel to the world in larger and larger portions, with each new deal generating a greater cash flow. Helbros came out with Evel Knievel watches. Krypton manufactured special Evel radios. Knievel hobby kits were pushed by the Addar company. Mego brought out a line of bicycle accessories. Leisure Dynamics claimed the rights to drinking straws. As the Snake River jump grew closer, more companies fought to come on board. It seemed that everyone who signed up with Knievel made a sizeable profit, but it was Ideal which seemed to benefit the most from the partnership.

Before signing up Evel, Ideal was in trouble. Many business analysts figured the company would either go under or be bought out by a rival. Then Evel jumped into the company's plans. Taking a last-gasp financial chance, they gave Knievel a $100,000 advance for the rider and motorcycle jumping toy. Costing fourteen dollars retail, the toy set would generate almost twenty million dollars in sales during its first eighteen months on the market. Suddenly, thanks solely to Evel, Ideal was very healthy.

Coming back to the table and cutting more deals, the toy manufacturer introduced Evel concepts for other toys, action figures, posters, and clothing. Six months before the scheduled Snake River leap,

Evel was as important to Ideal as the Mustang was to the Ford Motor Company. By early 1974 the company's best-selling item was its model of the skycycle Evel was supposed to use to jump the canyon.

Though *Business Week* had called the money-making ventures by Ideal and others "the marketing of suicide," these licensing companies couldn't have cared less. Predicted sales for Knievel licensed products in 1974 were over two hundred million dollars. With his cut estimated at between five and ten percent, Evel would be taking home ten to twenty million dollars off products marketed to children alone. No person in the world at that time could come close to this kind of sales. Yet even as kids badgered their parents for more Knievel toys, the media questioned how and why the man in the red-white-and-blue leathers had become a celebrity and a hero to America's youth. A greater deal of it was the fact that America needed a new hero. Another portion of this status was due to timing.

Today the marketing of Evel Knievel the hero probably wouldn't have happened. Too much is now known about every facet of a person's life. Yet in the early seventies, a person's private life was still private. Celebrities, politicians, and athletes could womanize and party and never be "outed" in the press. While it was true that Evel did like to drink, gamble, and spend time with the jet-setters of the era, he was just like many of the celebrities who were often lionized by the media. The main difference was that Knievel didn't play ball, run for office, or make movies; he won his fame by risking his life in the arena. The fact that his career choice was like no one else's in America made him much more marketable than a centerfielder for the New York Yankees or the star of a hot television show on CBS.

Still, many wondered if the demands and the risks he was taking were worth the millions he was now making. When asked about this, Knievel simply smiled and talked about his eighty-seven-foot custom yacht, a barn full of cars, hundreds of suits, the biggest and nicest house in Butte, a custom rolling one-of-a-kind truck/home for the road, numerous trips to Vegas each year to gamble, the ability to do anything he wanted and be with anyone he wanted. He could also point out that he was an idol to millions who had been disillusioned by things like Watergate and Vietnam. Meaning so much to his fans fed his spiritual lust for life and made him important in a unique way. So dangerous or not, Evel would not trade his life for anything. He was living his dreams and fantasies. Jumping a mile was a classic example of how everything he wanted in life was coming true.

For years he had dreamed of how big the marketing opportunity associated with a canyon jump might be, now he was being blown away because his dream hadn't begun to touch on the event's real potential. As the jump over the Snake River grew closer, he found that he could not focus on the details of preparing for the jump and still run the promotions for the event as well. He was going to have to have help.

In the past ABC Sports had covered many of his big jumps. This time the network couldn't come close to the price Knievel had put on the Snake River broadcast. He wasn't going to risk his life for anything less than several million dollars, and Super Bowls didn't even cost that much in 1974. When he got in his rocket on September 8, he envisioned the whole world watching, and he wanted to be paid well for that audience. After all, the previous year a live Elvis concert had been carried worldwide and viewed by more than a billion people. If the King of Rock could shake the world and not risk his life, Evel asked members of the media to think about what a famous man who was putting his life on the line might be able to do. The worldwide numbers could be huge. Unfortunately, few television executives had Knievel's vision. They saw the event as a one-hour segment of a sports show only. It would take an independent thinker to understand what Evel was offering.

Top Rank Productions, Inc. of New York, a company owned by Bob Arum, stepped up to the plate with an offer. It thought Evel's big event would play well on pay-for-view cable and closed-circuit television outlets. Arum, who was in at the beginning of selling title fights and other special sporting events on a pay-for-view basis, convinced Knievel that Top Rank could generate a lot more cash than a network broadcast ever could. How much money did Top Rank think they could bring in? Arum all but guaranteed fifteen to twenty million dollars. How much would Knievel and his representatives at Glass & Associates receive if that amount proved correct? In the neighborhood of sixty percent of the gross, or over six million dollars. With Arum, Knievel had a man who thought as big as he did. Evel liked that kind of large-scale, cutting-edge type of vision.

In March 1974, Evel had a bad landing as he leaped over ten Mack trucks in Fremont, California. Still, he managed to hold the bike and stop safely. A week later in Wisconsin he jumped a normal line of cars. Even though the cycle had mechanical problems, the rider stuck the jump. It was beginning to look like God was watching over Knievel, keeping him safe for the Snake.

In April Evel jumped ten Mack trucks at the Orange Country International Raceway in California. As thousands at the drag strip looked on, Evel made the leap look easy. He appeared to be hitting his stride at just the right moment. He looked to be a man in his prime and there was no doubt he felt his biggest dream was going to generate more money and fame than he ever could have believed possible. The nation was no longer laughing at him for wanting to leap a mile on a motorcycle, as a matter of fact, the country and the world were now getting excited by it. Still there were two looming questions, the first of which was could he do it and live.

The major reason the jump had been delayed until 1974 was the failure of test shots with the faux skycycle. Once he had found a place to stage a jump, Evel had gotten serious about finding a man who was capable of putting together a machine to make it over a canyon. Wanting the best man possible, he set to work looking for someone who had experience in the space program. Astronaut Jim Lovell, who himself was an Evel fan, told the stuntman about an engineer he respected who had once been on the Polaris missile team.

Robert C. Truax had worked with navy missiles as well as in the early development of NASA. He also told Evel that he was a past president of the American Rocket Society. Yet titles and past experience aside, the stuntman usually picked his team members based on either friendship or gut-level feelings. As there were no missile engineers in Butte, Evel went with the gut on this choice. Ultimately Truax was invited on board simply because he was just the type of guy Knievel liked.

Bob was not only a rocket expert, he was a plain-spoken, down-to-earth, and direct person. He listened well and understood that while he might be building a rocket, it still had to look something like a motorcycle. Evel explained that he expected not only make to it across the canyon, but he expected to live as well. While Bob could add the wheels and make Evel's contraption look something like a Harley with wings, getting the stuntman safely to the other side of the Snake River was going to be much harder. As a matter of fact, he encouraged Evel to just give up and forget the jump. When he discovered Knievel was determined to make good on his promise to the media and fans, Truax stayed on board to try to keep the rocketcycle from becoming a coffin. Yet with the limited budget he had been given, Bob knew he was fighting an uphill battle. He wished he had the budget that he had with the navy. Then he could have guaranteed success. As the parameters were now, he was literally building a spacecraft in a his garage.

At fifty-six, Bob Truax thought he had been introduced to every kind of man in the world. After all, it took some unique folks to serve in submarine duty. Yet when he met Evel, he knew he had found someone totally unique. Knievel was either the craziest or stupidest person Truax had ever encountered. Yet for the stuntman to have a chance of living through his dream promotion, Bob felt he was the only man who might be able to provide the motorcycle jumper with the edge he needed. Bob was also driven by the promised $100,000 bonus if Knievel did successfully jump the canyon in the skycycle.

Truax planned for Evel's rocket-bike to use a two-hundred foot ramp that was angled at fifty-six degrees. He elected to build the ship with a steam engine to reduce the chance of an explosion and fire on the ramp before takeoff. Needing five thousand pounds of thrust and at least three hundred miles per hour within seconds of leaving the starting point, what Bob soon discovered was that he was really building a bomb without the explosives. A parachute was included in the cycle to float the rider and rocket down to earth when the steam power was exhausted. On paper it all looked good. Yet even Bob didn't have much of a clue if it would work. After all, NASA and the navy had experienced several major blunders that had looked good on paper.

Truax explained to Evel the specifics of how the skycycle would work so many times that the stuntman could quote each detail of the story verbatim, but Knievel, a student of speed and power, recognized that Truax was just guessing. Evel could take some solace in knowing it was at least a more educated guess than the stuntman could have made by himself.

On April 15, 1972, Evel traveled to Snake River to watch Truax run a test jump with his first skycycle. The prototype took off with promise before suddenly losing altitude and speed and falling into the gorge not even halfway across the river. For Evel it became apparent that it was time to change the date for liftoff, for the engineer it was time to get back to the drawing boards.

On June 24, 1973, with a host of media watching, the team launched the second prototype. It also ran out of steam early. It would be months before a team found it downstream. If Truax was a genius, he hadn't yet revealed it to his boss. Putting on his best face in front of the media who had watched the test, Evel explained the drone wasn't supposed to fly across the canyon. This test was simply to evaluate needed thrust, rate of lift, and other very technical elements for the big jump. As he was already at the end of his budget, Knievel also announced that there would be no more tests. The next liftoff would be the one he was riding on September 8, 1974.

Though Evel only had so much money to devote to Truax and the skycycle, he was still living lavishly. If the contraption the engineer was building was going to kill him, Knievel wanted to make sure he enjoyed the last year of his life as much as humanly possible. That meant buying a lifetime of dreams and desires in just over a year.

After the failed test flights, the media repeatedly asked Evel if he were scared. The stock answer became, "I'm Evel Knievel, I'm not supposed to be afraid." This played well with his fans, especially the kids, but those who knew him well felt the man was more frightened than he had ever been in his life. Though he would not admit it, those close to him believed Evel viewed the rocket as a death trap. Yet flying coffin or not, Knievel vowed the event would take place on the latest scheduled date. He would not put it off again. With millions of dollars in contracts and a huge pay-for-view television production being marketed for Labor Day, the biker really had no choice but to go on with the show. In this case, John D. Rockefeller couldn't have reached into his deep pockets and given everyone his money back. As Evel would admit to *Sports Illustrated,* "I have created a monster."

Besides the obvious problem of simply living through the jump, the other stumbling block facing Evel would not be as obvious as a mile-wide gorge. It would arise because of the need to sell pay-for-view tickets around the country. A press tour set up to sell the show would ultimately go well, but because so much of his life and business were now being placed in the hands of people he didn't know well, Knievel would find himself eventually burned by a man hired to enhance the stuntman's heroic image.

Bob Arum convinced Evel he needed a publicity expert to come in full-time and put together a promotional campaign benefiting a hero. This person could put together the tour, notify the press, set up the interviews, and make sure that Knievel's name was kept out in front of the American public for the months before the jump. The man Arum chose for the job was an old friend from Los Angeles, Sheldon Saltman.

Saltman understood what was needed before he ever met Evel. Yet when the two men stood face-to-face in Butte, the promoter realized the star of his current project was a product worthy of his talents. Knievel was a publicity department's dream! The first thing Saltman noticed was the huge diamond ring Evel wore on his left hand. After the dazzling effect of the mass of diamonds began to erode, Sheldon noted that the stuntman was good looking, well spoken, and direct. At the outset, this job looked easy.

Sheldon made few bones about the games he played in the publicity racket. His luxury car even sported a personalized license plate that read, "CONMAN." Saltman was as good as anyone in the business and over the last few years had promoted everything from boxing matches to motion picture releases. He was a media shark. His ideas were big and his plans were grand. Yet from the moment Saltman began to visit with his new client, the promotional professional realized that Evel's plans were much more specific and much bigger than any person Sheldon had ever met.

Whenever Saltman brought up a problem in a city or with a media group, Knievel knew someone to call. Whenever the promoter came up with an idea for an entrance to a staged event, the stuntman had already thought of an idea that was even bigger. Sheldon quickly discovered that Evel knew more about promotion than most experts, so Saltman was going to have to work hard to keep up with the daredevil. In truth, his job should have been easy.

Sheldon had come on board late enough that he didn't have to inform the public who Evel Knievel was. A person could go into any store and find the stuntman's products. You could turn on the television and see Evel pitching everything from Right Guard to Ideal toys. In every town and city in the United States, kids were pretending to be Knievel as they jumped their bikes over ditches, curbs, toys, mounds of dirt, and anything else they could find. Promoting Evel was as easy as promoting Elvis. The whole show should have been getting Knievel to the microphone and letting him take over.

Saltman got to know Evel for the first time in the stuntman's hometown of Butte. In this area, where Knievel really was considered not only a hero, but a special friend to the community, the urban promoter couldn't have immediately understood the man or the town. What the city slicker saw were the rough edges of rural life. He saw poverty and despair. He viewed Butte as depressing and stark. The promoter was as lost in Butte as many of the miners who drank in the city's bars would have been lost in Hollywood. Yet not understanding Butte was just the beginning of Saltman's problems.

Evel Knievel was living larger than he ever had. He was now making hundreds of thousands of dollars a week and spending that amount just as quickly. Though Saltman probably didn't realize it, Evel was looking at a clock that might well be ticking down the last months of his life. He didn't have time to waste a moment. With death staring him in the face, he was naturally demanding. His friends in Butte accepted this facet of the Knievel personality because they understood where it came from. They ignored the profanity he used and the fact that he drank a bit more than he usually did. Faced with what he was facing, most of them would have run away and hidden until after Labor Day. Yet they all knew their friend well enough to know he didn't run. Never had. So he had a right to buy what he wanted, say what he wanted, and drink when he wanted.

As the days went by and Saltman saw more of Knievel, he seemed to become more fixated on the man's eccentric nature and big way of living. Sheldon had never known a man with so much stuff. Evel had a dozen or more cars, cases of various kinds of alcohol, countless rings and jewelry, as well as more clothes than the queen of England. The stuntman also carried around hundreds of thousands of dollars in cashier's checks, made out to Evel Knievel, in his wallet, as well as a role of large bills in his pocket. He seemed to have more of everything than any man the promoter had ever met. This included energy.

Sheldon was about the same age as Evel, but he couldn't keep up with him. Even with the cane and bum leg, Knievel moved quickly. He could play a round of golf in the time it took most men to complete nine holes. When the stuntman drove a car, he now pushed the pedal to the floor and got to his destination in a hurry. He drank quickly, ate on the run, and seemed as awake at three in the morning as he was at sunrise the next day. He seemed willing to bet on everything too. Sheldon was amazed that Evel would wager thousands of dollars on a round of golf or the spin of a roulette wheel.

Saltman had to figure that Knievel would change when they got out of Butte and into the big cities. He was expecting the man to settle down and be less conspicuous. Yet in New York, Evel was the same Evel as he had been in Butte. At a fight in Madison Square Garden, Knievel was the center of attention. At nightclubs and discos, the stuntman drew crowds like a magnet. Even the media fought to meet him. Saltman didn't really have to push any special buttons to sell Knievel in the Big Apple, all he had to do was turn him loose. Everyone wanted to pal around with the stuntman, even other stars who were usually surrounded by scores of people hanging on their every word.

When Muhammad Ali met Evel at a party, the talkative fighter quickly discovered he had an equal in the ability to gab and the ability to charm a crowd. After a few moments with Knievel, Ali told everyone, "This guy is the white Muhammad Ali." The stuntman shook his head and immediately interjected. "No, that guy is the black Evel Knievel."

For Saltman, who was used to working with people he fashioned and controlled to his own advantage, working with Evel must have been the most intimidating experience of his life. Evel designed everything he had his hand in. He designed the home he lived in to meet his and his family's needs. He designed to the last detail how each motorcycle jump he made was to be done. His clothing, jewelry and cars, they were all Knievel's design. And when it came to the press tour, Evel was going to have it to his specifications as well.

Rather than sleep and be well rested for a morning press conference, Evel would party at a city's best clubs and pull himself into the room just before the media began to ask questions. Saltman knew that the stuntman ran on his own clock and functioned just as he had in Butte, but he must have been surprised when he discovered Evel did this everywhere he went. If Evel was in a city, no matter what city, he acted as though he owned it. If there was something worth doing, he was going to do it while he was still alive and capable of enjoying it. Much more than any other man, Knievel was well aware that he might not pass this way again. So sleep was not nearly as important as experiencing everything there was to experience at each stop.

When dealing with media in Dallas, New York, Kansas City, and the more than sixty other major cities the press tour flew into, Evel was the perfect promoter. He knew all the answers, posed for pictures, told funny stories, and constantly came up with new ways to sell the Snake River event. Saltman found himself greatly admiring Evel the media star. Yet out of the public eye, Knievel's independence and bullying began to become abrasive to Saltman. He quickly grew tired of the way Evel naturally dominated every conversation, every meal, every moment of every day.

Providence, Hartford, Boston, Albany, Syracuse, Buffalo, the cities flew by day after day as each new battery of media bombarded Evel with the same questions he had been asked at previous stops. After a while it became boring and Knievel didn't like boring. It also began to seem like a waste of time.

On the tour the men would hit as many as four cities a day, always hopping on and off a small jet, trying to appear fresh at each stop. It didn't take too many days for the country boy from Butte and the city slicker from L.A. to realize that they were not good traveling partners. By the middle of the press tour it had become obvious to most that Knievel had liked Bob Arum, the folks from Ideal toys, and Harley-Davidson motorcycles, but he didn't have a very high regard for Saltman. The feelings seemed to go both ways.

Yet in truth, at the moment Sheldon Saltman's attitude was the least of Evel's worries. He had bigger things on his mind than a press agent who didn't approve of the way the stuntman lived his life.

While the press never picked up on it, Evel was deeply concerned about his wife and children. He had received threats that men were going to kidnap his family and hold them for ransom. He was constantly checking in at home to make sure things were all right. When he was in Butte, he was always looking out for suspicious characters. He even had nightmares about Linda and the kids being taken and killed.

Many of his friends felt the stuntman carried the huge cashier's checks in his wallet in case of a kidnapping. He could then easily lay his hands on the cash needed to pay for his family's release. If a possible kidnapping had been his only worry, then he probably could have easily dealt with it through a larger security force watching his home. Yet the family concern was just the beginning.

Evel was trying to take care of the details of not only the jump itself, but all the facets that made the jump possible. Even though few would have guessed it the way he was spending it, money was a big concern. Everything was costing a great deal more than he had expected. The ramp and rocket were eating up five or six times the money anticipated. So was everything else. Then there was politics, something he thought he had left behind at the Grand Canyon.

A group in Twin Falls was even trying to stop the jump by passing new city laws and regulations. He was hit with traffic restrictions, taxes, rest room ordinances, and security concerns. Every time he took care of one, another seemed to come up. Ultimately Evel was constantly battling forces that others should have been taking care of for him. Yet those in place to handle the problems always seemed to call him for advice. As the weeks streaked by the pressure on the man became almost unbearable. He was about to really put his life on the line and he was still having to deal with tiny problems that might derail the whole event. It was enough to drive anyone crazy.

There was no doubt that Evel's temper was now erupting more often than ever. He was constantly exploding over little things. This had become a very sore spot with Sheldon Saltman. Yet those who felt Knievel's wrath often failed to recognize the pressure he was feeling. In many ways he was living on death row with the whole world watching the countdown to his final days on earth. Who could deal with this situation and all the demands like a normal man, especially when he was brought new problems every hour?

Evel realized that he was often short with people. He knew he had little patience. He was a loner from a wide open part of the country who was now being forced to deal constantly with people and being pushed from place to place for reasons he often thought were stupid. This was not the way to live the last few months he was guaranteed of life. As he watched his life tick down, he tried to make a peace with Saltman by explaining why his life had made a positive impact on people.

"I've spoken out against narcotics and alcohol," he explained to the promoter. "I've spoken out for automobile safety and motorcycle safety concerning helmets and all that, and kids in this country look up to me. I'm not going to let them down. I'm not saying the canyon jump might serve a useful purpose, but the fact that I'm not a phony, I'll guarantee you, is a more useful purpose than the one Spiro Agnew provided this country as vice president."

It was obvious Evel now wanted to know his life had meant something. The publicist might not have understood the impact Knievel had had on his fans, but it was there. Thousands of kids wore helmets when they rode motorcycles only because Evel had told them it was the right thing to do. Others stayed away from drugs because he had sold the argument against narcotics use so well during his shows. His public image served as a real beacon when compared to the free-loving, drug-using rock stars of the era. He was a positive alternative to the world's negative forces. So who cared if he happened to get on his platform and gain the respect of millions doing something that in Saltman's eyes was very stupid?

By the second week of the tour, Evel was almost claustrophobic. He was tired of Saltman and dealing with the press. He was also tired of the games he was having to play each day. To get away from the rabble and keep from exploding, he snuck away by himself and visited a children's hospital in Akron, Ohio. With no press along for the ride, Knievel distributed toys and talked to severely ill kids for several hours. He came out crying. He had seen the faces of children who hadn't asked to face death and now were counting their time in weeks and months. After meeting the kids the stuntman finally thought he knew what real courage was. When he returned to the tour and his traveling mates asked him to talk about the experience, Knievel refused. Instead he just looked out the plane's window and kept his thoughts to himself.

By midsummer Bob Truax had tinkered as much as he could with the final rocketcycle. It was either going to work or not. Truax would have bet on the latter. He called Evel in for a private meeting and informed the stuntman the chances of surviving the jump would be under forty percent. Those odds were based on everything working the way they were supposed to. If something went wrong, then the odds of survival grew smaller.

Evel had spent one million dollars on a machine that really did appear to be a bomb carrying a rider. Yet he still had to sell the press on the fact that he believed in Truax and the skycycle. It wouldn't be easy.

As Labor Day grew closer, the national interest in the jump also grew. ABC News sent in their science reporter, Jules Bergman, to do a report on the technology that had gone into the cycle. Bergman, who normally covered NASA space flights, appeared very scholarly, but was not optimistic. Other reporters from all over the world came to file similar reports. Evel had what he wanted, the whole world was now focused on the Snake River and the stuntman from Butte. Yet it appeared more and more to be the end of a career, rather than a beginning.

In St. Louis a reporter asked Evel if he ever felt any fear. Knievel answered, "If I do, I'm not going to tell you. If I'm afraid, I'm not going to admit it, even to me. I'm supposed to be Superman, so I try and fool myself. But none of us wants to die. I have a death wish, but it involves a very beautiful woman when I'm a hundred and five years old; it doesn't involve the canyon when I'm thirty-five."

On July 4, Evel was the guest of honor in the Butte Independence Day parade. Yet even as he waved to the crowd and smiled, his wife saw a man who was more tense than she had ever seen him. The seriousness of the jump and the possibility that he might be living his last two months of life, were grating on him. And the demands continued to grow as the days quickly passed.

CBS *Sports Spectacular*, ABC's *Goodnight America*, and a host of other television shows scheduled interviews and appearances. Even though these programs took him away from his family and home, two things he now seemed to treasure more than he ever had in the past, Evel was always there giving all the right answers. If Saltman scheduled a media event, the stuntman performed on cue and like a pro. After a while Knievel lost track of how many times he had flown to Twin Falls and toured the jump site for the cameras. He also lost track of how many times he was called and informed that the site needed more Porta Potties, concession stands, security guards, camera platforms, roads, parking fences, and garbage cans. Every time he turned around, more of something was needed which required more of his money. In the past he had spent his earnings on things he and his family enjoyed, now it seemed like he was just throwing his cash away on things no one cared about.

Though he hadn't intended for it to evolve into anything other than a large version of his normal arena car jumps, by August Evel must have sensed that he had created a motorcycle version of Woodstock at Snake River. Because of the worldwide press and fan interest, Twin Falls was in a panic. Many believed that their town was going to be overrun with bikers. A few were predicting the community would be burned to the ground. Even the stuntman couldn't be sure that this wouldn't happen. After all, the Hell's Angels did have a large grudge against him. Who knew what that group would do if they rode into town for Labor Day weekend.

To make peace with Twin Falls, a community that was going to make millions off the jump, Evel finally agreed to sell no more than fifty thousand tickets. By admitting only that amount, the crowds would not be nearly as large as the quarter of a million predicted by the press, and the smaller number could easily be controlled. The guarantee of no more than fifty thousand calmed the public panic a bit, but people had still stocked up on firearms, ammunition, and fire extinguishers just in case.

For Evel, who was still working with Bob Truax to fix the problems with the rocketcycle and improve his odds of making the jump, more bad news came in the way of a call from Bob Arum. The pay-for-view giant had been informed that CBS was trying to lease the land on the opposite side of the Snake River and televise the event live on their network. As war between the close circuit and free TV outlet broke out, CBS took a unique approach to gaining a legal right to televise the jump. The network was calling Evel's stunt a news event. Certainly the way that it had been promoting the event had entered the area of news reporting, but was it really the same as covering the president or a war protest? The courts ruled in favor of Arum. Just like a Sinatra concert or a Major League Baseball game, Evel's jump was legally entertainment. Thus exclusive rights could be sold and CBS could not override those rights. Still, the battle took time and energy away from areas that should have been receiving attention. It had been another problem for Knievel to worry about.

For Evel the countdown of his life was ticking ever so much closer to the event he had been teasing people with for years. With each day his patience was also wearing thinner. Everyone wanted him to do something. Saltman, Arum, those at the jump site. Truax, and a thousand others whose names he barely remembered all had a job for him to do. One morning, as he drank a glass of milk, the stuntman finally exploded when he received yet another interview request from Saltman, "I've got a lot of things to put in order before I die on September eighth," Knievel thundered.

Evel also had another very difficult jump scheduled in Canada. This time he would jump over thirteen Mack trucks and his two sons would perform before the jump. What he couldn't have guessed was that the Snake River or the line of thirteen Mack trucks were not destined to cause him nearly as much pain as the man Bob Arum had brought on board to make Evel look good: Sheldon Saltman.

15

Evel Meets the Snake

There was no way anyone associated with the show that was surrounding the Snake River Canyon should have allowed Evel to book a jump at the Canadian National Exposition on August 20, 1974, less than three weeks before the big event. Yet the Canadians offered so much money, Knievel didn't feel he could turn them down. The unexpected expenses and overruns at the canyon had severely cut into his funds. Though he had spent the last year of his life spending as if he had an endless cash flow, he needed this paycheck just to make up for what the Snake was taking from him everyday.

Almost thirty thousand fans gathered at the C. & E. Stadium on that hot summer night. They had all come out just to see a performance by the man the announcer introduced as the "Last of the Gladiators" and "King of the Daredevils." Decked out in his red-white-and-blue leather jumpsuit, Evel looked like a hero. Yet for those who were close enough to really study him, he also appeared older than he had just a few months before. His hair was grayer, his weight down, and his face a bit drawn. The stuntman looked like he had been through Hell and back since his last jump. In many ways he had.

After mentioning to the crowd that this might just be "the last performance I might ever make," Knievel introduced his sons. Kelly was now fourteen, Robbie eleven. Dressed in leathers patterned after their dad's costume, the two popped wheelies and thrilled the crowd with a show that belied their years. The boys performed like seasoned riders. As Evel spoke of them to the audience, he choked a bit on his words and a tear caught in his eye. It was obvious that he was proud of them. It was equally obvious he loved them very much.

In the stands that night, Linda Knievel and nine-year-old Tracey watched in silent anticipation. Even though both of them had reservations about what Evel did for a living, on this night they were united as a family in a very special way. For the first, and perhaps the last time, the Knievels were a family act. Even Linda had to admit she was proud of her boys as they drew the heat of the spotlight in the large arena. Still, as the kids finished their prepared act, she prayed that this would not be the night they all watched their father die.

When Kelly and Robbie rode out of the arena, Evel strolled back to the microphone. Wearing a short cape and carrying his helmet and cane, the showman seemed to walk with a singular purpose. As he addressed the crowd, every eye was on him, every ear trying to catch each word he said. At this moment the ticket buyers who filled the arena treated Knievel as if he were the wisest and most important man on earth.

"Every year I go to Indianapolis as a part of the A. J. Foyt pit crew," he began. "They do a wonderful job there. I want to tell you something about qualifying at Indy that might help you relate to another problem that is plaguing us now. There are some drivers who don't use the fuel that Mr. Hullman requires at the track. They cheat and add nitro to try to get an edge. You know what happens? Those cars run real fast for about five laps and then blow all to Hell. That is what will happen to you if you use drugs. You will run real fast and then blow all to Hell."

After sharing the story on drug use and encouraging every child in the audience to stay away from using drugs of any kind, Evel then talked about the canyon he had "bought" in Idaho. He pledged that on September 8 he was going to jump that canyon. He added, "The only way they are going to get me out of the air is to shoot me down!" The crowd roared. For the stuntman the adulation was much needed. He had recently been labeled by a host of ministers, members of the press, and some promoters as a fool, a suicidal maniac who deserved to be locked away from children. Yet as the kids hung on his every word, and as he gave them something worth remembering and using to live a better life, Evel could feel as if he had again defeated his critics. He wasn't a fool, he was a showman who stood for things everyone should stand for.

"You hang onto your seats and I'll hang onto mine," the stuntman concluded when the cheers died down, "and we'll get this thing done!" His words indicated that he would be carrying everyone on the bike with him that night. Most had so much faith in Knievel, they probably would have accepted the ride too!

It had been just another typical Knievel prejump motivational speech, but tonight it seemed to mean a great deal more to him and the crowd. Everyone knew that this could well be his final hurrah. Even if he made it over the Mack trucks that loomed in front of him, there was the Snake River just ahead. Odds were, if one didn't get him, the other would.

As usual, ABC-TV was there, this time with Keith Jackson doing the commentary. Jackson played the danger of leaping thirteen huge trucks for all it was worth. Yet the veteran commentator didn't really have to tell the viewers Evel was putting his life on the line, they already knew it. That is why they were watching and why many of them were also looking forward to Labor Day.

At the Expo it took Evel a few moments longer to get ready than it normally did. He made three different practice runs, each time passing to the left of the takeoff ramp to check his speed and the way the bike was running. Before he finally signalled to his crew he was ready, he returned to the designated start line and bowed his head. He always said a prayer before each jump. He had done this on each jump for the last few years, but this time his talk with God seemed to take a little longer and cover more ground. When he finally looked up, a few claimed they could see tears in his eyes.

The crowd was ready for a jump, but Evel approached the ramp again, this final visit as more of sightseer than a stuntman. Slowing coasting to the top of the red-white-and-blue angled ramp, he looked at the long row of huge trucks almost as if he were counting them to make sure no one had snuck in an extra. From the ramp he could see that there were only thirteen, and he had jumped that many before. The distance he needed on this night was almost forty feet less that what had been demanded of him when he had attempted to leap the fountains at Caesar's Palace. This jump should have been almost routine. Yet there was so much riding on it and all of these invisible pressures were riding on Knievel's shoulders as well.

If Evel failed and crashed, if he was severely injured, all the money and preparations that had gone into the Snake River event would be lost. Not only would Knievel find himself in financial hot water too deep to swim out of, but so would Bob Arum and scores of others who had invested in the jump and the jumper. So while this Mack truck jump might have been just another ordinary stunt for the rider, the pressures were far from routine. And pressure, Evel knew, had caused many men to fail to accomplish even the most elementary things. How many golfers had missed two-foot putts because of the money riding on their stroke? How many basketball players had blown easy layups with a championship on the line? And none of them were looking at death the way he was!

Going over a mental checklist, Knievel made the jump in his mind. He knew the speed he had to have and he was sure the bike was in top condition. He saw himself flying over the trucks and sticking a perfect landing. Finally he decided he was in control and it was time.

Roaring to the ramp, Evel lifted the bike, stood on his pegs, and flew well past the huge trucks. Landing perfectly on his back wheel, easily setting his front tire down a split second later, the stuntman had done just what he knew he could do—he had flown more than 110 feet. Turning and riding his bike back to the top of the landing ramp, he got off and was greeted by the sight of streams of adoring fans jumping out of the stands and racing across the infield toward him. The police were simply outmanned. They could do nothing but watch Evel be engulfed by hundreds of people caught up in worshipping the man who had now become not only an American hero, but a hero for Canada as well.

With the Expo jump behind him, Evel could again turn his full attention to the Snake River. Until the final few days he was all business. Yet in the last week before he was to risk his life in an unproven rocketcycle, the stuntman was hardly concentrating on his big jump.

Evel had decided the jump should just be the capstone of an entire week of activities. Pulling a page from his past, he sponsored five days of moto-cross racing. Even while that was going on, he was out at the Twin Falls airport welcoming the folks who had come in to play in his golf tournament. He even managed to put Bobby Riggs and Joe Louis in his foursome. This time, for the sake of good sportsmanship, Evel assigned stakes of just ten dollars a hole for the game between the men. As always, Knievel left the clubhouse with the most money in his pocket. Of course the old fighter and tennis player were not the only ones gambling this week.

Besides Ideal and the other mainstays of Evel's large endorsement world, Chuckles candy had signed up for the big show, as had Toyota. Billboards and displays for the various companies had been placed wherever there was a chance a pay-for-view camera might get a shot of them. If Evel made it, they could all count on millions in sales. If he didn't, then they might all have a lot of stock that would be associated with a funeral.

From seemingly out of nowhere, an Evel Knievel Museum came to life just outside the jump site. It was filled with photos, motorcycles, and even the first skycycle, the one that failed to make it halfway across the canyon. It seemed that the bruised and dented rocket bike had been found by fishermen and fished out of the Snake River just in time for the big show.

Evel tossed a huge party in Butte for all of his out-of-town friends. More than five hundred showed up. The host spent more than $15,000 as he escorted his guests from bar to bar and showed them all of the sights of his hometown. Everywhere they stopped there was partying and laughter. On that night, Evel told a lot of great stories, showed a few good dance steps, and picked up every tab. He didn't look like a man who thought he was going to die, but he couldn't run from the odds forever. Even he had to stop and consider them from time to time.

At one function, less than a week before the jump, Evel explained he wanted to be buried in his Kenworth truck with all his bikes and clothes. He wanted the big rig's air horn to stick out of the ground so he could let everyone know when he was ready to come back. While Knievel smiled, more than a few guests shook. They wondered how he could be so cavalier about the fact he might just die.

As the day for the jump grew closer. Evel began to slow down. He stopped partying and making jokes. He also ceased being an outgoing host and began to withdraw to his family. He even told those he had put in charge of everything from security to concessions to solve their own problems. It didn't seem he had any time left for anyone but those closest to him.

As the days flew by quickly, the stuntman wished he had spent more time at home with family and less on the road. He had redis- covered just how much he loved his wife and children. He also was realizing that he might never get a chance to see any of them grow beyond where they were right now. The thought of missing so much of their lives haunted him more than the thought of missing the rest of his.

As the star of the show started to become introspective, the crowds began to arrive for the races. It didn't take long for pay-for-view head Bob Arum's men to notice that these fans were not at all like the family groups Evel usually performed in front of. These people were dirty, grubby, and disrespectful. By the middle of the week it was clear that several thousand bikers who were even worse than those who rode with the Hell's Angels had come to town for the jump. These folks were walking trouble. They were looking for a fight.

One of the first steps Arum's people took was putting up new fences in an effort to help crowd control. Even with these chain link barriers in place, there still simply weren't enough security officers to break up any large-scale violence. As more and more unsavory types rode in, many respectable people who had come to watch their hero began to leave. They were scared and probably had a right to be. Many of those who were walking all around the jump site considered rape a sport.

In an atmosphere that was beginning to look a lot like a low-rent Woodstock, Evel came out for a round of interviews and publicity shots the day before the jump. As Jack Perkins of NBC News watched Evel sit in the skycycle, he matter-of-factly told his viewers, "It's Evel Knievel versus the Snake River Canyon, with the Snake River Canyon the sentimental favorite."

Everyone who observed Evel and Bob Traux talk that day at the rocketcycle could sense the stuntman was not in a good mood. Though he normally would wait until every photographer had gotten the shot he wanted before leaving, on this day Knievel pushed past several in an attempt to get away from the site. He even jabbed one cameraman with his cane, knocking the man down and breaking his camera. The stuntman appeared to be hostile and ready for a fight. At this moment the cycle gang had enough sense to steer clear. If they hadn't, Knievel might have taken them all on.

Back in his trailer, just a few feet from the spot where he would risk his life in less than twenty-four hours, Evel was upset. He was sincerely sorry for his behavior. He hoped that people would try to understand what he was going through. Even for this man who always seemed to gravitate toward the spotlight, there was now a desire to have no part of it. All he really wanted was to go home and be with his family. He wished that people could understand that. He had realized too late that he should have spent his final day away from everyone but Linda and the kids. Nothing in the way of press demands should have been scheduled for September 7.

That night in Twin Falls the rougher elements of the crowd who had come to watch the jump amused themselves with booze, drugs, and sex. Women were being used, abused, and passed around. Motel pools turned into skinny-dipping parties. Though no one was burning the town, everyone's doors were locked and guns were loaded. Most of those in Twin Falls had gotten to the same point as had the event's star, they just wanted to get this thing over and be left alone.

The morning of the jump a mob of about five thousand drunken bikers went out of control. They were mad over the price of food and beer, so they simply took over several stands and helped themselves to anything they wanted. When they were empty, the roughnecks burned them and then highjacked two semis full of booze. As a few of the bikers had guns, local law enforcement officers decided it might be better just to let them have their way rather than try to defend the grounds. The law argued that after they got drunk the gang would be easier to handle.

The television crew was worried this miniriot would grow and spill over into the areas now fenced off and reserved for production and the jump itself. If the rabble forced themselves into those areas, then there would be no television to cover the event and no jump at all. These rag-tag rebels, the very type of bikers whom Evel had been preaching against for years, were now close to taking over his whole show.

Don Branker, who was heading up operations for Don Arum, decided not to wait on the Twin Falls authorities to figure a way to stop the riot. Branker took things into his own hands. Driving up the river, Don found a camp with another mean-looking group of bikers and hired them for his security team. Within an hour the new security guards had the drunken bikers under control. Finally things seemed ready for the jump.

More than a hundred members of the press from all over the world showed up early. As they checked out the skycycle one more time, they hardly noticed the destruction that had been wrought in the wee hours of the morning by the angry bikers. What the media noted were scores of helicopters and about 25,000 spectators. They also observed that the weather seemed perfect for the jump.

Under a cloudless sky, a strong breeze was blowing a mini-dust-storm across the canyon and right at the site. Soon everyone was covered with a fine layer of grime. With the temperature quickly rising into the nineties and the beer having been consumed during the riot, the major concern for most of those gathered became quenching their thirst and washing their faces.

Robert Craig "Evel" Knievel had other things on his mind. After breakfast with his family, he took a last walk around his home and property. He appeared to be a man facing execution. A student of history, Evel might have even recalled the way that Field Marshall Rommell had been ordered to die by Hitler's high command. Though not as certain of death as the German officer had been, the stuntman knew his chances were long indeed.

As the family left the home to board a plane and then a helicopter to get from Butte to Twin Falls and the jump site, Evel cornered Kelly and asked him to return to the bedroom and do a favor for his father. Racing back into the house, the son found a framed picture of the Snake River Canyon. Hanging the aerial shot over his parents' bed as he had been instructed, the fourteen-year-old boy then rejoined his family. In what he fully expected to be his last act in Butte, Evel had left the picture for Linda. On it he had written, "My Darling Wife Linda, I Love You, Bob."

Everyone on that final family trip felt sure that Evel was going to die. Linda, the three kids, and even the stuntman couldn't find any words of encouragement to share with each other. They all knew the two test flights had failed miserably. What chance did this one have? Yet even in the face of this, there was no way that the stuntman was going to back out. Even if it meant his death, he was going to try to do what he had promised for the last seven years. With no rain in sight, it seemed even God wasn't going to get in the way of Evel's suicidal effort.

Arriving at the site, Evel retired to his trailer and changed into his red-white-and-blue leathers. Coming out, he waved to the crowd and quickly made his way to the Skycycle 3. Sitting in a chair hung from a crane, he was lifted into position and then transferred to the cockpit of what looked like little more than a white bomb topped with a painted blue field filled with white stars. "Evel Knievel" was spelled out on each side of the cycle in gold block letters, and several sponsors' logos had been painted on the back of the projectile. As he was belted into what he now believed was little more than a colorful death-trap, he must have felt like a man sitting in the electric chair. When a priest came up and gave him last rites and prayed with him for a final time, the claustrophobic fear of death must have been all-consuming. It was just past 3:20 in the afternoon.

Over the public address system, a song about Evel's exploits was played and then the crowd heard the taped voice of the stuntman reading one of his own poems about his life. Finally the local high school band played the national anthem. When the pomp and ceremony was complete, Bob Truax visited with Evel one more time. Truax wanted the stuntman to stop the jump. The engineer felt the wind was blowing too hard in the face of the ship. When Knievel refused to get out of the craft, the two went over the last-minute prejump checklist, which was probably more "hope you make it" than things the rocket builder wanted Knievel to remember. As Truax walked away, the stuntman found himself completely alone while millions around the world looked on.

The heat inside the tiny cockpit must have been stifling. With the sun beating down on Evel, his leather suit pressing against his body, the feeling of being roasted alive along with the overriding presence of death would have forced most men either to tears or a race to unbuckle the safety belts and rush away from the vehicle. Yet Knievel stayed.

He would later say that while he waited for liftoff he was haunted by the look in his family's eyes when he had left them. They thought they were saying good-bye to him for a final time. They believed that they would be planning a funeral before the day was out. Putting Linda and the kids through this kind of situation was something he now wished he had never done. Nothing was worth having your family look at you like you were wasting your life and walking away from them for no sound reason.

As he waited for the temperature of the steam to hit 700 degrees, the amount Truax figured was needed to provide the thrust to lift the cycle over the canyon, Evel prayed, "God, take care of me."

As a hushed crowd looked on and millions more watched in theaters and homes, the television team of David Frost, Pittsburgh sports anchor Lee Arthur, and Jim Lovell, tried to explain what should happen next. On the screen a digital clock counted down the last minute before liftoff. Inside the cockpit the thing Evel would later say that was constantly going through his mind was the singular thought, "I am a dead man. I don't have a prayer."

At 3:36, the countdown reached zero, Evel hit the fire button and the X-3 lit up, steam shooting out the rocket's tail. In the blink of an eye the craft began a quick climb up the steep ramp. For a second it appeared that Truax's machine might just have the thrust to get its rider to the other side of the Snake River, but about two-thirds of the way up the ramp, the drone parachute blew. At just the moment the engine was trying to lift the skycycle toward the clear blue heavens, the chute was pulling it back to Earth. With the large piece of nylon dragging behind him, there was no way that Evel was going the make it across the river.

The skycycle turned on its side and the canyon wall was suddenly all the stuntman could see. As the main chute popped out and the rocket ran out of steam, Evel and the craft dangled from the lines, slowly drifting down into the canyon. As it descended, the vehicle kept scraping the near wall and the crowd pushed a fence down to race to the canyon's edge and see what had become of their hero. If it hadn't been for the motorcycle gang who acted as security guards standing firm between the crowd and the canyon, many would have probably gotten too close to the precipice and fallen a thousand feet to their death. As it was, only Evel was in danger of losing his life.

As the skycycle disappeared, a strange silence fell over the crowd. Most didn't know what to do. No one could guess what had happened to the daredevil. Even the television announcers were at a loss. All they could say was "The ship is going down."

As he fell closer to the river, Evel was frantically trying to get out of the cockpit. When he couldn't jerk free from the safety harnesses, he tried to cut himself out. As the Snake rushed up to meet him, the stuntman knew he was going to go into the water. As he was tied to a ship that wouldn't float, Knievel was sure he would drown. He didn't want to die like that. He would have rather blown up. However, he was helpless to escape from his red-white-and-blue coffin as it raced to the embrace of the river. The same river that had claimed both the test-flight vehicles, not giving them up for months.

Because of the strong wing blowing across the canyon, the skycycle was slowly being pushed across the river. By the time it hit the bottom of the canyon, the vehicle had come to rest halfway on the shore rather than in the deepest part of the Snake River. Knievel could thus extract himself with no panic and no fear of drowning. As he waited for a raft of rescuers to come up the river to his point of impact, Evel was thrilled that he had survived.

From the rim of the canyon it appeared as though the stuntman had gone down in the water. His family was horrified to think that he was drowning and there was nothing they could do about it. For several long minutes everyone held their breath. Then came the news from the rescue boat, Evel was alive and well.

Truax realized the reason the drone parachute blew out at takeoff was a simple electrical problem that had been overlooked. A minor adjustment could have easily fixed it. Yet maybe without this act of God, Evel wouldn't have survived the ordeal. To the deeply religious Linda the mishap was an answered prayer.

As a helicopter brought him back to his family and a television interview, certainly Knievel had nothing for which to apologize. He had given the jump his best shot, he had tried to do what he had promised to do, the fact that he hadn't made it meant little. Trying was what mattered. It was how he judged everything he did.

"I'm glad to be back in one piece," he told the press. Evel then matter-of-factly added, "We should have run one more test."

Over the next few days some reporters questioned if the American public had been ripped off. They thought the jump over the Snake River had been a farce. They even accused the stuntman of pushing the parachute button as soon as he hit the release switch. Evel didn't apologize for not making it to the other side of the Snake River or for not getting killed trying. He later said, "If I had made it, everyone would have said that it was easy. If I had died, then everyone would have said, the daredevil died. How I ever lived is a miracle!"

Life was suddenly sweet for Evel Knievel. When he hugged Linda and the kids he was weak-kneed with the joy of being with his family again. He couldn't wait to get back to Butte, to take some time off and treasure another sunset and the next sunrise.

The state of Idaho put up a monument to honor the daredevil's effort. To Evel this piece of stone cemented his image as a hero. The Snake River, like the fountains in Vegas, had not been a success in the conventional way Americans had always viewed success, but for the stuntman, each had offered a challenge and a risk. He had faced the challenge and survived the risk.

Yet while the jump had not injured Evel, a person inside his camp would soon deeply wound him. He would soon discover a man he had confided in would forever change the stuntman's life and alter his image.

16

Time Overtakes Evel

Though many had predicted a quick descent for the stuntman, Evel's star didn't become tarnished after the Snake River Canyon jump. Even though there was a great deal of debate on what the event meant to Knievel's bank account—he claimed he took in more than six million dollars, others reported as little as $250,000—the marketing bubble that was Evel had not burst. If anything it was growing. Once again failure had been a good career move for the daredevil. He was proving the long-held axiom that people respect any and everyone who gives each opportunity his best shot. Yet the fans who stayed most loyal were those kids who were riding bikes and dreaming about someday owning a motorcycle.

Children's author Jay Scalzo wrote a juvenile biography on the stuntman for Grosset & Dunlap's Tempo Books imprint. Junior high kids read Scalzo's work in huge numbers. However, the real story about Evel Knievel was not really in a book, it was at the cash register. AMF Bicycles, Ideal Toys, and more than two dozen other companies were still turning Evel's name and image into tens of millions of dollars in sales. There were lunch boxes, action figures, clothing, notebooks, sheets, pillow cases, and a hundred other items with the stuntman's image pasted all over them. Once again, not making the landing but having the courage to make a promised jump had helped the man be embraced by an even larger group of fans. It seemed as long as he had the physical ability to jump a line of cars, he would always be able to make money with his motorcycle.

After performing in front of thousands of thugs and riffraff bikers who had tried to upstage his Snake River rocketcycle show, the "King of the Stuntmen" was called to perform at the home of the queen herself. London, England, wanted Evel to cross the ocean and jump double-decker buses on the hallowed grounds of Wembly Stadium. After he completed his British show, there were multimillion-dollar offers from all the other major cities in Europe. Evel was going international and his financial experts thought Knievel might be able to make $25 million before he returned home. However, when the cult favorite landed on English shores, he was greeted by such apathy that the potential of huge profits seemed much more fantasy than reality.

The Knievel bandwagon hit London a week before the jump. As soon as he was on the ground Knievel realized that his performance, as well as the whole tour, was in trouble. Only a few thousand tickets had been sold for the Wembly jump. It seemed very few British people knew who this American king was. Before he arrived, even fewer cared. The staid English didn't seem to have much use for anything as barbaric as daredevils riding motorcycles.

Evel spent a week walking the streets of London, touring the sights, playing golf with celebrities and common hackers, and talking to every television and newspaper reporter who asked for an interview. From time to time, just to prove how really crazy he was, he drove on the wrong side of the streets and insulted the legendary British snobbery toward America every chance he got. The wilder he was, the more press he received and the more interest he generated. The bloke was crazy, most thought. But he seemed to have such a good time living on the edge, that he also fascinated them. He even reminded old-timers of the American soldiers who had lived in their country during World War II.

In five days tickets sales for the daredevil's jump went from under seven thousand to over one hundred thousand. By the day of the event, there wasn't an empty seat left. When the stuntman finally suited up for the event, he found out that he had drawn a larger crowd than any major soccer contest ever held in Wembly.

On May 31, 1975, the day of the London performance, the row of red buses had been lined up, the Snake River skycycle had been mounted and displayed, and Evel stood ready to greet a gathering of English fans who were now crazy about him. What made the adulation even more special was that no publicist had created this frenzy, Evel had done it by himself. Yet even as the crowd chanted his name and sang cheers to him, Knievel was wondering about his reasons for jumping again. He had real doubts about his ability to stick his landing. "Don't know why I continue to do this," he told one reporter, the concern written all over his face.

Evel had reason to worry. The motorcycles that had been sent over from the U.S. for the jump were geared wrong for this unique setup. There wasn't anywhere in London to get Harley-Davidson parts, and the new gears never arrived from America. Thus, the stuntman didn't have the proper equipment to do the jump, but he also felt he couldn't back out after the week he had spent selling the show and turning the English people on to his act. As he watched one hundred thousand eager Evel converts wait for him to make his appearance, Knievel once again saw death staring into his face. Soon most of America would see the grim reaper stalking the stuntman too.

As had been the case for almost all of his big jumps over the past three years, ABC-TV was on hand covering the event live for *Wide World of Sports*. Though Evel's leaps in the past had been ratings winners, some wondered if the Snake River failure had tarnished his drawing power. Would the American public continue to turn on their sets to watch the stuntman jump over something as seemingly mundane as a line of passenger buses? ABC had taken the risk based on instincts. The network's instincts were well founded; the program would be the highest rated *Wide World of Sports* ever aired, even stomping Ali's biggest fights.

As the clock ticked down to showtime, Evel passed on his traditional white leathers trimmed in red and blue. Instead he slipped into a blue jumpsuit with red and white stars and striped trim. When he walked out looking like a living version of the Union Jack, his new British fans went crazy for the Yank. It seemed that even across the

Atlantic he still knew how to win people over to cheering his every move.

After his routine of stunts and a speech, Evel raced up a ramp that led to the upper reaches of the stadium. Though he had a little more distance for takeoff, this jump had much the same look as one he had made two years before in the Los Angeles Coliseum. Like that previous effort, for the Wembly jump to be successful, everything had to go perfectly. As the gearing had already screwed up the needed parameters, this stunt became little more than a wing and a prayer. Rather than put off the crash he knew was waiting for him, Evel simply signaled his crew and let it rip.

As he barreled down the ski jump–style ramp, then along the long boards of the takeoff ramp, the biker could see that he was in trouble. He just couldn't generate enough speed. Yet there was no way to pull out. If he tried to stop the Harley before liftoff, he would be sure to have a terrible wreck. At least if he jumped he stood a chance that his skills might guide him to a rough but safe landing on the far side of the buses.

There were thirteen buses at Wembly, if there had been one fewer he would have made it. It was number thirteen that spelled doom for the rider.

The Harley came down hard on that final bus, with both the front and back wheels hitting at almost the exact same moment. The bounce created by the simultaneous impact tossed Evel over the handlebars. He struck the front wheel just before hitting the ramp. It then became a race between the stuntman and the cycle to see who would stop first.

In most of Evel's crashes the bike had remained upright on its wheels. This time, because he had bounced off the front tire as he flew off the seat, the Harley turned upside down and then on its side as if mocking Knievel's fall. It appeared to be a perverse version of the cat-and-mouse game a teenage Bobby Knievel had once played with the Butte police. Twice the motorcycle skidded hard into the stuntman. When Evel finally rolled to a stop, the bike landed on top of him. Rescue crews had to lift the heavy Harley off Evel, then turn the bike's racing engine off before they could even check on the fallen rider.

Team mechanic John Hood was the first to arrive by the stuntman's side. Medical crews got there a few seconds later. ABC's Frank Gifford sprinted up next, network cameras right on his heels catching every painful moment. Back home in the States, Knievel's fans were close enough to their fallen hero to hear him moan in agony. A badly injured Evel seemed in shock. It didn't look like he knew where he was. After a quick initial examination, an ambulance crew lifted the biker off the pavement and onto a stretcher. Yet at a moment when many thought he was dying, he waved off the doctors and the ambulance and demanded to be helped back to his feet. He didn't want to leave Wembly yet. He had something to say.

Frank Gifford was one of those whom Evel tried to drape his arm around as he struggled from the stretcher. Slowly, with a stunned crowd cheering, the gimpy American daredevil made his way to the landing ramp and demanded a microphone. As the now silent one hundred thousand looked on, Knievel, obviously in great pain, addressed his new fans.

"Ladies and gentleman of this wonderful country, I would like to tell you that you are the last people in the world who will see me jump again. I am through." His voice indicated that he meant it too.

Every part of his body was bruised, there were more than a few cracked bones and a major concussion, but Evel's most severe injury at Wembly was a broken pelvis. He had snapped it completely in two. For a couple of days after the crash he was in such great pain that he wasn't even aware of what was going on around him. He didn't know millions in England and the United States were praying for their hero. Yet by his fifth day under the British doctors' care, the stuntman realized that he had misspoken. He was recovering so quickly that he decided he wouldn't retire. He might not have been able to continue his European tour, but he still believed he had a few more performances left in his body.

Almost four months later on October 25, a now-healthy Evel journeyed to Kings Island amusement park in Cincinnati to jump not thirteen buses like he had failed to leap in London, but fourteen. Once again before the event, Knievel was nervous and worried about the distance. Yet this time, outfitted in his white leathers, he at least seemed to feel he had a prayer. The staff at Kings Island had bent over backwards to make the stunt as safe as possible. Because there was lots of room for takeoff and landing, his ramps were much more traditional too. This was no jump that began on a ski jump ramp.

As the fourteen Greyhounds, a large live audience, and ABC's *Wide World of Sports* waited, Evel gassed his engine and roared down a long approach ramp. In picture book fashion, he gracefully flew through the air, landing the back wheel first well beyond the final bus. In a little more than a blink of the eye, Knievel had made the last big jump of his career look easy. Thousands of fans saluted him again and ABC pulled an even greater market share than the network had at Wembly. He was a certified and bankable hero. Many were convinced this Superman of motorcycles could jump forever. Yet Evel was feeling the wear of a dozen years and three hundred jumps. After Kings Island, he again announced his retirement.

Still very much a hero and an American icon, TV shows like *The Bionic Woman* now used Evel as a guest star to increase ratings. He usually played himself. Talk shows such as *Dinah* and *The Tonight Show* booked him whenever they could too. He was colorful, outspoken, and bluntly honest. He was always entertaining and so honest with his thoughts that he usually said something that offended someone. So Evel made for not only a great interview, but good audience numbers as well.

Jumping on board Evel's express train at last, Hollywood couldn't help but remember just how much money the George Hamilton bio on the stuntman's life had generated, so it decided to put Knievel opposite supermodel-turned-actress Lauren Hutton and see if he could ride his name to box office magic. Besides Hutton, Gene Kelly and Red Buttons also co-starred in *Viva Knievel*. In truth the movie was probably as good as most of the action flicks of the period and Evel did well for his first time in a major starring role, but his fans didn't want to see him playing himself, they wanted to see Knievel being himself. Though the plot of *Viva Knievel* had the stuntman jumping in a number of great action scenes, fighting drug runners, and playing a wonderful and colorful hero, Burt Reynolds didn't have to worry about Evel becoming the "King of the Box Office."

A year after he had announced his retirement at Kings Island, on October 29, 1976, the stuntman was talked into coming back for a final hurrah at the Seattle Kingdome. Evel wowed his fans by clearing seven buses inside. But it was an ugly jump. He didn't get the speed he needed to fly through the air in the graceful fashion his fans were used to seeing. He nose-dived just after leaving his first ramp. Though he somehow managed to land the bike safely, the Harley's frame cracked on impact, and the stuntman knew that age had finally caught up with him. He finally began to believe that after a dozen years, he just couldn't do it anymore. In his words, "I was getting scared to pull the trigger."

CBS convinced Evel to go out in style with a leap over a tank full of sharks in Chicago. The network thought Knievel's leap would help sell its special on live daredevil stunts. In dress rehearsal the day before the broadcast, the producers talked the stuntman into trying the jump for real. The network wanted to make sure all their cameras were in the right places. The results were disastrous. Evel crashed as he came down, not only badly injuring himself, but hitting a misplaced cameraman as well. It was the first time the rider had ever hurt anyone but himself on a jump.

The accident was even more horrific because his daughter, Tracey was there watching her father perform. As he lay motionless, the girl didn't know if Evel would even live. The set was utter chaos. Finally a VW ambulance arrived and carted Knievel to the nearest trauma unit. The doctors assured Linda and Tracey that the man would live, but he would be laid up for a while.

Knievel broke both arms and his collarbone and suffered a severe concussion. The cameraman lost his eye. It would be over twenty years before the Fox network turned daredevil performances into ratings magic. Ironically, the man who drove those shows' ratings would be Robbie Knievel.

Unable to work and in great pain, Evel was once again having to let his bones heal. About all he could do was spend time with his family and complain. This lack of action and mobility bored him. He needed to be on the move doing things. Thanks to his many endorsements, at least he and his family had an income even if Knievel was unable to really get on with his life and his work.

If the injuries and lack of activities weren't bad enough, a former employee turned on Evel. The stuntman was caught completely unprepared for a Dell paperback book, *Evel Knievel on Tour*, that presented Knievel as anything but an American hero. Sheldon Saltman, the publicist whom Bob Arum had teamed with Evel for the Snake River promotion, had penned his memories of the press tour before the canyon jump.

The story Saltman wrote not only attacked the stuntman's character but alleged drug use and presented bizarre pictures of Knievel's family life. In the past a host of magazine and newspaper stories had revealed that Evel drank quite a bit and had been known to womanize, he had even spoken about these shortcomings on talk shows, so this bit of news was hardly worthy of much attention, much less a book contract. However, the fact that Evel, who was proud he was a role model for the antidrug movement, had been accused of using narcotics horrified the stuntman. When Saltman intimated that Knievel mistreated his wife and hated his mother, it was more than the stuntman could stand. Evel saw these as out-and-out lies. In his mind, Saltman had only been able to make money from their relationship by painting the story with far more color than had been there. In other words, Evel thought the writer had lied.

Others backed Knievel's version of his life. Close friend and ABC commentator Frank Gifford went public with his support for the stuntman. "Evel does not use drugs," Gifford had told the press. While it was true that he was a chauvinist, Evel also took offense that anything he did implied that he didn't love his wife, mother, children, grandmother, and everyone else in his family. He had honestly told scores of people what a wonderful woman, mother, and wife Linda was. He had never intimated that he was angry with his parents for giving him up as a small child. He understood their plight.

Even though Evel still had casts on both of his broken arms, he was so outraged by *Evel Knievel on Tour* that he called a friend and they made a trip to Los Angeles. The duo tracked Saltman to the Fox studio. Evel confronted the writer in a yard outside an office. As his friend held Saltman, Knievel used a baseball bat in an attempt to break Sheldon's arms. It was supposed to be a symbolic act based on the philosophy of "an eye for an eye and a tooth for a tooth." The stuntman thought that by smashing Saltman's arms, he would make the publicist think before ever writing another word about anyone else. Evel accomplished his goal and fractured Saltman's left arm and wrist. If Evel hadn't been handicapped by his own two broken arms, he might have done even more damage. The thirty-nine-year-old stuntman then simply walked away. He didn't run, he didn't try to hide. When an arrest warrant was sworn out, the police had no problem finding their man. Knievel didn't resist the arrest, but he refused to offer any feelings of guilt about the assault. He had responded to an attack on his character just like his friends in Butte would have. He had taken the law into his own hands, sought out the man who had wronged him, and taken revenge.

Evel Knievel on Tour was in reality an uninteresting book about an event that was three years old. It was doubtful that it could have done much long-term damage to Evel's career. The paperback was not going to be read by that many people. As smooth as Evel was in front of the cameras, he probably could have defused the whole things with a press conference and a few interviews. In two months it would have probably been forgotten. Yet by literally taking the law into his own hands, Evel would cost himself millions. As he awaited trial, most of the companies who used his image dropped him.

On October 14, 1977, supposedly after drinking a half bottle of Wild Turkey whiskey, Evel appeared in court. He was sorry for embarrassing his family and letting down his fans, but he still wasn't sorry about what he had down to a past employee who had turned on him. As his attorney, Paul Caruso, began to set in motion a plan to justify the attack and have his client's record wiped clean, Knievel vetoed it. The stuntman simply stood up and said, "I want to plea guilty because I am guilty of the charge. I did it." There would be no trial and no sensational media coverage. The court proceedings took less time than any of Evel's performances.

Exactly one month later, Knievel again made a court appearance to be sentenced. Due to his guilty plea and the fact he would not apologize for the attack, the judge had little choice but to sentence Evel to three years probation and six months in county jail. Though gong to prison meant losing his freedom, the retired stuntman shrugged it off. "The judge was a good and fair man," he told the media as he readied to spend the next five months of his life behind bars.

As Evel traded in his tailored clothes for prison garb, *Evel Knievel on Tour* was all but forgotten by the public. Saltman's book quietly disappeared from the shelves with few Americans ever having read it. Rumor had it that Knievel had bought every copy he could find and had them destroyed.

During his time in jail, Evel discovered that he just thought he had known mean people when he had grown up in Butte. In the cells all around he discovered individuals who were crazed with evil. They talked about killing others as if it were a sport. They had no morals or convictions, only a lust for blood and power. Knievel, who had never shied away from a fight, cut a wide path around the psychopaths he met in the Los Angeles County Jail. As a matter of fact, Evel was so good he was released a month early because of his model behavior. Yet there wouldn't be much on the outside for the man to look forward too.

Before he returned to Butte. Evel informed the press that he still had no regrets over taking a baseball bat to Sheldon Saltman. He added, "If I had it to do it over again, I'd break both of his arms." He even told *Newsweek,* "I should have killed the little bastard." Five months in jail had not mellowed the stuntman.

Not long after Evel came home, Robbie, who was now jumping motorcycles on his own, moved out. Even though he was only sixteen, he just couldn't take his father's demands. The son didn't feel the older Knievel had the right to tell him what to do. Stubborn like his dad, Robbie may have wanted to follow in his father's professional footsteps, but he wasn't about to have Evel tell him how to do it.

With Kelly now grown up and Robbie having left, the big home in

Butte was quiet and lonely. Things were tough too. Money wasn't flowing in anymore. The endorsements had dried up. Evel was selling some of his possessions for cash. He was also having to make token appearances and do stunts at small venues just to pay his bills. Worse yet, when he had been rolling in dough in the days just before the Snake River jump, he had spent more than he had. Now creditors were starting to ring his bell and threaten him with lawsuits. In the midst of all the madness, Linda gave him some good news. She was expecting a baby.

Alishia, the forth of the Knievel children, became a beacon in an otherwise darkening world. The beautiful baby seemed to bring out a softer side in the stuntman. Now when he played golf or spent time with his friends, he bragged about his little girl more than he did the things he owned, the people he knew, or the jumps he had made. Yet with another mouth to feed and with little money in the bank, Evel couldn't live on his past accomplishments. He needed to get back in the public's eye and generate some revenue.

Looking for the hook to revive his sagging fortunes, Evel came up with a new idea for a stunt. He wanted to jump out of an airplane without a parachute. In what seemed like a made-for-television concept, he drew a mental picture of his falling 35,000 feet with five other jumpers. They would open their chutes at five thousand and then the stuntman, with no parachute or any other safety equipment, would guide himself down to earth, trying to land on one of fifteen one-hundred-foot-high stacks of hay. If he managed to hit the top of a stack, he felt he would survive, but his spleen would probably rupture on impact, therefore he thought he would have it removed a few months before jump day.

The haystack story did get some press, but no one in Las Vegas or anywhere else seemed to want to gamble on it. Evel was now old news in most people's minds. The world had changed and moved on to other things and was finding new heroes.

Still gambling in Vegas and on the golf course, still painting when he was at home, still being Evel whenever he got the chance, the stuntman pretended to be on top of the world even when his world was crashing down around him. As he looked at some of the toys and products that had once trumpeted his name, he wryly noted, "A hero in the United States is the shortest-lived profession anyone could participate in."

17

The Worst of Evel

Even though he had made probably as much as fifty million dollars over the last decade, Evel Knievel was now all but penniless. The stuntman had never expected to live to see forty. He had fully expected to die as a result of one of his stunts. So he had spent his money as if he wasn't going to know tomorrow. Somehow his body had survived thirteen major surgeries and almost forty broken bones, but now that body would not allow him to get back on a motorcycle and perform even modest stunts. So he was not only financially broke, he was physically broken.

One very bitter pill Evel had to taste was realizing how severely the attack on Sheldon Saltman and the jail time that followed had damaged his reputation and career. Many of the companies that once catered to his every wish now wouldn't return his phone calls. With creditors at his door and hounding him everywhere he went, he was faced with the prospect of losing everything he had; his cars, boats, planes, and even his home. In his mind, this was all Saltman's fault.

Declaring bankruptcy, Evel watched as almost all of the things his blood, sweat, and broken bones had purchased were sold at bargain basement prices to people he didn't even know. All but deserted by the jet-setting friends who had once been very glad to help the stuntman find ways to spend his earnings, he was now almost as alone as he had been when he began his career. It was a tragic turn in a uniquely American success story.

As Evel moved from a life of luxury to a modest existence in his hometown, three things gave him great solace. The first was his daughter Alishia, a child he saw as an angel sent from God. The second was playing golf, a game he thought was the "greatest in the world." The last was his art.

A longtime friend of Knievel's, western artist Black Jack Ferriter, had long tutored the former daredevil in painting. Except for a few basic lessons on color and brush technique, Evel needed very little teaching. His paintings, once just a novelty described by the press as an outside interest, had blossomed into beautiful works of fine art. His studies of Native Americans, wildlife, and rugged Western scenes were often breathtaking. So magnificent was some of his work that close friends had trouble believing this macho man had such a natural flare for creating such beautiful art. So in the beginnings of his darkest days, art brought perspective and peace to Evel's life. Yet these three calming elements were simply not enough to get him through his next set of trials.

For almost fifteen years the stuntman's life had seemed scripted in Hollywood. He had become an American success story. He had lived like a king. He had constantly faced and beaten death. He had become a hero all over the world. Yet by 1981 Evel's dream had become a nightmare. Everything he had treasured seemed to be turning to dust before his eyes.

Sheldon Saltman, the writer of *Evel Knievel on Tour,* took Knievel to civil court. The author, whose arm was fractured during Evel's 1977 attack at the Fox studio, was now demanding a financial settlement for damages. With Knievel still unrepentant, a sympathetic court awarded Saltman thirteen million dollars. The only satisfaction the retired stuntman could gain from this judgment was that by having already declared bankruptcy and lost everything of value he had ever had, he didn't have a single dime left for the writer. Saltman's victory was therefore not only symbolic, but ironic. The money had disappeared because of the writer's book and the attack that followed. If the book hadn't been written, Evel would have probably still been an endorsement king and could have paid the damage settlement. Of course, without the book there would have been no attack and no court case. Round one of Evel's financial wars could therefore be declared a draw, with both parties losing but able to declare a moral victory.

In 1983, the Internal Revenue Service dropped a new bomb on Evel's world. An audit had found that the man who had been hailed as such a patriot during the dark days of war protest and draft card burnings had failed to pay $1.6 million in taxes on earnings during his heyday as a performer. An angry Knievel fought back, producing checks that showed he had paid the government millions. However, just like when he tried to get permission to jump the Grand Canyon, he had little success with the government. Within four years, not only was the IRS demanding that original amount but another $2.5 million as well. Everything that Knievel owned or earned quickly had a lien slapped on it. Uncle Sam literally owned Evel now. Evel lost round two of his financial wars to the IRS.

At the same time the IRS became interested in Knievel's returns, so did Montana. His home state found that Evel owned them $390,000 and they sued him for the amount. Disgusted and unable to pay, the stuntman pulled up stakes and left Butte for life on the road. He was now the loser of the third round of financial wars.

The Legends group had become interested in Evel's art. Providing him with a luxury touring bus and trailer, they set up showings for Knievel all across the country. As a part of the agreement, Legends owned rights to all the stuntman's art. The new deal gave Evel a salary, the freedom to travel, and once again a spotlight to shine on his work. *People Weekly* did a feature on his art, as did countless local papers. Some of his paintings went for more than ten thousand dollars. Signed prints of his art were priced at more than two hundred dollars. This facet of his talent brought back a bit of respect for the onetime icon. Yet he was still a long way from the fame he had known in the seventies, and the IRS was getting a cut of everything he was making.

Since he release from jail and his retirement from jumping, Evel's drinking had become a much bigger part of his life. Even he admitted that he was drinking too much. Constant hangovers reminded him of that fact. Much more than anything else, it was the booze that was ruining his relationships with his family. Robbie had hinted at that problem being the driving factor in his falling-out with his father. Tired of feeling bad, tired of not having control over his life, Evel looked for a reason to sober up.

It was largely because of Alishia that Knievel tried to quit. The little innocent girl was the only one who had the guts to take his whiskey bottles and pour them down the drain. If anyone beside Alishia had attempted this act, it would have probably sent Knievel into a rage. Yet when his daughter gently tried to steer him in the right direction, he listened. Evel went through weeks of suffering withdrawal as he tried to get rid of alcohol's powerful hold on him. Thanks to Alishia, for a while he made it. During those days he gave God and Alishia all the credit for his being sober.

In many ways these days of sobriety, when a humble Evel displayed his art and traveled with his wife and daughter, were the best he and Linda had seen in some time. In a biographical documentary made when he was successfully fighting his addiction to liquor, Knievel stated, "I would have never succeeded without my wife." Later in the film the legend also took the blame for any problems his family had encountered over the years. He declared that everything had been his fault. Yet the pressures of life, especially those brought on by his constant pain and financial problems, eventually drove him back to the bottle. This time the drinking would cost him a great deal more than money.

In 1986, while in Kansas City, Evel had been drinking and was arrested for soliciting an undercover policewoman. The embarrassed Knievel paid a two-hundred-dollar fine. This event, compounded by so many others in the past, was probably the blow that finally ended his union with Linda. Though she would not seek a divorce, she and Alishia moved back to Montana and left Evel alone on the road.

To many across the country Evel was either still a star or a curious novelty. He was especially popular with those who followed the stunt career of Robbie Knievel. On several occasions father and son tried to work out their differences so that the elder stuntman could appear at Robbie's shows. Evel was there in November 1985 when his son jumped thirteen buses at the Los Angeles Coliseum. More than a decade before, the Coliseum had been the scene of one of Evel's own big jumps. Rather than allow Robbie and his crew to work out the details as they had for scores of shows over the past several years, Evel tried to get into the mix and even stop the jump. He didn't like the setup. When he was given a microphone and allowed to address the crowd, the elder Knievel told them that the stadium's management was screwing his son around. He just didn't see how Robbie could make a successful jump within the parameters determined by the venue. Robbie jumped anyway, taking his hands off the handlebars in midflight and then sticking his landing perfectly. The crowd roared and an obviously concerned Evel was relieved.

Four years later, after several more years of going their separate ways, Evel again joined his son, this time at Caesar's Palace. Robbie was going to repeat his father's most famous jump by leaping the famous Las Vegas fountains. While Evel readily and enthusiastically admitted pride in all his children—by now Kelly was a successful businessman and Tracey had gone into full-time Christian service work—he didn't like the fact that Robbie was jumping at all, much less at this site. It scared him. He didn't want to lose his son over something as unimportant as jumping two fountains.

In Vegas, as he had in Los Angeles, Evel argued with his son over the jump's setup. Evel felt that a landing ramp would be necessary to have any chance at surviving the leap. Robbie wanted to come down directly on the parking lot. In this case the wisdom of age was served as the team set up a landing ramp for Robbie. It was a fortunate move. Like his father the younger Knievel easily cleared the fountains, but without the ramp he probably would have come down far too hard to control the landing. With the ramp in place Robbie made it looked easy. The elder Knievel was just thankful there hadn't been a rerun of what had happened to him in 1968.

Evel would take credit for keeping his son from breaking his neck at Caesar's Palace, and he probably should have been singled out. However, the Vegas jump would spell the end of the two generations of Knievels appearing together. Robbie, who had only broken two bones in his hand during his entire history of jumping, simply didn't feel he needed his father to boost his career and gate. In truth, he didn't want Evel's advice either. The elder Knievel sensed it was time to let go as well.

The separation from Linda, the fact that his children were more closely aligned with their mother than their father, as well as the fact that he was no longer the name-drawing superstar he had once been was hard on Evel. Though usually surrounded by a lot of old fans at his art exhibits and when he went out of the town and partied, Knievel was very much a lone wolf again.

Evel had once said that there were five things in life that counted. The first was believing in God. The second was being a good and loving son to one's mother and father. The third was being a good husband. The fourth was being a loving and good father. The final thing was being a true friend. In the bleak days that closed out the eighties, Evel knew he had been a good and loyal friend to many, and he readily admitted a belief in God, but in some ways he had fallen short of his own ideal for the other three important factors of having a happy and successful life. He was paying the price for his short-comings now, and it hurt much worse than having lost his money and his career.

Evel had been down in the arena countless times. On every occasion he had gotten up. He was down again, but this time he hadn't been put there by a bad landing during a motorcycle stunt in front of a national television audience and thousands of concerned fans. This time Evel Knievel had been knocked down by his own life choices. Would he find the strength to get back up with no one but himself looking on?

18

Evel Cheats Death Again

By 1990 Evel was living a life very isolated from his family. His recreational outlets were principally gambling and golf. In many ways it was the game played with a small white ball that had become his salvation. The old Knievel, the one who faced death in the arena and met every challenge with a unbreakable spirit, was brought to life each time Evel took to the links. The very competitive nature of the game itself, that fact that it was really a sport where an individual was not only trying to beat other men and women, but also trying to bring out the best in himself—to top his last performance—fully defined the passion that had always driven the man. To make each contest even that much more interesting and give himself an extra incentive to win, Knievel liked to gamble on every hole and every game. His life had always been about beating the odds, and on a golf course he would bet to beat the odds even if he was playing Jack Nicklaus.

Nicklaus had once wrote about Evel, "he makes the game's so-called hustlers look like penny pinochle players." Knievel had always played life as big as he played golf. He had held nothing back and had taken every opportunity to challenge himself, usually by having taken the road less traveled, the hard one, the one that offered the most resistance but the largest rewards. Over the last decade, he had gambled and lost much more than he had won.

As bleak as the eighties had been for the retired stuntman, the new decade seemed to be offering some forgiveness to him. The episode that landed him a jail term had now been all but forgotten. His son Robbie's continued success jumping even longer distances than Evel once had kept the Knievel name alive. Most importantly, for many kids who grew up the late seventies and early eighties, Evel was still a hero. In these baby boomers' minds, the excitement of watching Knievel jump at Caesar's Palace, Wembly, or King's Island was still a very powerful memory. So was remembering riding an AMF Evel Knievel bike or playing with one of Evel's Ideal Toy Company's action figures. These items, along with everything else that ever carried his endorsement, were now some of the most popular and expensive items offered at antique and collector shows.

The rebirth of interest in Evel's career brought about a dramatic change in attitude from scores of marketing-savvy companies and businesses. Realizing that to many young people Knievel was the symbol for Las Vegas—two decades before he had won the right to jump the fountains at Caesar's Palace with the promise of luring customers to the city that never sleeps—Maxim Casino made Evel their television spokesperson. He was the company's point man who convinced tourists to step into this up-and-coming gambling house. In the perfect marriage of pitchman and pitch, Evel described Vegas as the place with no limits.

Harley-Davidson brought Evel back too. He appeared not only at their stores, but signed autographs at promotional outings at the company's new line of eateries. The company, which was making a comeback of its own, wanted to link with a man who defined the positive side of biking.

A luggage company used Knievel and lampooned his image in a spot that showed a suitcase being tossed from an airplane and landing on a highway. Then the case opened, Evel's head popped out, and he delivered a funny line. The implication being that the line of luggage was just as tough as Evel himself.

Soon Little Caesar's Pizza signed him up. Knievel's affiliation with the Caesar's name was just too good for the chain to pass up.

Choice Hotels got on board too. After all, who knew more about traveling than the "King of the Stuntmen"? Then came a brilliant bit of inspiration: someone figured out they could even exploit all the times Knievel had been hurt.

In one of the more unusual business marriages of any age, the Stimulator, a strange little device that claimed, when used properly, to relieve pain from certain areas of the body, called upon Evel to promote their product. For many people who were suffering chronic pain from arthritis and other ailments, Evel Knievel was someone to whom they could easily relate. If this device helped him cope with all the pain he must be feeling as the result of his injuries, then surely it could help them with the problems they had. The folks who marketed the Stimulator had obviously guessed right when they had hired a man who had publicly broken so many bones. After Knievel began to pitch them, millions of Stimulators were sold through television and print ads.

Though it wouldn't mean as much money as many of his other endorsements, ESPN using Evel to push their X-Games series may have been the most important. In the commercials Evel called the young men who slid down mountains on snowboards and performed other equally wild stunts, "crazy." Millions tuned in to view the games simply because the daredevil thought these athletes and their events were extreme. What could they be doing that would shock the man who had tried to fly over a river in little more than a bomb with wheels? What viewers and Knievel were surprised to discover was that the athletes who played in the X-Games had long embraced the stunt-man as their hero and role model. As would soon be obvious, so had a lot of other people.

Much like Mickey Mantle and other old baseball stars, Evel's come-back was driven by a thirst for times when things were less compli-cated and heroes were easier to define. What this meant for Knievel was not only a chance at new ad revenue, but an opportunity to go to card and collectible shows and meet his still-loyal fans. Signing photos and other items for cash, Evel was a hotter ticket at these events than almost every other sports hero or television personality. Many approached his booth just to introduce their children to the most courageous man they had ever watched perform. Even Knievel had to be shocked at how many still lionized him as a champion.

Besides card shows and casino openings, Evel was also a huge draw at celebrity charity golf tournaments. For Knievel nothing could have been better than having someone pay him to play golf. Yet he had no way of knowing that in 1991 the game he loved would give him a second chance at experiencing love.

Krystal Kennedy was an energetic, shapely, tanned, blond professional golfer when she ran into Evel on a Florida course. She was also engaged and only twenty-one years old. Too young to have been born when Evel jumped the fountains at Caesar's, Krystal probably didn't remember seeing any of the man's best work. Yet in spite of their three-decade difference in age, she liked him.

For a week they visited, got to know each other better, and played a lot of golf. When it came time for Evel to move onto his next personal appearance, Krystal took her engagement ring off and joined him. From that moment on, they were inseparable.

Kennedy was a woman who would stand up to Knievel. He could not run her over. Bound and determined to get him into shape, she watched his drinking, tried to change his diet, and pushed him to exercise more. By and large it worked too. Evel quit drinking hard liquor, lost weight, and began to look as if he was ready to perform again. Yet while he showered his lover with gifts that included large diamond rings and the two often walked hand in hand at appearances, Krystal and Evel, who both prosessed strong personalities, often clashed too.

In 1994, in Sunnyvale, California, police were called to a domestic disturbance in a motel. It appeared that Kennedy and Knievel had fought and the retired stuntman had struck the former professional golfer. Though the woman refused to press charges and the man sincerely apologized, the cops still searched the room and the couple's car. In the vehicle the officers found several firearms. In court Evel was ordered to do two hundred hours of community service for a weapons violation.

In spite of that one run-in with the law, the couple appeared happy and well suited for each other. Evel's timing in love and life might have been off in the 1980s, but by the middle of the 1990s, Evel

Knievel was back in rhythm. He was also again a star. Knievel was so popular with the junior high set that new versions of his old action figures were released on the market, a line of new Evel Knievel stunt bicycles sold as fast as they could be made, and he was in heavy demand for personal appearances in spite of fees that even the stunt-man viewed as outlandish. *Sports Illustrated* and *People* checked in for a visit, as did a host of other periodicals. Web sites including one that he sponsored, had popped up everywhere, all seemingly online just to trumpet Knievel as a legend. With a beaming Krystal almost always by his side, it did seem that these were the best of days for Evel. He was now making big paychecks and not having to break any bones to earn them. Yet underneath the veneer of success, there was one very troubling sign.

Though he was only in his late fifties, Evel looked much older. His hair was white and the pain from his many operations could be seen on his face. He was a man who had always shied away from drugs, even most prescribed by doctors, and the only relief he often could get for his intense suffering came from sipping a beer. This didn't help much either. If the fans who constantly sought him had known what he was going through each day, their admiration for the retired stuntman would have increased tenfold. Arthritis had so crippled his body that the once elementary act of getting out of bed and getting dressed took more out of Knievel than a day of manual labor did for most people. Playing eighteen holes of golf, all the time joking and telling stories, should have been impossible for a man in his condition. Yet with the courage he once saved for his jumps, he not only played the game, he played it well and without complaining.

On a golf course in 1997, just about the same time that Linda finally divorced him, Evel fell. When he hit the ground he fractured his hip. The orthopedic surgeon who was called in on the case said he had never seen a man in this much pain. Rather than put the surgery off until Evel was healthier, as would normally have been the case, the doctor ordered an immediate hip replacement operation.

Just as he had when he was at the peak of his career, Evel healed much more quickly than a normal person. Though it had been predicted he might be on crutches for as much as six months, within half that time Evel was back on the golf course. His renewed vigor also put him back in the motorcycle business.

The California Motorcycle Company signed Evel to design and produce a motorcycle they would market and sell as a limited edition model. When they were built, the legendary stuntman signed each bike personally, thus adding to the model's appeal as a motorcycle collector's dream. Not only did he endorse them, since the surgery he had been riding one of them. Though the vigor in his voice and the energy in his step indicated that Evel was off the floor and ready for action, he was about to be hit with an even larger challenge than a broken hip or jumping a mile over an Idaho river.

In the spring of 1998, Evel's heath really seemed to be slipping. Taking even a sip of alcohol made him choke and throw up. He often couldn't keep his food down. Weak, almost twenty pounds under his ideal weight, he had an unhealthy skin tone, and the spring that had recently been restored to his step was now gone. Even his voice, always dynamic and strong, was now sometimes little more than a whisper. Checking into a hospital, a worried Knievel thought he might be dying.

Tests conducted by specialists did not bring any positive news. Evel was gravely ill. Hepatitis C had infected his liver. The disease, which is chronic and fatal, was eating him alive. Without a liver transplant, the stuntman probably had less than a year to live.

The doctors told Knievel he had probably contracted the illness through a blood transfusion during one of his many operations. The hepatitis had remained dormant for a some time, but now was attacking with a vengeance.

When Evel left the hospital, he felt like a dead man. With the possible exception of the skycycle ride at Snake River Canyon, Evel had never felt so close to death. In the past, when he had been jumping, he knew he could die, but he always believed that his skill, talent, and luck would save him in the end. Now, for the very first time in his life, there was nothing he could do. It was out of his hands. Only a team of doctors and a donor's organ could buy him another chance at life. Going home to Clearwater, Florida. Evel golfed when he felt

218

well enough; when he was feeling bad he prayed and counted his blessings.

Knievel felt blessed that Robbie had called him the previous Father's Day. The two of them had set aside their past differences and had pledged to restore not only a relationship, but a friendship. Since that call it had become very easy for the two stuntmen to share almost anything.

Evel had also reestablished a good relationship with his ex-wife and other three children. He had publicly said that he admired Linda a great deal. He said again and again, "Living with Evel Knievel was never easy." Whenever he returned to Butte, he always took the time to visit with his ex-wife.

His kids were all special now too. Kelly, the businessman; Alishia, the little angel who was now growing into a beautiful girl; and Tracey, a dynamic Christian who had worked as a missionary. At this time not only was Tracey building a deep bond with her dad, she was praying for him everyday. Evel had to figure that if God listened to anyone, it would be Tracey. If they found a donor liver, Tracey's prayers would have at least been a part of the reason.

The man who had gained so much fame as a daredevil was also grateful that so many kids again called him a hero and an idol. This rebirth of adulation had come to mean so much to him that he even spoke to the press about the problems he had with alcohol. There was little doubt that his drinking had helped create his condition, he said, so now he preached to his fans not only to stay away from drugs, but from booze as well. If he died before they found a liver for him, at least he could be satisfied he was again trying to make a positive impact on kids' lives.

As Evel faced death, he also began to speak about his belief that his spirit would continue. He didn't understand exactly how or in what form, but he just knew that when the body died, the essence of what made him special would not pass away. It would remain alive.

"Dying is a part of living," he explained to A&E network's *Biography* series. "You just have to accept God's way."

Evel might have accepted and believed that his spirit was eternal, but he wasn't going to give up life as he knew it without a fight. On his Web site he posted a letter that spoke of his need for a liver. "We are awaiting a donor of a liver that will be a suitable match for my blood type, O positive, the most common type in this nation. I will try to do my part by maintaining my positive attitude that I have always preached that has worked so well for me throughout my life." He also urged as many people as possible to register as organ donors.

In early January 1999, Evel was admitted to Tampa General Hospital suffering from dehydration and exhaustion. The Hepatitis C was now beginning to go into its final stages. Just as he had once stared across a line of cars and wondered if he could stick a landing, Knievel now looked down a road that didn't even promise tomorrow. He wondered if this was one landing he would even have a chance to stick. Though he vowed to stay alive until doctors found a donor organ, many thought the gladiator's time on Earth was now numbered in just days.

Somehow Evel rallied, got out of his hospital bed, and was home in less than a week, but he knew without the transplant he still might die at any time. On February 2, 1999, his special beeper went off signaling the opportunity for a second lease on life. When he checked in with his doctors, they informed him he was next on the list and they had a liver that was a positive match. The liver was his!

Yet as he considered what this meant, Evel also discovered that a young man who was further down the list was going to die, probably within hours, if he didn't get a liver too. Telling his surgeons he felt pretty good, Knievel made a huge leap of faith. Gambling with his life one more time, he gave up his spot in line in order that a man he had never met might have another chance at life.

A week later his beeper went off again. This time the liver would be his. A man less than half Evel's age had tragically died. He had signed his donor card. Because of that signature and his family's wishes, Knievel was being given the most precious gift in the world.

The operation was so successful and Evel's recovery so smooth, that two days later he was up dressed and allowed to watch his son, now known professionally as Captain Robbie Knievel, perform a live "Death Jump" on the Fox television network. Robbie was going to take off from the roof of one of the twin Jockey Towers and land on the other tower's rooftop. More than two hundred feet below him, thousands had gathered to watch the daredevil perform without a safety net. To successfully make the leap, Robbie, outfitted in a white leather jumpsuit adorned with stripes and stars much like the ones his father had once worn, was going to have to leave his takeoff ramp at more than a hundred miles an hour, fly 130 feet in the air, and then stop his bike before flying off the top of the second building.

As were the millions who watched the broadcast and the thousands, including the stuntman's mother and Robbie's own two beautiful daughters, Evel was nervous. He believed there were too many risks involved in this leap. Just seconds before Robbie was to begin his rush to the takeoff ramp, Fox showed a live shot of Evel in his room. When they did, the Vegas crowd went crazy. Just like Joe Dimaggio, the elder Knievel might have been retired, but he was still considered the greatest. It was Robbie's jump, but the old man was still the champion in the people's eyes.

Robbie easily made his leap between the towers, and everyone, including his father breathed a sigh of relief. While the fans went home to consider their jobs and the other details of their normal lives, Evel realized his son would soon jump again. This thought scared him. Rumor had it the next jump would be over the upper reaches of the Grand Canyon. When Robbie took to the sky at the canyon, it would put his father through Hell like only a parent could know. The veteran stuntman now fully realized what his own family must have gone through each time he made another death-defying leap. It was terrible.

Ten days after his five-and-half-hour transplant surgery, Evel was released from the hospital. As he readied to leave, he held a press conference. Jubilant but humble, he looked and sounded a decade younger than he had just a few weeks before.

"Sometimes good guys do finish first!" he began. "I'm one hundred percent better and looking forward to living a long time!

"As soon as I am well enough I am going to contact the donor's family to thank them personally and also give my condolences for their loss. I now have a new best friend and I don't even know him. He gave me life."

As he had never had an insurance company that would write him a health or life policy, he then quipped, "The operation cost me about four hundred thousand—but every dollar was worth it!"

At the conference Evel also gave the hospital one of his signature California motorcycles. Hand painted in his traditional stuntman colors of red, white, and blue, his name emblazoned in gold lettering on the side as per Knievel's instructions, the $25,000 bike would be used in a raffle to raise money for organ transplants.

Evel concluded the news conference by stating, "I'm thankful to God Almighty for everything I've faced. I've always tried to stand against the wind, I've had everything in this world that it has to offer to a human being. I'm proud that I was born an American. God has been good to me and I hope and I pray that my spirit will go on and that I'll win again."

For a man so close to death so many times, life had now become very sweet. Evel Knievel, who had faced every challenge head-on, now had taken a leap of faith and found a greater purpose. As a transplant survivor, he seemed ready to take the fight for more donors to the national stage. He seemed ready to use his talents and fame to help others jump over death and land safely in life again.

A few weeks after he left the hospital, Evel rode one of his limited edition motorcycles on a stage in Las Vegas. Riding another California model was Robbie. Side by side the Knievels drew a huge applause. His blue eyes sparkling, his gaze fixed on those who were cheering him, Evel was back in the spotlight and healthy again. Somewhere in the back of the room the Grim Reaper must have been wondering what he would have to do to finally get his chance at the daredevil. How many more times could Evel Knievel possibly beat the odds and escape death's clutches?

As he waved to his fans and planned a busy year of personal appearances, product endorsements, golf, and charity endeavors. Evel Knievel, American hero, had to be struck by something he had told A&E's *Biography* just before his transplant. "I lived a dream. It has been a wonderful dream!"

And he took millions along for the ride.